'All parents across all cultures and countries can relate to the challenges in parenting teens. In this clearly written book using everyday language, Sheila Redfern has managed to produce the guide that caregivers have been waiting for. Grounded in evidence-based practice and filled with relatable real-life examples, she provides compassionate guidance for increasing our capacity to understand and respond to our teens' behaviours. This is a must-read book – not only for parents and caregivers, but also for the professionals who support them.'

Carla Sharp, PhD, *John and Rebecca Moores Professor at University of Houston*

'Understanding the neuroscience of the changing teenage brain can really help parents to empathise and connect with their teenage children. Sheila Redfern is an inspirational psychologist with a truly engaging story to tell about parenting, growth and how to nurture the growing teenage brain.'

Sophie Scott, CBE FBA FMedSci, *Professor, Director, Institute of Cognitive Neuroscience, UCL*

'Shepherding a young person through the tumultuous journey of adolescence and early adulthood is arguably the most challenging and emotionally charged responsibility many of us undertake. Redfern brilliantly applies the developmental science of mentalizing – the ability to understand and interpret the thoughts and feelings of young people, as well as recognizing their impact on our own mental states – to construct a powerful and coherent parenting approach. This comes into play especially when dealing with adolescents who seem determined to disrupt any form of such consistency. In this landmark book, Sheila Redfern deploys her remarkable clinical acumen and her innovative model of Reflective Parenting to help navigate this often-daunting task. Redfern's work brims with practical solutions to the manifold problems parents are likely to face, drawing from her wealth of insight and extensive clinical experience. It's a book that not only understands the trials and tribulations of raising adolescents but also provides effective strategies to handle them. Whether you're striving to guide a young person as they grapple with the complexities of growing up or seeking to offer the most effective support as they stride into adulthood, this book is a priceless tool. I firmly believe it's the finest guide presently available, offering an enduring and invaluable contribution to the field of parenting adolescents.'

Peter Fonagy, FMedSci FBA OBE, *Professor and Head, Research Department of Clinical, Educational Psychology, University College London: Chief Executive, Anna Freud, London*

HOW DO YOU HUG A CACTUS? REFLECTIVE PARENTING WITH TEENAGERS IN MIND

Have you ever wondered what's going on in your teenager's mind? This engaging book will give you the tools to understand just that to ultimately help you keep the close connection you both need during these tricky years.

Following on from her acclaimed book for parents of younger children, Sheila Redfern brings the reflective parenting model to parents of teenagers. Teenagers can be experienced as prickly and hard to get close to – like a cactus – but Dr. Redfern shows us how this stage of your child's life can be more enjoyable and connected than you'd imagined. Rather than focusing on their behaviours, this book emphasises how we can teach teenagers to manage their feelings and relationships in safe ways. It advocates theories underpinning reflective parenting – mentalizing, attachment and neuroscience – as essential for building resilience and security in young people, which is crucial through the storm and stress of adolescence. Chapters are filled with everyday, relatable scenarios and practical advice on pressing issues such as self-harm, social media and gaming, risk and ASD. There is also a chapter devoted to adoptive parents and foster carers.

This practical guide aims to help readers become more reflective and available as parents and understand what might be in their teenager's head. It also serves as an essential resource for clinicians working with families.

Sheila Redfern, PhD, is a consultant clinical child and adolescent psychologist at Anna Freud, London and the director of Redfern Psychology. She has worked with children, adolescents and their caregivers in mental health settings for thirty years. She is a parent to three boys.

Sheila Redfern
Photograph by Sonia Weir

HOW DO YOU HUG A CACTUS? REFLECTIVE PARENTING WITH TEENAGERS IN MIND

Sheila Redfern
Structural Edits: Claire Cross
Cartoons: Kiriko Kubo

Routledge
Taylor & Francis Group
LONDON AND NEW YORK

Designed cover image: ©Kiriko Kubo

First published 2024
by Routledge
4 Park Square, Milton Park, Abingdon, Oxon OX14 4RN

and by Routledge
605 Third Avenue, New York, NY 10158

Routledge is an imprint of the Taylor & Francis Group, an informa business

British Library Cataloguing-in-Publication Data
A catalogue record for this book is available from the British Library

Library of Congress Cataloging-in-Publication Data
Names: Redfern, Sheila, author.
Title: How do you hug a cactus? : reflective parenting with teenagers in mind / Sheila Redfern.
Description: Abingdon, Oxon ; New York, NY : Routledge, 2024. | Includes bibliographical references and index. |
Identifiers: LCCN 2023047530 (print) | LCCN 2023047531 (ebook) | ISBN 9781138310742 (hardback) | ISBN 9781138310766 (paperback) | ISBN 9780429459245 (ebook)
Subjects: LCSH: Parent and teenager. | Parenting.
Classification: LCC HQ799.15 .R43 2024 (print) | LCC HQ799.15 (ebook) | DDC 649/.125--dc23/eng/20231017
LC record available at https://lccn.loc.gov/2023047530
LC ebook record available at https://lccn.loc.gov/2023047531

ISBN: 978-1-138-31074-2 (hbk)
ISBN: 978-1-138-31076-6 (pbk)
ISBN: 978-0-429-45924-5 (ebk)

DOI: 10.4324/9780429459245

Typeset in Sabon
by MPS Limited, Dehradun

CONTENTS

PROLOGUE

As a consultant clinical psychologist with over 30 years experience working with children and adolescents in mental health services, and a parent to three teenagers myself, I am endlessly fascinated by the importance of family relationships to young people's mental health. I have particularly loved working with adolescents over the years and find their energy, humour and strong opinions re-energises me in my work. Recently, I was at a school show, produced, directed and starring teenagers from years 12 and 13 at our local school. The shouts, cheers and unbound enthusiasm for their friends in the audience as the teenagers took to the stage was massively uplifting and infectious. I was so struck by the sense of camaraderie and fierce loyalty this crowd of 17 and 18-year-olds showed for their performing friends – sweeping the rest of us along with the force of their enthusiasm for a good time. Whenever I'm in a room full of teenagers, I seem to find myself laughing. Why then, do teenagers get such a bad rap?

What is it like being a teenager in this social media-driven age? Anyone between the ages of 15 and 21 will have experienced two to three years of their adolescent development spent locked down in their home. Home for many adolescents might have been a comforting sanctuary, though it could also have been a place of occasional, or more constant, loneliness, and for some, even violence, neglect and/or deprivation. Whatever the environment, there is little doubt that the Covid-19 pandemic has had a huge impact on adolescent wellbeing. We are only just finding out the extent of this impact, but early research findings tell us that young people have struggled greatly with increased anxiety; and while the relaxation of lockdown has been a huge relief for many, it has been an extreme challenge for adolescents who were already struggling with their social relationships.

What I discovered, and what runs through this book, is that the teenage voice is intelligent, insightful, emotional, and complex, and we parents can oversimplify this voice, even mocking it as though the teenage voice shouldn't be taken seriously. I love working with teenagers and, in my view, they are a much-maligned group. The stereotype of a teenager is of a difficult, somewhat prickly and uncommunicative person who is always hard to get close to – a bit like a cactus. I am pleased this book gives me an opportunity to open up a greater curiosity about what goes on in the teenage mind, instead of conforming to "typical teenager" negative stereotypes. Attributing a behaviour or personality trait to "just being a teen" is as meaningless as saying "he did that because he's a Scorpio."

While we are going to spend time understanding the experiences of teenagers, including some examples of the impact of the pandemic on your teenager's development (for they may have been approaching adolescence during the period from 2020–2023), this is primarily a book about *your* experience. What is it like to parent an adolescent? What has your experience been like, and what do you struggle with? What feelings does it bring up for you and what are your hopes and fears for your teenager? This is not a book to tell you how your teenager should behave or how to change their behaviour. The approach I'm going to share with you, though, will help to bring about a greater understanding of your teenager and, ultimately, may hopefully help to change some of the aspects of their behaviour you might be most worried about right now. The two main things I would like to help you achieve are, first, to learn how to regulate your emotions when you are parenting your teenager and, secondly, to bring about a greater connection between you and your teenager. Parenting is one of the hardest and also one of the most joyful experiences you will have, whether you're a biological parent or a family relation, carer or adoptive parent. I'm going to speak to your experiences and, using my own curiosity, encourage you to reflect on what it's like for you to parent your teenager. I'll also help you engage your curiosity about both yourself and your teen, to help you work through some of the challenges this period of life brings with it.

In my experience, working with parents and carers, I see that, almost without exception, parents I work with are trying their very best. However, I have worked with many parents who have really struggled to connect with their children because of reasons such as their own childhood experiences, current circumstances, or past trauma. Sometimes their struggle has been related to their teenager experiencing mental health problems that they feel completely unprepared for. Whether you had a difficult childhood yourself, or one that you consider to be fairly ordinary, there is no doubt in my mind, after my many years of clinical practice, that your state of mind is crucial to how well you understand your teenager, the way in which you interact with them, and to how they will turn out.

I've found through my clinical and academic work that there are two main types of books about parenting. The first takes a cookbook approach, telling you what to do; the second is more theoretical, focusing heavily on the psychological theory of development. Neither type properly addresses the relationship between you and your teenager or acknowledges that your relationship with your teenager is unique and individual to you and them. I've studied many psychological theories of human development – psychoanalytic; cognitive and behavioural; systemic and neurodevelopmental. It seems to me that what's missing is a book that helps ordinary parents put these theories into practice. It was this frustration that influenced me to write a book for parents that explored the model of understanding human relationships known as "mentalization," and showed parents how to bring this practice into their everyday interactions with their teens, using a practice called "reflective parenting." So, while this book does have some elements of the cookbook and shares what I consider to be some useful tools, it also brings a theory to life in a way that will help you improve your connection with your teenager.

I am going to take you through a series of stages which I hope, by the end, will lead to a place where you feel you've got a better understanding of both your teenager and your own response to them. Crucially, by the end of this book, you should have some more ideas about how you can connect with your teenager, because if adolescence is characterised by one thing, it's the separation of parent and teenager. You and them.

Each scenario is a composite of people I have spoken to and worked with and, while no single scenario represents one person, I have further anonymised the details by giving a different name to each teenager and parent. I'm aware that there will be many concerns you may have about your teenager which I either don't touch on, or go into detail. For example, you may have a teenager with ADHD, or OCD, and I don't go into these and other specific mental health concerns. I do speak more about teenagers with ASD and teenagers in care, because these are areas of special interest to me and where I have a depth of experience. However, the principles of reflective parenting, and the approach I bring to life in this book, are applicable to you in your parenting of any teenager and will give you a different way of approaching your relationship, no matter what their difficulties.

Identity

The personal pronouns used in the book refer to the gender identity assigned at birth to the teenagers and parents in the scenarios. I have used he/him/his and she/her throughout the book, but there are scenarios where the teenagers' or parents' identity may have changed from their assigned one at birth, here I have used "they/their." The teenagers and parents represent the cultural and ethnic diversity of the population I have worked with and live amongst.

ACKNOWLEDGEMENTS

This book is dedicated to the memory of my beautiful, late mother, Marian Redfern. Without her enduring love, optimism, and belief, I wouldn't have been able to write my first book or have continued with this one after her death in 2020. She continues to be the most inspirational woman I've ever known. I feel lucky to have had a mum and dad who taught me so many interesting things in life. My thanks and love go to Rich, Gabe, Joe, and Will for being so encouraging when it was hard to balance parenting, life, and work on top of writing – you are my whole world.

I am indebted to the wonderful community of friends and parents who have contributed to this book by generously sharing their own experiences; Alison Rogers, Sam White, Anna Motz and Annaliese van den Berg in particular, but also so many parents in Furzedown (Tooting) who shared their experiences of parenting teenagers with me. Thank you to all of you. Thank you to colleagues at Anna Freud for speaking about their clinical work and personal experiences; Peter Fonagy, Dickon Bevington, Tessa Baradon, Michaela Biseo and Theresa Schwaiger. Special thanks to Laura Talbot for working with me on the networks chapter – I am so impressed with your work and thinking. I am grateful to the editorial team at Routledge and extremely thankful to Claire Cross, whose brilliant editing and thoughtful reflections on my work have been invaluable.

Finally, and most importantly, I would like to thank all the teenagers I've worked with clinically over the years, my own children and their friends and the fantastic young people in my local community, including Maia Frost, whose moving, funny, brilliant, and insightful perspectives on their teenage lives have kept me energised in this work for so long.

INTRODUCTION

Becoming a parent to a teenager

Think back to when your child was just two years old and you're watching them run along the pavement ahead of you. They run with that determination and self-confidence of a toddler who feels fully in command of where they are going, without any sense of danger whatsoever. As they run on, you laugh at the joy of their determined running and giggling, but suddenly see they are getting dangerously near to the road. An articulated lorry is hurtling down the road, the driver high up in his cab; surely he can't see you from up there? Within a split second, you pelt towards your child, shouting "STOP! STOP!" at the top of your voice; you reach out to grab them by the collar of their coat, yanking them back towards you, and then firmly take their hand. Their carefree behaviour is suddenly interrupted by your firm hand and authoritative voice. You have them back by your side, and with a bit of wriggling and writhing around as they try to break free from your grip again, you walk hand in hand along the road – your heart rate gradually slowing down – until you reach the park.

There's no question about who is in charge in this scenario. Who is responsible for the child's safety, who is being listened to, followed, complied with, and looked to for rules and guidance about how to navigate a way around the world.

Now think about another scenario. It's thirteen years later, and your, now fifteen-year-old teenager is heading out. You've heard via a couple of other parents that a school friend is having a house party while their parents go out for the evening. When you ask, your teenager reluctantly gives you a few names of who will be at the gathering. Your teenager has a large, heavy-looking sports duffle bag with them. When you ask what's in it, you're told it's

DOI: 10.4324/9780429459245-1

"just stuff," and off out the door they head. You might feel worried out of your mind that the party is going to be awash with drugs, alcohol and hormonal teenagers seeking sex. Do you feel anything like the same compulsion to shout the same loud "STOP" that you yelled thirteen years ago? There's no way that "STOP!" is going to work in this situation as it did when they were dangerously near the road, but your sense of anxiety might be around the same level. So, what do you do?

What does being a reflective parent mean?

The core purpose of this book is to help you become more reflective in your parenting of your teenager. The theories underpinning reflective parenting – mentalizing and attachment – are seen as essential for promoting resilience and security in young people. Teenagers who have been parented in a reflective way are better equipped to navigate their way through life's joys and difficulties. When anxiety is at an all-time high in our society, particularly for young people, never has there been a more important time to help our teenagers learn how to develop the relationships and mental resilience they need to deal with life's uncertainties. When I talk about reflective parenting, I'm referring to the type of parenting that focuses not just on what your teenager is doing – on their observable behaviour – but what is going on in their mind – the inside story of their behaviour. Reflective parents think and speak in a way that refers to states of mind. For example, a reflective parent would say, "I think my son/daughter is feeling anxious about his future and I'm worried that I won't be able to reassure him that it's all going to be okay. I'm not sure why they are in their room so much, but I'm guessing it feels too overwhelming sometimes to face going into school." You will notice that there are references to thoughts and feelings in these two sentences. The parent isn't too sure what is going on with their teenager, but they are interested and curious about them, and they reflect on their own state of mind – distinct and separate from their teenager's. A parent who was less reflective might say, "My son/daughter stays in their room too much and they need to understand that it's important to get out of their room and just go to school. It won't help hiding from the world." The focus here is on what their teenager is doing and not what they are thinking and feeling. The reflective parent can see that their teenager is not coming out of their room for a reason, linked to how they are thinking and feeling. This parent is likely to respond to their teenager's feelings and help them with those first, which opens up the possibility to them changing their behaviour. The parent who is focused solely on the behaviour will try to fix that behaviour, leaving their teenager not feeling understood or unable to manage the feelings that lie underneath.

Reflective parents are equally likely to be in touch with their own thoughts and feelings and to have some understanding of how their own state of mind affects their interactions with others. When you are being a reflective parent, you are mentalizing – simultaneously being aware of what's in your own mind, and putting yourself in your teenager's shoes by being empathic and curious about their mind. None of us can be a reflective parent all of the time, because our emotions rise and fall along with events that happen in our lives and as a result of the support (or lack of) that we get from other people. This book will help all of you to understand how to regain your ability to be reflective and connected to your teenager and also to understand why you sometimes struggle to do this. It is not a book about blaming parents, but about having compassion for yourself and how to develop an understanding of yourself as a parent in order to bring that emotional understanding to your relationship with your teenager. As a result, they will develop greater resilience and security for life. In Chapter 1, we explore reflective parenting in more detail, but first let's look at the theory of mentalizing, and how this important skill can help you in all your relationships.

Understanding mentalizing theory

In the literature on child psychology, it's well established that adolescence is a period of great tension – between a desire for independence and autonomy, and a feeling of still being dependent on parents and other authority figures, when, in fact, peers and social networks are far more appealing to teenagers. It is a time when it's vital to an adolescent's development that they show you they are not the same person as you. They need to do this and at the same time stay connected to you. Understanding this dynamic can help you think about what's going on with your teenager in the above scenario. Throughout this book, an exploration of your relationship with your teenager and how to understand the world from their viewpoint will help you think about how to approach these common adolescent situations.

Much research focuses on the experience of the adolescent, with some taking a mentalizing-based approach – that is, looking at our ability to reflect on the thoughts and feelings of both ourselves and others, discussed later in this introduction and throughout the book. Research published in 2016 by UK psychoanalyst Peter Fonagy and his colleagues looked at the importance of improving a teenager's own ability to mentalize. It demonstrated how the greater a teenager's ability to do this was, the less distress they felt when faced with the demands of adults, and the more emotionally resilient they became.

A type of treatment known as mentalization-based treatment (MBT), originally developed by Peter Fonagy and psychiatrist Anthony Bateman (1) in the treatment of borderline personality disorder, has since been further developed by clinicians and researchers worldwide to help tackle a wide range of mental health difficulties in both adults and children, including in adolescents who self-harm.

However, very little MBT work has focused solely on the experience of parents and carers, who are the people with the most influence over adolescents and so best positioned to develop their mentalizing skills. They are also the source of much of the relationship conflict, as well as emotional intimacy, experienced by adolescents. For those teenagers receiving therapy, strengthening the mentalizing skills of their parents means they are more likely to benefit from the interventions as they feel understood by both their therapist and their parents. It's the availability of *both* minds that helps increase their sense of trust and restores their ability to regulate their emotions more successfully.

How can this book help you?

Caring for a baby, toddler or young child presents enormous challenges, both practically and psychologically, to many carers. For most of us, parenting is an expedition into the unknown with relatively little equipment to get us through. When writing this book, I started to reflect more on the challenges facing parents when their child reaches adolescence, particularly as my own children were growing up.

When I had finished writing my first book, *Reflective Parenting* (2), aimed at parents of young children, I was with a group of friends, all parents, and one of them said, "So when are you going to write a book to help me with my teenagers, Sheila? The first book is a bit too late for me!" At the time, two of my own boys were already in their teens and I had been starting to think about how the whole concept of mentalizing with teenagers is such a different ball game from doing this with young children. For a start, my teenagers didn't seem to be quite so receptive to my curiosity about their minds! I had been doing a lot of reading about adolescent brain development, and felt relatively informed about what was going on for them neurologically, hormonally, and even developmentally, but how could I use this to work out what I needed to do as a parent? That was a different challenge altogether.

This is a book for any parent who is curious about the impact of having a teenager in the family and wants to understand how the practice of mentalizing can help them maintain a connection with their teenager through what often feels like a rollercoaster ride through the adolescent years.

When parents have serious concerns about their teen's mental health, seeking professional help and advice is key; in this case, finding a therapist who uses an MBT approach can help teens feel that their thoughts and feelings matter. Often, though, concerns are less acute and parenting teenagers is about the day-to-day struggles in your relationship with them and worrying about how their lives are going to turn out. When you're worried about how your teen is coping with the demands of life, simply being available – while acknowledging that they will often want to turn to peers first – can help them navigate problems and keep you connected. Taking a mentalizing approach, which will be explored throughout this book, can greatly enhance your connection and can be vital during the adolescent years.

There are no perfect behavioural or emotion-management strategies for parenting teenagers that you can refer to which will quickly fix the problems as you are experiencing them in your relationship. There is some help at hand though. By using a set of "reflective parenting" tools set out in this book, you will learn how to develop both your own self-awareness as a parent of teenagers, and also an increasing awareness of the thoughts and feelings of your teenager. Reflective parenting complements other tried-and-tested parenting methods you may have used throughout your child's life. The beauty of learning this technique is that it will bring about a greater connection between you and your teen, and hopefully even a calmness and enhanced understanding of your relationship. Most of the time, we all tend to wing it. I muddled my way through most situations with our own teenagers, never completely sure if I've got it right or not, and they certainly let me know when I've got it wrong! But sometimes they let me know when I've got it right, when there's a closeness and trust in our relationship. We then find that we have very special times when we've tried mentalizing the situation and ourselves rather than trying to just do something; stepping in without thinking.

Throughout this book, we'll reflect on some common scenarios between parents and teenagers and tune in to your own state of mind during these times. This in turn will help you understand the feelings and intentions behind the behaviour of your teenager that you find challenging, worrying and perplexing.

These two processes, reflecting on yourself and on what you think might be going on inside your teenager's mind, particularly when you feel like you are going out of yours, will help you manage situations you previously felt were beyond your control.

How can this book help your teenager?

In May 2018, there was a story in the news about a 30-year-old man, Michael Rotondo, who was ordered by a judge to move out of his parents' home in Camillus, New York, where he had been living rent-free for nearly a decade. This high-profile story began a discussion about a syndrome referred to as "failure to launch." This syndrome was said to be a phenomenon associated particularly with millennials, who for a range of reasons, including financial, social, and political, struggled to make the separation from their parents' care. In the 2018 book, *Property* (3) – a compilation of short stories by the author, Lionel Shriver, a chapter titled *Domestic Terrorism* – depicts a 32-year-old, Liam, who refuses to leave the care of his parents and live independently. While this is considered a problem for millennials, it also raises interesting new challenges for parents. Fear of too much independence and risk-taking might strike terror into the hearts of most parents of teenagers, but there is a new fear lurking around how much have we enabled, or prevented, our teenage children from developing the independence needed to navigate their way through life's problems without our support? Despite there being very serious practical obstacles facing our older adolescents compared with when we were their age, such as astronomical rents, enormous student loans, frozen pay scales and houses they can't afford, there may be some parental obstacles, too. Your role in helping your teenager become resilient, independent and secure in their adult life is more challenging than ever given the increased stresses they face.

The statistics from the UK NHS research on child and adolescent mental health show that in young people aged 17 to 19 years, the rate of mental health problems rose from 1 in 10 in 2017 to 1 in 4 in 2022 – the biggest challenge to mental health being anxiety and depression. The focus in reflective parenting is on keeping a connection with your teenager and helping them to manage, sometimes overwhelming and unwanted, feelings. This is one of the most important skills for life you can teach your teenager.

Failure to launch

Failure to launch is also about lacking the tools to make the transition from adolescence to adulthood. As parents, it is our job to help our teenagers and young adults navigate their way through life's transitions, helping them pick up some of the tools to do this on the way. In Sweden, there is a term for the type of parents that fail to facilitate this transition. They are called "curling parents" – a reference to the Olympic sport of ice curling. Just like in the icy sport, curling parents smooth the way for their children. They sweep away any obstacles and make life easier. Life is so difficult anyway that they feel it is helpful to try to cushion the blows for their children. Are there any negative consequences though? Aren't these parents just trying to help and support their adolescents in a harsh and expensive world? The signs from Sweden are somewhat more disturbing. Psychiatrist David Eberhard observed, "Young people in Sweden tend to be very disappointed in life, especially in their twenties. While there is a falling rate of suicides, there is a huge rise in suicide attempts, especially among girls aged 15 to 25."

Providing a safe harbour

This push-pull between holding on and letting go is one of the central themes of parenting adolescents. When your child is younger, it's easier to demonstrate your love and be the rescuer, and in adolescence, you've got to be more like the safe harbour rather than the lifeboat; a metaphor I learned from my colleague in this work with risky adolescents, Dickon Bevington. It will help you to think of framing yourselves as the safe harbour, moving out of the lifeboat you were once in with your younger child where you had the role of making it all better. Moreover, it's not helpful to your teenager to stay in that role as it's absolutely vital they learn how to navigate this potentially stormier period of their life.

Reflecting on thoughts and feelings alone is not the type of parenting being advocated here. Boundaries still count, and so does parental authority. There is no one-size-fits-all parenting manual but all parents can use the framework of reflective parenting to help navigate teens through the adolescent years. Parenting during adolescence sees a shift from the early years when you had to constantly make decisions about the right way to raise your child – how to feed, clothe, educate and nurture them, help them socialise and set limits. In this next phase of their development, you might start to ask your teenager how *they* are going to navigate a problem. This book will explore a different method of parenting where, instead of worrying about how *you* are going to come up with all the solutions and suggestions for life's challenges, you are going to support your teenager to come up with their own ideas about how they are going to meet challenges when these arise. By drawing out from your teenager how they are planning to solve difficulties, without pointing out flaws but simply offering another perspective of any potential downsides, you will learn how to mentalize yourself and your teenager in a way that helps them to thrive, gain independence and develop skills for life, while staying connected to you.

What is mentalizing?

Imagine you are walking through the centre of your hometown or city. As you walk down the main road towards the town square, you see a man dressed in shorts and a baseball cap looking at his phone. He looks down at his phone, then walks off in one direction, only to consult his phone again, look up in the direction of an important local landmark in your town, and then look down at his phone again, while starting to walk more purposefully in the direction of the town centre and local landmark. You might conclude from watching this scenario that the man is a visitor to the town and not local. As you see him walk one way, then the other, noticing his face change from somewhat puzzled and confused to confident, you conclude he was lost, has now located where he wants to go and is heading in the right direction.

This whole sequence probably occurred unconsciously in a matter of seconds. So, how did you do this? Are you a mind reader? Well, not exactly, but you are probably pretty good at reading other people from the way they look, behave, and move. This ability, to read other people and attribute thoughts and feelings to them, is known as mentalizing. You do this every day without even thinking as it's a completely normal human response. It's how we make sense of the world and the people in it, and how we get along with others from day to day. Non-mentalizing gets us into arguments, and even worse, on a mass scale, it can lead whole countries into war, and puts us at the opposite end of religious, political, social and sexual views of many different spectrums. If we started to mentalize those with opposing social, political or religious views to our own we might not end up agreeing with their perspective at all, but we would go further towards understanding them, and in doing so, might be able to have a more reasoned conversation with people who don't share our views. We might even end up empathising with the opposite view to our own occasionally. In our daily lives, whether at work or in daily encounters, we may often deal with people who have opposing views. When we're curious and open to getting to know people better, we can often gain insights into how events in their lives influenced their thoughts and actions.

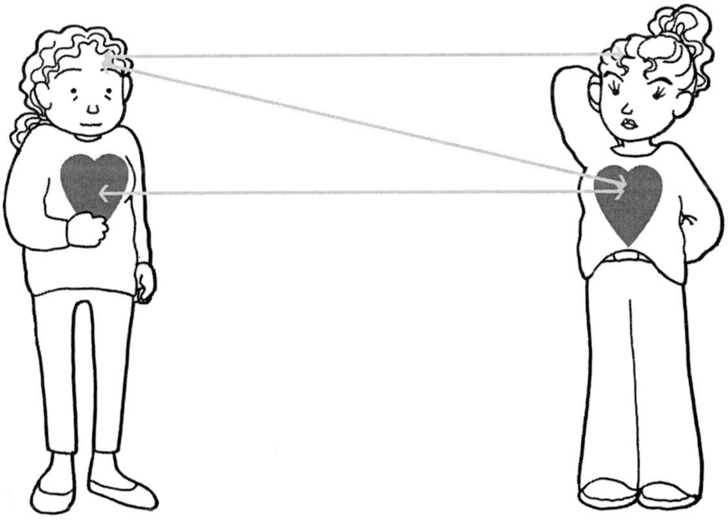

Figure I.1

How does reflecting on ourselves and other people work?

We may have to make difficult decisions in our working lives that may meet opposition. While we might disagree with others, learning to empathise with another's view is crucial. For example, say I'm working with a parent who hates social services because he feels they have taken his child from him, I don't need to agree with his view of social services and their staff, but I do have to empathise with his view and validate his statements at the very least to think about how I might help him. The same applies to teenagers. If we don't start to see things from their perspective, even though we might totally disagree with their views, we won't get very far when we want them to listen to us. The ability to mentalize, for both parents and adolescents, is central to how we communicate with each other and can be considered key to how we navigate a way through even the toughest of times, for both us and them.

So, what happens when we fail to mentalize others? Isn't the scenario about the tourist just obvious? Well, yes, and no. It's true, we all make inferences about other people's behaviour all the time. If your partner walks in the door from work with a loud sigh and dumps his bag heavily on the floor, you might quickly assume that he's had a bad day. But we don't always get it right, and we're not always in the right frame of mind to start wondering about what other people think and feel *at all*. You probably won't be surprised to learn that a sleep-deprived parent, woken for the third time that night by her crying baby, is compromised in her ability to think about what the baby might be thinking or feeling. Equally, the angry parent who has lost his car keys and is late for a presentation he's giving at work to 100 visitors from out of town, isn't in an ideal frame of mind to wonder about what's going on for his teenage son that day. So, our mentalizing capacity fluctuates depending on our emotional states. For example, when we're stressed, this is described as a state of high arousal. In this situation, our mentalizing capacity is reduced. Conversely, when we feel calm, our mentalizing capacity increases. This is an important concept to hold on to and we will look at it more throughout this book, particularly noticing the things that increase or decrease our capacity to mentalize.

Where does this ability to reflect on ourselves and other people come from?

We all learn about our thoughts and feelings from our very early attachment relationships, mainly the one with our main caregiver. When we feel upset, hurt, angry, or hungry, our caregiver (usually, but not always or exclusively our mother) will hopefully respond to us, and in that response tell us a bit about how we are feeling. Let's imagine, you are a small baby and you are feeling cold and uncomfortable because your nappy is wet and your blanket has come off while you were wriggling in your sleep. You cry to let your mum know that you are uncomfortable, because you don't yet have the words to tell her. She comes towards you, sees your face is upset and copies (or mirrors) your upset face saying, "Oooh, what's wrong? Are you sleepy?" She puts the blanket back over you, but this isn't what's mainly on your mind, you are still wet and uncomfortable, so you cry a bit more. She comes back towards you and picks you up saying, "Let me look at your nappy, oh you're wet. That must be uncomfortable. Let me change you and make you comfier and warmer." Her face is now smiling as she changes you on the mat and she soothes you with her voice, saying, "That feels a bit better now, doesn't it?" She snuggles her face into your tummy to give you a comforting kiss, lays you back down in the cot with a soft smile and says quietly, "now, time to go to sleep. I love you." Similarly, when as a baby you feel hurt, hungry, or frightened, you cry to signal to the person who looks after you that you need them to respond. A pattern emerges where your parent turns to you and tries to understand what's causing this suffering and to respond to that. Over time, a baby instinctively feels, "when I don't feel good, I cry, mummy understands that I need help, and she responds to me. When I suffer, I can tell mummy how I feel, and she can help me and make me feel better."

In this everyday exchange with a small infant, there are a lot of different things going on in it, most of which seem automatic. When the mother picks up on the baby's discomfort, she is telling the baby, "I am trying to guess what it is you're feeling"; she puts some words to this which express emotions such as, "uncomfortable" and "wet." These fit with what the baby is feeling, so the baby has a sense her mum can understand her mind, and she gives some words to the emotions she experiences. This gradually helps the baby to build up an understanding of what's going on in their own mind and, at the same time, gives her a message that her mum is able to understand her. This is the foundation of what we call "secure attachment" (see box in this chapter) and it helps with the development of mentalizing. In these types of interactions, babies learn about thoughts and feelings in themselves as well as in their caregivers.

In everyday life, we won't always be able to respond to our baby's needs. Say you have just had a row with your partner, it will be much harder to turn your mind immediately to your baby, and the same applies to your relationship now with your teenager. If these are just occasional moments, but the majority of the time you are responsive, warm and available, your baby – and later your teenager – is safe in the knowledge that they can still rely on you to be available *most* of the time.

If we imagine a different scenario, where the mother says to the baby, "what are you crying for? I've told you to go straight to sleep and not to make so much noise" and instead of mirroring her baby, she scowls at her, or perhaps laughs at her distress. In this scene, the baby becomes confused about their feelings. They had a bad feeling, but it hasn't been mirrored so they can't understand what it means. When this type of interaction happens frequently in a child's life, they grow up confused about thoughts and feelings, in themselves and in other people. It will be much harder, but not impossible, for this person to mentalize when they grow up. We will look at this in more detail in Chapter 9.

Before we learn how to reflect

In our first few years, we are building up the skills that allow us to reflect on our own and others' states of mind and it takes up to six or seven years before we have a more complex understanding of them. How our capacity to mentalize develops depends on the quality of the experiences we are having with our main caregivers. The more secure these attachments, the earlier we will develop this ability to understand the state of mind of other people (4). Prior to this, we are operating in what are called *pre-mentalizing* modes, of which there are several types. When we are babies, we are operating in a pre-mentalizing state referred to as "teleological mode," which means we understand something based on its results. So, in the scenario above, we are too young to understand the full extent of our own thoughts and feelings and what our mum is thinking and feeling; all we know is, "If I cry, she comes and comforts me. I get my nappy changed and a blanket put over me and I feel better."

When we become toddlers, we start to understand mental states (thoughts and feelings in other people and ourselves), but we don't yet understand that what we are thinking and feeling isn't in other people's minds too. You see this when toddlers are covering their eyes with their hands. They think, "Because I can't see you, you can't see me!" This mode is called *psychic equivalence* mode – the reality as I see it *is* the (only) reality.

As we get a bit older, around five years old, we develop a greater ability to play and start to use play symbolically. For example, we might pretend a banana is our phone and the cardboard box is an office desk we are pretending to work at, and this form of pre-mentalizing is called *pretend mode.*

When we reach around six or seven years of age, if the important adults looking after us have been easy for us to understand and they have responded to our needs, we start to be able to integrate these different modes into a way of being that helps us to begin to understand and interpret other people's behaviour – in other words, we start mentalizing. When we have this skill, we can develop relationships more easily, understanding other people and maintaining friendships.

Where a child doesn't have this secure early experience with their caregiver, they are more likely to use these *pre-mentalizing* modes to explain other people's behaviour. Equally, we all revert back to these *ineffective mentalizing* modes at times of high emotional arousal; for example, when someone important to us has let us down, we might be so upset we can only think, "If I message them to say I'm upset, they will have to message back and if they don't, then I know they don't really like me" (teleological mode). Adolescents are much more likely to slip into these ineffective mentalizing modes and your job as their reflective parent is to help them recover their capacity to mentalize – that is, to regain awareness, understanding and control over their emotions.

What happens to reflecting in the teenage years?

In adolescence, we will come to understand throughout this book, how teenagers are more likely to lose their ability to be reflective because of changes in their brain. They frequently return to these pre-mentalizing modes in states of high emotional arousal. For example, you might see your teenager acting like a toddler when they are angry with you for not understanding or agreeing with them, and they slam their door to show you how they feel, unable to put it into words. This is an example of an inability to mentalize and, while it happens to all of us some of the time, it can happen to teenagers a lot. Let's look more at how and why this happens.

Our ability to reflect on the thoughts and feelings of others also fluctuates with age. Mentalizing is a crucial capacity for humans mainly because we are *social* beings. If we didn't understand anything about other people's behaviour, in terms of the type of thoughts and feelings that might be behind it, then it would be impossible to make any sense of their actions. The behaviour of others would appear entirely random, confusing even, and we would be left in a state of misunderstanding. People on the autistic spectrum have great difficulty with this because the structure of their brains means that their capacity to understand and relate to others is compromised, although not non-existent. Chapter 5 on socialisation explores the issues that are particularly relevant to parenting a teenager on the autistic spectrum.

Thinking about your teenager's development – a time of transition

So much is changing in an adolescent's brain and body during this period of development, as discussed in Chapter 1, and it is helpful to mentalize what this is like for teenagers. This is not just a time of physical and neurological change, but also of great vulnerability. It's during this period of development that teenagers are much more likely to engage in risky behaviour and develop a mental illness. Naturally, this is at the root of a great deal of parental anxiety. Sarah-Jayne Blakemore (5), a neuroscientist at University College London, has studied adolescent brain development and its link to risky behaviours and reports on some interesting findings. In one interesting study in Blakemore's book, on mice and alcohol consumption, it was found that adolescent mice will drink more alcohol when they are in the company of other adolescent mice than with their own peers.

The evolutionary explanation for this is that humans and other animals need to develop enough so that they can eventually live independently from their parents. This is of course quite culturally specific, and it is the norm in many cultures for adults to live at home with their family well into adulthood. In addition, today, factors such as the high cost of living can impact the opportunities for living independently even when young adults want to do so. That aside, if an adolescent is going to become independent from their parents, then they need to affiliate with their peer group. During this stage of development, it's of paramount importance to your teenager that they become themselves, that is, they become a relatively autonomous individual who can survive without you and become established in their own social hierarchy.

It's only in the past 20 years that we have understood that the brain changes after childhood into adolescence. Prior to this, professionals in the field had been working on the basis that once the brain is fully formed, we could interpret behaviour based on a combination of genetic and environmental influences. This relatively recent discovery, that the brain continues to change into adolescence and early adulthood, and that this period of heightened plasticity in the brain, has triggered a whole new field of behavioural science regarding adolescence. In Chapter 10, we will think about the struggles of adolescence that continue well into the early twenties. These struggles clearly don't suddenly end when your teenager reaches eighteen. We used to think that our capacity to think about the thoughts, feelings, intentions, and desires of ourselves and other people stopped developing in childhood and was fully formed by around age 7. We now know that this capacity to mentalize goes through further changes, with peaks and troughs during the pre-adolescent years and into early adulthood. While we are still studying adolescent brain development and learning about the changes that occur during this period, it's important to bear in mind, that the changes that take place during the teenage years are very much influenced by our environment and experiences and not just by changes taking place in the brain. We will look in more detail at brain changes in adolescence in Chapter 1.

Family life

Family life is one of the places where mentalizing is the hardest. Peter Fonagy and Liz Allison (6) said "there is no context more likely to induce a loss of mentalizing than family interactions. It is within the family that relationships tend to be at their most fraught, their most loving and their most intense emotionally; in other words, the family is an environment with the potential to stimulate a loss of mentalizing in one or more members of the family, on a daily basis." This is because when there are multiple minds in one place, and when the intimacy of relationships in the family produces strong emotions, there is more likelihood of a raised emotional temperature in which people feel misunderstood, misunderstand others and get into conflict. Combined with the difficulties that adolescents have while their brain develops in mentalizing other people's perspectives as well as understanding themselves fully during this period of development, it's clear that this is a uniquely complex stage of the parent-child relationship.

Mentalizing your adolescent and staying connected involves some or all of the following:

- Always stay in touch. Staying connected to your teenager is very important and recognising their need for independence doesn't mean they can't stay connected to you.
- Be available to your teenager at the time they need you. This won't work by setting a time that suits you for a catchup, so be prepared for some very late-night chats. Be there if needed, in the background – "I'll be in the room at the back if you want me."
- Be aware that your teenager is sensitive and vulnerable to criticism (despite an often tough exterior), especially anything that feels critical of their identity or appearance. Avoid comments like, "you'd look better with your hair off your face." Instead, affirm something you know is important to your teenager, e.g. "those jeans look really great on you."
- Don't take insults or rejections personally. This isn't about you, it's about them. Learn to suck it up and mentalize yourself through it.
- Prioritise focusing on your teenager's relationships and on being relational, rather than behaviour-focused. Make any time you can, even just five minutes in the car on the way out, to connect with your teenager every day. They need this connection more than they can show you.
- Check-in on your teenager and don't leave your teenager alone for long periods, thinking they are ok is not a good idea. Make sure you say hello and goodbye when they come and go.

- Establish a connection after a separation or rupture. Focus your attention on reconnecting and free yourself from distractions (get off your phone!).
- Allow your teenager to be dependent at times. This is not encouraging dependency, rather it's allowing their natural dependency a place to express itself and for you to give the warmth, security and comfort that is needed at any age.

How the book is organised

Each chapter includes an example or two of parents and teenagers and models a mentalizing stance in thinking about each of their perspectives on the same scenario. The scenarios are followed by a series of questions, designed to prompt you to reflect first on yourself and then on the teenager in the scenario. By learning to adopt this mentalizing approach, you will start to think and feel a little differently about yourself and your teenager. This will not only help you regulate your emotions (which may be very strong) more successfully, but will also bring about a greater feeling of being understood in your teenager, who as a result will feel more closely connected to you. Through this greater connection, you will be able to support your teenager in their life choices and through the inevitable difficulties during this period of their lives.

Throughout, the voices of teenagers are included, both as recipients of their parent's attempts to understand them, and the voices of teenagers speaking about the issues they face and how they want a parent to be, and not to be. Through focus groups and consultation, the adolescents in this book add their own voices to the argument for being a mentalizing, reflective parent and help the reader understand that the need for a secure, reflective relationship in which they feel understood and validated is just as important in adolescence as earlier on in childhood. It just needs to be done in a slightly different way.

1

REFLECTIVE PARENTING DURING ADOLESCENCE

Understanding and nurturing connection

"You're not me"

A group of parents are sitting around the table in my house, talking about the things that concern them about their teenage children. I have invited them to be part of a focus group to help me understand the current parental concerns about teenagers – this is outside of my clinical work. Stories are shared; some have us in stitches, and other ones leave us feeling unsettled, upset, and without any real answers. There seems to be a strong need to share, to say "It isn't just my teenager who does this, is it?" and, "Am I the only one who has gone for 24 hours with barely a conversation with my son/daughter that wasn't about 'what's for dinner?'" Also, "Are they going to be OK if I let them do that?"

Two things strike me most at the end of this evening. One is that people want to go on talking and sharing. The other is that although we've all spent a long time talking about our teenagers, very little time has been spent talking about ourselves and how they make *us* feel, or what specific things *we* do that make our teenage sons and daughters appear so worrying or difficult to us at times. No one says anything like, "For me, I worry so much about drugs and alcohol because my dad used to drink too much." There is no self-reflection. There seems to be an unspoken feeling left in the air after the meeting is over; a sense of disquiet that we aren't perhaps as connected with our teenagers as we might like to think we are. There are so many worries left hanging about things that can potentially go wrong. The biggest worry is about our teenager's mental health; what if they are just extremely unhappy and we don't know how to make them

 DOI: 10.4324/9780429459245-2

happier? I held many more groups like this one with other parents, which all had a similar focus.

This chapter looks at why mentalizing is so important when you are parenting your teenager, and how taking a reflective parenting stance (discussed later in this chapter) can help you to feel a closer connection and greater understanding of what your teenager needs. Before I go through the model of reflective parenting – which runs throughout the rest of the book – first, it is important to explore why mentalizing is so helpful when we think about adolescent development, both for helping us navigate the risk-taking behaviour of teenagers that's so familiar to us, as well as provide the opportunity to build their resilience, which is less commonly understood as a concern.

What's happening in your teenager's brain?

Being aware first of the important neurological changes that are taking place in your teenager's brain can be incredibly helpful as this can help you to understand your teen and their behaviour and in turn, figure out your response.

There are three basic biobehavioural systems that enable humans to adapt to our complex social environment: First, there is the reward system that is involved in producing rewarding experiences associated with relationships (including parent-infant and infant-parent and romantic attachment relationships) and also rewarding experiences associated with experiences of autonomy and a sense of being in control of our actions; second, there is a mentalizing, or "social cognition," system. This is human-specific and lies behind our capacity to understand ourselves and others in terms of our feelings, wishes, desires and values, referred to as "intentional mental states." In their 2018 work, Peter Fonagy and Patrick Luyten (1) discuss how our uniquely human mentalizing system is essential to our understanding of a complex interpersonal world. Third, the stress/threat system – this helps us to deal with distress following a threat.

During adolescence, these three biobehavioural systems are being reorganised in the brain and, put very simply, this reorganisation of the systems leads to patterns of thinking, behaviour and responses to others, including parents, which may be difficult to understand, seem illogical, highly reactive or self-destructive. I would encourage you to try to reframe your understanding of these behaviours and emotional responses as adaptive instead of disruptive. The major developmental changes that take place in adolescence are significantly related to the structural and functional reorganisation of these reward, mentalizing and stress systems. Take, for example, an adolescent's typical lack of communication with parents or other authority figures. From our adult–parent perspective, we see this as rude, arrogant and/or self-centred. From an adolescent's perspective, if they feel under excessive stress in a relationship, the reward system, explained below, is affected and their capacity to relate becomes impaired (Figure 1.1).

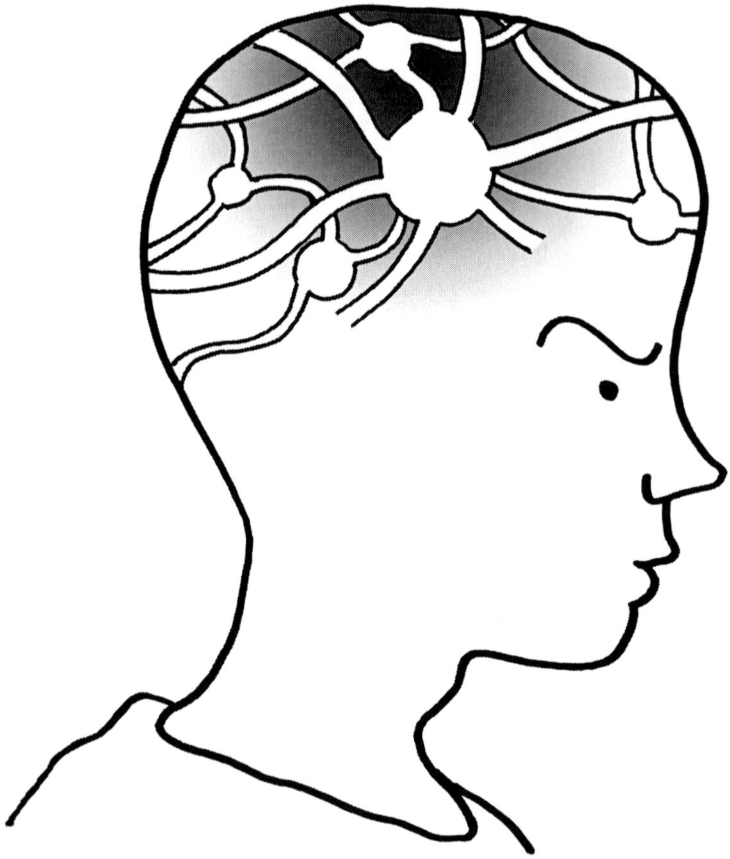

Figure 1.1

Understanding the reward system in the brain

The reorganisation of the reward system in the adolescent brain and how this affects behaviour is still relatively poorly understood. Dopamine – a type of neurotransmitter, or chemical messenger, that the body makes and the nervous system uses to send messages between nerve cells – plays a key role in how we feel pleasure. It's a big part of our unique human ability to think and plan. It helps us strive, focus, and find things interesting. We do know that in adolescence the lowest levels of dopamine are found in striatal regions of the brain and the highest levels of dopamine are found in the prefrontal regions of the brain.

The changes in the adolescent brain result in what the psychologist Linda Spear described as a "mini-reward deficiency syndrome". What this looks like in adolescents is something that may be very familiar to you: a teenager who is easily bored, coupled with frustration at their strong need for belonging among peers and a sense of achievement. The status associated with these often gives rise to intense feelings of rejection and failure, leading to subsequent frustration and aggression. Such feelings can lead the adolescent to engage in compensatory behaviours such as risk-taking, substance abuse and oppositional behaviour.

Brain development and parenting

What is the relevance of understanding brain development to your relationship with your teenager and the model of reflective parenting? How does this basic understanding of what's going on in your teenager's brain help with your understanding of them and how you might parent them differently? I am talking to my 15-year-old son about what plans he's made for his exam revision in Year 10 and he appears not to be listening to me. I ask, "have you got a revision plan? You don't sound very organised." He fiddles with his hair and gives me a blank look so I repeat the question, re-working it to ask, "Are they on your mind? Are you worrying?" He replies, "I was just thinking about my hair." It's hard to understand as a parent that this statement isn't a reflection of how my son feels about his exams but more a reflection of where his focus lay in that conversation. The neuro-developmental changes that are behind his distraction include changes in the rate at which the amygdala and prefrontal cortex develop. The prefrontal cortex is the regulator of impulsive and emotional actions (made by the amygdala) and in later life helps us to make thoughtful decisions. In adolescence, the amygdala grows at a faster rate than the prefrontal cortex and can often lead to rash and impulsive decisions being made. In the case of the teenager thinking about his hair, the amygdala is activated so he is only thinking about his immediate feelings and not the longer-term, more logical issue of his exams.

To avoid overreacting in a way that provokes conflict, which creates distance and can lead the teenager to reject the parent's input, this is a great opportunity to mentalize yourself as a parent and consider your own thought processes during this exchange and consider how you tackled the question of exam revision. What do you think about how you tackled the question of exam revision? What were your own thought processes during this exchange? When you start to do this, you manage your emotional response better and this makes it less likely that a situation between you and your teenager will escalate.

Our expectations of teenagers

The rapid speed with which the brain changes in adolescence can help you understand why your teenager doesn't always respond to you as you would like. We place a lot of expectations on teenagers to make adult decisions because of changes taking place in their bodies as well as their age, when they haven't reached that point of maturation and their brain is still developing. It would help if we in fact revised our expectations and instead helped them to make decisions in their lives. We often seem to act on the understanding that what teenagers want is to be left alone, because the bedroom door is shut, the earphones are plugged in, etc. Leave them in their room, they'll be alright. The evidence points to the opposite and your teenager's need to know you are available is crucial. Despite appearances, they do need our help to make decisions and therefore mentalizing their perspective – and our own as their parents – can help you to support your teenager effectively.

Mentalizing in adolescence

As humans, we need to mentalize to be able to communicate effectively within complex social systems and collaborate with others. The degree to which we're able to mentalize can also give rise to self-consciousness and enable our imagination. However, although this might sound helpful, hyper-mentalizing (where we over-attribute extreme states of mind to others) can increase our risk of suffering mental health problems. For example, if self-conscious emotions such as embarrassment, shame and guilt become excessive, this can interfere with our ability to cope with everyday stressors. By the same token, imagination, which we think of as a positive characteristic, may cause adolescents to become negatively aware of the difference between how they would like to be ideally and who they are, and can lead to unhelpful comparisons with others who seem to have an "ideal life."

As with the stress and reward systems, the mentalizing neural system undergoes a significant reorganisation in adolescence, as mentioned in the introduction, which means that the mentalizing skills of adolescents are therefore temporarily disrupted. Though not conclusive, various theories suggest that there is a "dip" in social cognition – how we process information in social contexts – (2) that can affect how accurately teenagers are able to mentalize (3). While further work is needed, the rapid brain changes in adolescence that affect how teenagers relate to others and their desire for autonomy and achievement can mean that mentalizing is challenging during these years. This is particularly true for young people who experienced adversity in early childhood, some of whom may have grown up in environments that lacked a secure emotional attachment to a parent or caregiver.

The challenges of being a teenager

Being an adolescent is not easy. If you cast your mind back to when you were a teenager, you will probably remember that it wasn't all fun. If we look back through the records of young people being referred to social services, these suggest that it's harder than ever to be an adolescent today.

This period of development presents such a challenge to young people because they are trying to establish themselves as independent and autonomous with their own individual identity, separate from their parents. The feelings that arise when dealing with relationships can leave young people feeling overwhelmed or hopeless. The complexities of relationships are difficult for adolescents to deal with because of their reduced ability to mentalize at this age. This can increase any existing feelings of self-hatred as relationships fill them with a fear of being rejected, not liked, or not as good or attractive as other people. On top of this, a tendency to overthink the reasons behind others' actions can lead to further feelings of inadequacy, self-doubt and self-hatred. When these feelings become too intolerable and overwhelming, instead of keeping them in, which feels unbearable, they often respond with impulsive, acting-out behaviour. For some this might include self-harm or avoidant behaviour, such as missing school, avoiding starting new close relationships after important ones end, and staying in their rooms for long periods.

Why it helps teenagers to mentalize

The aim of helping teenagers practice mentalizing is to restore their ability to understand what's going on in other people's minds and appreciate different perspectives, as well as understand what's going on in their own minds. Once this balance is achieved, the teenager's ability to mentalize – to think about their own and others' thoughts, feelings and intentions – is enhanced. Increasing the capacity to mentalize helps reduce the level of conflict in families and other close relationships. This theory is backed up by evidence that shows that the capacity to mentalize protects our ability to function socially and emotionally.

A 2006 study by Hauser (4) followed 150 young people admitted to a mental health unit. This found that at the follow-up 10 years later, a surprising number of these young people were functioning extremely well and the common protective factors they all shared were:

1. an ability to reflect on their thoughts, feelings and motivations.
2. a sense of their own identity and a feeling of responsibility for their own actions
3. an ability to reflect on the minds of others.

These were characteristics that were thought to be present in the adolescents prior to them suffering a mental health problem and were seen as significant to their recovery and later resilience. The research tells us something very important about these qualities – all indicative of mentalizing – in our parenting of our teenagers.

Figure 1.2

The aim of helping teenagers practise mentalizing is to restore their ability to understand what's going on in other people's minds and appreciate different perspectives, as well as understand what's going on in their own minds.

The following common adolescent scenario shows how easy it is for teenagers to experience lapses in their ability to self-reflect or think about others when they're in a state of heightened anxiety (Figure 1.2).

Stepping into the shoes of an adolescent

David is a 17-year-old in year 13 at school. His racial identity is black British and his family are working class and describe themselves as a close family.

David has heard from a mate in his class that a friend of his is having a party on Saturday. He goes on social media to message the host of the party to see if it's cool for him to come to the party with his friend. He doesn't get a response for a while, so he messages other people who are going to the party to find out what they are wearing as he's worried about standing out. He gets a response confirming the location of the party and invites his friend over to his house, who is closer to the host, so he's got someone to go with, and they start drinking at David's house before the party. To distract himself from the nerves of going to the party, he drinks more than he usually does, which is more than he can handle.

When David and his mate arrive at the party, he scans the room and realises that he doesn't know as many people as he thought he might. He latches on to the only people in the room he knows and starts to feel self-conscious. He thinks, "No one knows who I am. People are thinking, 'Why is this guy here? Who does he know?'" David starts to feel anxious. He checks the time to see how long he's been at the party and notices time is going slowly. He realises that his shirt is creased and pulls it down to make it less creased, becoming increasingly agitated.

He pretends he needs the toilet and checks his hair in the mirror. He wishes he'd had it cut. Going back into the room, he finds one of his friends on the sofa so he sits down next to him and gets his phone out. On his phone, trying to look busy, but aimlessly flicking, he looks up and sees everyone else chatting, drinking, dancing and smiling. He starts to feel his hands getting sweaty and "knows" that everyone is looking at him. He feels panicky and has a strong urge to leave the party. He calls a minicab and goes home.

When he gets home, he feels the panic building even more as he gets a load of social media messages from his friend asking where he's gone. He makes an excuse, saying he felt sick, then turns his phone off. However, he finds his breathing is getting faster, his hands are sweatier and he's in his own head and he feels trapped by the anxious thoughts circling in his head. He lies on his bed feeling confused and convinced that other people can see his unease and will think it's a sign of weakness.

What is going on with David?

Now, let's practice mentalizing David.

1 David doubts his attractiveness when he sees other friends talking to girls. He thinks about what others think of him; for example, "What's this guy doing here? I would never talk to him, he's not my type."
2 He overthinks what other people are thinking about him and his own place in the room.
3 By drinking to manage his nerves, he moves from a state of anxiety to feeling low and close to depressed as the sedative effects of alcohol take hold.
4 He doesn't want any involvement from his parents but needs a good friend he can trust to distract himself from the stress, anxiety and overthinking. A friend could calm him down.

This scenario and our attempts to mentalize it raise one of the crucial differences between mentalizing an adolescent and mentalizing a younger child. When we think about the mental states of younger children, we can act like detectives, looking for clues behind the behaviour; actively tuning in to the possible thoughts and feelings behind the behaviour. Working with parents of adolescents and being a parent of three teenagers myself, I am extremely conscious of the fact that this curiosity is often most unwelcome and intrusive and the last thing a teenager wants is to feel that their parent is searching for clues and telling them they know how to solve their problems. As adolescents are keen for a sense of autonomy, they need to feel that they don't *have* to depend on anyone else to solve their problems, but rather that they can experience a sense of control themselves. It's important therefore to understand this position when mentalizing your teenager.

What could David's parents do?

Let's try to mentalize David's parents. When David's parents notice he's back early from the party and seems out of sorts, they could try to help him feel close. Depending on their parenting styles, they might feel immediately worried about David and leap to conclusions about his anxiety, worrying it is part of a much bigger problem. Equally, they might not see what's behind David's withdrawal and tend to leave him alone in his room, assuming he'll be fine. David's parents should avoid probing into the situation that has caused him so much anxiety as this will only make it worse. The opportunity to talk about the situation will come if David's parents just make themselves available, listen, and then wait for David to talk if he wants to. Most importantly, they should make themselves available without intruding. It might feel tempting for his parents to give him lots of advice about how to handle social situations, but they need to understand his perspective and what it felt like being in a room full of friends when he felt so self-conscious and self-critical.

David's parents could tentatively ask:
Were you in the mood to go to that party?
Was it difficult not knowing many people there?
Did you contact a mate when you felt bad?

Stepping back

In mentalization-based therapy for adolescents (MBT-A), the aim is to increase the young person's awareness of the minds of others and for them to become more mindful of themselves and self-aware. In doing this, adolescents become less impulsive, take fewer risks, and are more balanced in their thoughts and feelings about themselves and others. In the scenario above, we might imagine that if David was able to manage some of his doubts about his place at the party (which might be triggered by a number of factors, such as his past experience of relationships or lack of them, his racial identity in the group, and his self-focus on his appearance) he would, in turn, be able to lower his anxiety levels. Your role as a parent is vital in helping teenagers learn how to mentalize, and you can model and teach this by becoming a more mentalizing parent yourself.

While the "intrusive" curiosity used to mentalize young children might need to be kept on the back burner, it's extremely important for your adolescent to feel understood. Taking your teenager's perspective – stepping into their shoes and imagining just what something is like for *them* – is probably more important at this stage of development than at any other time. Part of feeling understood might involve you having to step back, as adolescents frequently don't want parents to get involved in sorting out their problems.

I'm not you. You're not me

Mentalizing is all about appreciating that people's thoughts and feelings are separate and distinct. Nowhere is this more relevant than when thinking about parenting during adolescence, when separation from parents and a sense of autonomy and distinction from others is extremely important to a teenager's development. In this regard, taking the mentalizing stance of a reflective parent can be extremely useful to you and your teenager. This type of parenting will help you to understand and connect with what's going on inside your adolescent's mind. This, in turn, allows them to feel a sense of independence and distinction from you because they feel increasingly understood by you. Reflective parenting also helps you to reflect on, and understand better, what's going on in your own mind when your children reach this age. Mentalizing yourself helps you to regulate (or manage) your own feelings, which is crucial if you want to avoid escalating negative cycles of conflict between you and your teenager.

One message that adolescents communicate both consciously and unconsciously to parents is, "You're not me." The child that once didn't want to leave your side and clung on to you as you dropped them at the school reception class, is now the young person who asks you why you need to know where they're going. One parent at my focus group with local parents recalled walking into the kitchen where her adolescent daughter was just hanging out, to be greeted with the question, "Why are you here?" Was this an existential question or an irritated response to sighting a parent in an adolescent's space? It was hard for her parent to know what was a fitting response, so she backed away.

While it may not always feel this way during adolescence, your importance in their life, as the secure base from which they can explore the world, is as vital as ever; there are just different ways you need to go about keeping this sense of security in their minds. A younger child needs to know that their parent is always holding them in mind, but adolescents can find this extremely intrusive. As a parent of a teenager, what's most helpful is to think about the thoughts, feelings and intentions behind their behaviour. As part of this mentalizing approach, it is vital to your teenager's development that you recognise and fully validate their need *not* to be you, even at times when you recognise parts of yourself in their behaviour – for example, when you were an adolescent.

When we think back to our own teenage years, it's likely we can recall times when we felt bored and restless. Tuning in to some of the feelings we had as adolescents is an important part of the self-reflection – or self-mentalizing – that we need when thinking about our teenagers. Some of these memories are also a useful aid for empathising with your teenagers and putting yourself into their shoes. Conversely, other, more difficult, memories might make it harder to disentangle your own experience from those of your teenager.

Security

Adolescence is classically known as a period of storm and stress during which young people strive to be individuals, separate from their parents and relationships outside of the immediate family become of paramount importance. These relationships and the meaning teenagers attach to them seem absolutely vital to their survival and ground them in who they want to identify as; however, parents are still needed just as much as when they were toddlers, ensuring comfort and protection, and at the same time promoting exploration. During adolescence, we just don't want to recognise this and, importantly, it is much harder for the adolescent brain to acknowledge the thoughts, feelings and perspectives of other people. This goes back to the differences between adult and adolescent brains. Adults think with the prefrontal cortex, the brain's rational part. This is the part of the brain that responds to situations with good judgment and an awareness of long-term consequences. Teenagers process information with the amygdala. This is the emotional part. This leads teenagers to be preoccupied with their own emotions – particularly when they have an overwhelming emotion – and less able to tune into other people.

For you as a parent, providing a secure base takes on a different form when your children are older. It might feel at times as if you are the only one who wants this attachment, but it is as essential to your adolescent's sense of security as it was when they were little. A healthy attachment with your child during adolescence comes about when both you and your teenager manage to redefine your relationship by taking into consideration the social, cognitive and emotional changes taking place at this time that mean teenagers need to assert themselves as individuals. In Chapter 2, we will look at attachment theory in more detail, particularly how it underpins many aspects of our parenting. Suffice it to say here, attachment underpins the development of our understanding of our own mind and other people's – underpinning mentalizing.

Threats to security

Tensions in adolescence arise frequently when a young person develops their independence and individual, separate, identity. Your teenager is making a clear statement that they are separate from you and need you less. If this process isn't understood by the parent, this is a threat to the closeness of the relationship between a teenager and their parent. Another threat emerges when parents identify so much with their own adolescence and have failed to move on developmentally from this so that they can't sufficiently parent. The parent may jeopardise their child's development and fail to protect them properly. The real adolescent in the family does not want or need an adolescent parent who can't take on the adult authority role. For example, where a parent's own emotional needs aren't being met, either through their current circumstance or from their early childhood experiences, or both, they may fill this void through excessive use of alcohol or drugs. As they focus on their own needs, they're unable to provide an appropriate level of responsibility for their child.

Parents who think of themselves as their adolescent's best friend can also pose a threat. Is this what adolescents need from their parents? Being on their side, showing you understand and take on board their perspective is important, but being a best friend implies being on the same level as them and being like them. It can be hard for some parents to take on a more authoritative, adult role. This is particularly evident where parents still need some of their own adolescent needs to be met. This could look like a parent who is quite focused on gratifying their own need for excitement, attention or entertainment, or one who wants to ally themselves with their adolescent by pursuing adolescent activities with them. The chief problem with this behaviour is that not only does it prohibit the adolescent from being able to separate out from their parent, which is essential to their development, but it also severely compromises the parent's capacity to offer protection and proper caregiving to the real adolescent in the family. In the most serious scenarios, a parent whose own adolescent development was thwarted can potentially neglect their own child and actually put them at risk.

Reflecting on parenting teenagers

Asking ourselves questions about our own parenting can help us examine our own approaches. Do you feel comfortable with being part of an older generation who doesn't always "get it"? How do you feel when your teenager doesn't want to share all the details of their life with you? How we approach this stage of parenting and understand our own emotional responses to having teenagers is such an important part of parenting adolescents. Without this self-reflection or self-mentalizing, the risk is that we can either become too distant from our adolescents or get so close that we become intrusive and stifle their need for autonomy and independence. Learning to mentalize can help us strike this tricky balance. It's a tricky balance to strike, but one that learning to mentalize can really help with. The following chapter (Chapter 2) looks at how to start mentalizing yourself – to reflect on your own thoughts and feelings – as a parent of an adolescent.

What does being a reflective parent mean?

Being a reflective parent means being able to mentalize yourself and your teenager – that is, think about your own and your teenager's thoughts and feelings. Not necessarily at the same time, but certainly as distinct and separate minds and people. If we're doing this reasonably well, then we would expect to be mentalizing around 30% of the time. After all, it would be a bit strange to be constantly reflecting, we'd never get anything done! This balance between action and reflection is important and necessary as the job of being a parent is about *doing* as well as reflecting. It can also be difficult to mentalize accurately at times. This can mean that you might feel confused about when your teenager wants to be close to you. You might feel confused about when they want to be close to you or more independent and distant from you, and it's easy to get this wrong. In other words, the change from a young child who needed you to reassure them to an adolescent who, even when they could benefit from your help and actually needs you, fights against this need and fails to express it, presents a real challenge to your parenting during this stage of your child's development.

The tools and techniques for reflective parenting

Employing the set of practical techniques, or tools, set out below, can help you to make sense of the ideas around reflective parenting and learn how to mentalize both yourself and your adolescent.

As well as helping you mentalize in everyday scenarios, these tools can also help you recover your ability to mentalize after the most stressful times, when your capacity to mentalize can be hampered/reduced after the most stressful times with your teenager. In the following chapters, everyday scenarios will highlight how you might use the tools below to maintain your connection with your teenager and support their mental health.

Make use of the following tools to help you practice reflective parenting and navigate your way through your teenagers' lives:

- **The emotional thermometer** (Figure 1.3)

Emotional arousal is a way of thinking about the level of our current thoughts and feelings. It is also a way of describing how strong our feelings are. The "emotional thermometer" is a way of being aware of your "temperature," or emotional arousal level, at any given moment. Thinking about your emotional thermometer is part of self-mentalizing and can be used alongside a tool like the Parent MAP (described below).

It's normal for our emotional temperature to ebb and flow throughout the day. There will be times when we are in just the

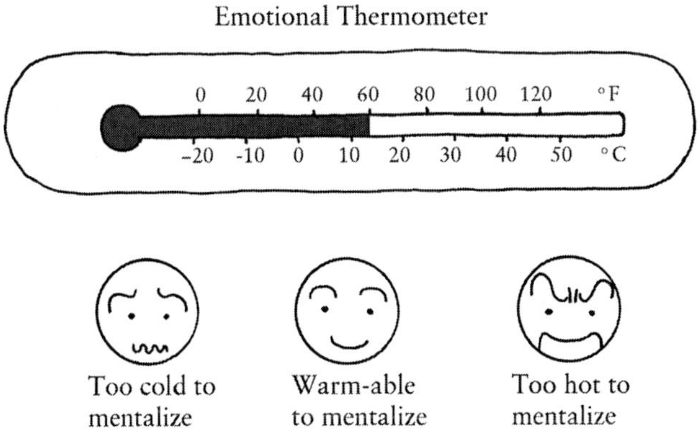

Figure 1.3

right range – when our emotional temperature is warm – to be able to reflect on our own thoughts and feelings and on our teenager's, but this will only be possible about 30% of the time. The emotional thermometer helps us to be aware of our ability to mentalize and in a particular moment what might be influencing us: are we too cold or too hot, and what do we mean by that? Perhaps we were distracted or tired, or something's going on that means we're just not able to bring enough attention to our teenagers. Or we might be a bit switched off and that means that we're too cold to think clearly about how our teenager is feeling. At other times, perhaps we just had a blazing argument with someone or a case of road rage and that's put us in a place where we're too upset or too emotionally aroused – too hot – to mentalize. Good mentalizing – reflecting on our own and our teenager's mind – will happen when we're in that warm spot in the middle. At the extreme temperatures – when we are too hot or too cold – this is not a good time to act or try to intervene with your teenager. At these times it will be hard to understand your teenager's feelings and you might say or do something that makes things worse, causing your teenager to shut down, or explode at you.

Checking in with your emotional thermometer can help you find the right time to speak to or respond to your teenager. So, for example, when you notice that your temperature is either too hot or too cold, you can take a step back until you can regulate your emotions, then return to a conversation or situation. When you learn to manage your emotional arousal in this way and get into the "warm" range you are more likely to understand your teenager's thoughts and feelings, along with your own. You can also apply this thermometer to your teenager to assess whether they are too hot or too cold and therefore unlikely to engage constructively with you; or suggest they might use it to help them recognise when it's a good time to talk something through and when it's best to wait.

- **Mentalizing Adolescent Parenting: the Parent MAP** (Figure 1.4)

This tool is a way of reflecting on yourself – how you currently parent and how you want to parent your teenager. Building your understanding of parenting is a work in progress. As well as the influence of past experiences and your family history and social identity, your current circumstances and state of mind also influence your parenting at any given moment. All of these factors go into making you the person and parent you currently are.

Figure 1.4

Research has found that it's just as important to reflect on yourself as a parent as it is to reflect on your child in terms of the impact this has on the quality of your relationship and their consequent behaviour. A series of studies in 2012 and 2017 carried out by Suchman et al (5,6,7), found that where mothers were able to "self-mentalize," the quality of their interactions with their children during play was significantly better than that of mothers who were better at just mentalizing their child. This evidence strongly points to the importance of reflecting on your own mind as a parent as an influence on the quality of your relationship with your teenager. Throughout the book, you will learn to mentalize your own thoughts and feelings as you reflect on your response to certain scenarios and where these responses come from.

- **Learning to reflect on your teenager: using the Parent APP**

Three qualities are key to mentalizing your teenager, which can be encapsulated in a handy acronym, the parent APP, which stands for:

A – Attention and curiosity
P – Perspective Taking
P – Providing empathy and validation

These three qualities are the main principles involved in taking a reflective parenting mentalizing stance towards your teenager. The first principle is about taking a step back, looking at what your teenager is doing and being curious about them both implicitly and explicitly by voicing curiosity, rather than telling them what you think they are thinking and feeling. Without taking this attentive and curious stance, you can be perceived as thinking you know your adolescent better than they know themselves, which is extremely annoying for your teenager.

The second important element to mentalizing your teenager is the ability to listen and try to understand their perspective without imposing your own (until it's needed and you are clear it will be well received).

Finally, it's very important to empathise with and validate your teenagers' thoughts, feelings, and experiences. Empathy has a more emotional quality; it is a *felt* expression of your understanding and compassion for someone else's experiences. It also has the power to deepen a feeling in someone else and/or make that feeling bigger, so it's important to gauge when empathy is helpful and when it might lead to feelings becoming too overwhelming. Try not to say "At least" at the beginning of an attempted empathic statement; for example, responding to, "I feel really upset I got a B in my English A level" with, "Well at least you passed it." A more empathic response would be, "I'm sorry you didn't get the grade you wanted and deserved. You worked so hard for it."

Parents often worry that empathising is somehow letting their teenager off the hook. A sentiment might be, "I need to tell him he should have studied harder and not spent so much time with his girlfriend." Will this motivate an adolescent to study harder and get better grades next time? Or will it instil a sense of shame and of not being good enough? Empathy, no matter what age your child is, is a powerful communication tool, "I can see what you're going through and I feel bad for you. I believe in you, and I want you to feel good about yourself and your work. I trust you, and you can trust me to get it."

Validation is a more cognitive process and can have the impact of regulating more difficult-to-manage feelings. For example, imagine your teenager expressing her outrage at the fact she was left out of a group chat. Validating this feeling as something she has a right to feel has the impact of both reassuring her that you understand and also helping her to control a potentially spiralling and overwhelming feeling.

- **The two-hands approach – helping your teenager develop a sense of agency**

When applying reflective parenting to younger children, a technique called the "two-hands approach" is used. The idea is that one hand mentalizes the child's behaviour – that is, works out the intention, thoughts and feelings behind it; while the other hand sets out a consequence, or action, from an authoritative perspective that is clear to the younger child.

The principle behind this tool is that children need to both feel understood in their behaviour and also feel contained in the boundary and rule setting that parents bring to the relationship.

In adolescence, this model is applied slightly differently. The reflecting, or mentalizing, "hand" is still just as important. The other hand is more concerned with modelling and setting out a pathway from adolescence to adulthood. It serves the same purpose of containing the young person as the model did with the younger child, but the boundary setting is designed to help the adolescent make informed choices and develop a sense of agency – that is, a sense of control, as opposed to simply following a set of rules or guidelines set out by the parent.

What does reflective parenting look like?

Reflective parenting is about being aware of your own mind while noticing and showing your teenager that their thoughts and feelings are different and separate, but of great interest to you. The parent MAP and parent APP tools help you to do both these things simultaneously and these two things help you and your teenager to feel connected and your teenager feels understood and supported by you. Let's look at the difference between taking a reflective, mentalizing approach to a conversation with your teenager, and a non-reflective, non-mentalizing one. Scarlett, aged 14, has just found out she was left out of a group chat about a shopping trip on the weekend. She saw some pictures of the group of friends on someone's story, including her best friend, Holly, after the friend had told her she couldn't meet up with Scarlett that weekend because of a "family event." Her mum finds her lying on her bed, holding her phone, crying.

Non-reflective parenting	*Reflective parenting*
Scarlett, why are you crying?	Oh Scarlett, something upsetting has happened
They did what? Well, get rid of them, I never did trust that girl, Holly. She's mean.	I'm not surprised you're so upset. That's hurtful.
You don't want to be friends with girls like that. You can't trust them.	Holly meant a lot to you. I'm so sorry.
Why did they behave like that? Did you do anything to put them off?	It's hard to understand why they would do that. You were stuck at home while they were out, that's so hard.
Stop crying now. They're not worth it. You're better than them.	You wanted to be part of the group so much. I wonder if there was something else going on for Holly? She's been a good friend in the past.

Some of the main differences between Scarlett's mum when she is being a reflective parent, compared with a non-reflective one include:

- Instead of giving commands (non-reflective), she describes how Scarlett is feeling.
- Instead of putting her own opinion across (non-reflective), she empathises with Scarlett's feelings and perspective (she uses her parent MAP to mentalize herself and manage her own feelings, and the APP to mentalize Scarlett).

- Instead of asking "why" questions (non-reflective), she validates Scarlett's feelings and acknowledges her struggle to understand "why" her friends behaved how they did.
- Instead of trying to shut down Scarlett's feelings (non-reflective), after empathising with her feelings, she tentatively wonders if there is a different perspective to the way Scarlett sees it currently (reflective).

What reflective parenting feels like for teenagers

When Scarlett feels her mum's empathy for how she's feeling, it allows her to open up more about what has happened. She experiences her mum as being attentive and curious to her feelings and perspective, without feeling her mum is judging her or her friends. It wouldn't help her for her mum to take a position against her friends as they are hugely important to Scarlett. Instead, her mum validates how important they are to Scarlett and, once she feels validated, she is able to start to think together with her mum about any other possible ways of viewing her friends' behaviour. Scarlett is so upset and confused about why her friend lied to her and why the group went out without her, that it's impossible for her to think clearly, so more questions from her mum at this point would aggravate her and she might shut down. When her mum listens and understands how much her friends mean to her, she can contemplate another point of view on the situation. Her mum doesn't impose the view on her that Holly is mean and this allows Scarlett to still feel hurt but hold on to her wish to be friends with Holly.

Reflections: When do you parent at your best?

A good place to start when thinking about anything you want to work on in terms of your parenting is to ask yourself this question: "When do I parent at my best?" It's not something we are often asked, and for that matter are even less likely to ask ourselves. Instead, parenting often feels full of self-criticism and judgements by and of others. In groups with parents where we explore reflective parenting, this is the question we think about first. One dad said he thought he was really responsive to his children's passions and ambitions; for example, if they wanted to do an art-based creative activity, he found he could get seriously interested and involved because this was something that he found interesting too. On the other hand, with one of his daughters, who hates school, he felt it was very important to give her the opportunity to do things that she's good at and to validate her. He said he is always eager to do this, and I wondered why. He reflected that he was encouraged by his mum to write, so referring back to his own experience of being parented, he was trying to do the same for his teenagers, and a part of this involved his feeling that he never really fulfilled his own potential. We can see that his current parenting both reflects the positive experience he had with his own mother (where his interests were encouraged) and also some attempt to fulfil an unmet ambition in himself via his own daughter. Asking him to reflect more deeply on his own thoughts and feelings might help him to separate out his own unfulfilled ambitions from his wish to support his daughter. We will look in more detail at self-reflection as a parent in Chapter 2.

Supporting your teenager's mental health

Looking back to the discussion between the parents at the start of this chapter, the conversation moved to the topic of mental health and parents started talking animatedly about their fears for their teenagers. One mum said that her worry stems from anecdotal reporting that kids can get into terrible trouble and have suicidal thoughts without the parents having any idea. "Adolescent girls", said one dad, "are particularly moody and quite changeable. What looks like a deep concern one moment is suddenly gone, so it's hard to know what's important and what isn't." They all talked about their struggle with not knowing at what level they should engage with any particular mood and when they should feel worried, concluding that it feels very hard to know in the moment as moods seemed to vary and swing so rapidly from low to high and back again. One dad concluded that just making himself available by saying, "I'm here if you need me" felt really important. Most parents agreed that all of this can feel hard when the bedroom door is literally closed in their faces. However, the overall metaphorical message seemed to be, "You can close your door if you like, but I'm keeping my door open."

When the discussion moved to thinking about mental health issues such as depression, it was clear that a mentalizing approach –

thinking about their teenager's thoughts and feelings – was very helpful. Parents spoke of, "Just talking to them and telling them they can't solve something on their own" and, "Trying to listen to them and not jump to conclusions on what it was about." It became obvious that things improved when parents engaged with the problem, but only to a level that didn't feel intrusive to their child, for example, by asking them repeatedly. In the following chapters, mental health difficulties will be explored, as well as everyday problems, looking at how reflecting on both yourself and your teenager can help them regulate emotions and keep you closely connected.

The parent partnership

When parents are together, the tension in their relationship can impact the mental health of teenagers. Most children feel they have a responsibility to make their parents get on. Teenagers are still able to develop a new narrative about themselves and their future and these narratives are in a constant flux to justify the present. When a group of adolescents were asked how important it is to them that their parents get on, 75% said it was an important factor in their own well-being. Asked the same question, parents said that they thought the importance to their adolescents of them getting on well as parents was around 15–20%. This significant difference highlights the discrepancy between what parents think their relationship means to their adolescents and how their adolescents think of them, and what their teenagers *actually* feel. Often parents express how their teenager is "not really interested in anything outside of themselves" or is "so wrapped up in their own world that they don't notice what else goes on in the family." In reality, their adolescent is taking in everything and very aware of the family dynamics, but just not expressing this. Your relationship with your teenager's other parent is important to so many of the areas of an adolescent's life that we will keep returning to it in future chapters; thinking about how it influences their social world, their mental health and their transition to adulthood.

Some of the concerns parents express about their adolescents

When asking parents in a focus group about the things that were uppermost in their minds when it came to their teenagers, some key themes emerged:

- Immediate safety
- Gangs and knives
- Drugs and alcohol
- Mental health problems
- Road traffic
- Immediate threat and immediate safety
- Death
- Illness
- Attitude towards parents
- Respect (and lack of)

All these themes and more are explored in the scenarios of teenagers and parents throughout this book.

The adolescent perspective

I am sitting around my table again, this time with six teenage lads, all around 15–16 years old, asking them about their views of their parents and parenting in general. What I'm struck by first is just how thoughtful and opinionated they are, and how willing they are to speak to me about this subject. What impresses me most is how much it appears that this stuff really *matters* to them. I'm asking them about themselves and their parents of course, but the responses I get back are so much more than this. They speak about parenting in general, about what it means to be a "good" parent, and the influence this has on them and others they know. They talked about their parents and what they feel are the issues that in *their* minds currently preoccupy parents when it comes to their teenagers:

The first thing that came into James's mind when I asked about how parents approach parenting teenagers was; "When they try and get in touch with you, you know they want to know where you are, but when you try to get hold of them... ... you can't find them! They expect you to reply instantly, but it doesn't work the same way for them!" James went on to say, "They only want to know where I am because they want to know what time to get the food prepared! They don't really want to know or are interested in how I am or what I'm doing." This comment was interesting because it highlighted the importance of attachment relationships. He was articulating his need to know that his parents are there if he needs them, even if he doesn't want them around him all the time.

Another boy in the group, Sam, said, "When I get home from school and no one's in, I'm like 'where are you?'. They are usually at a movie or out for dinner, but they don't tell me. It would be good to know."

Here are some of the other themes that emerged:

- Parents repeat instructions over and over. They need to understand we get it the first time.
- Some boundaries are helpful. We don't know what to do without them.
- Total control is too much. They don't need the amount of detail they ask for.
- They do need to care about where we are and what we're doing, but shouldn't get overinvolved.

These are clearly just some of the many themes teenagers think about when it comes to how they want (and don't want) to be parented. Depending on their early experiences with you, their friendship group, and the other important influences on their life, it will be individual for each teenager. When I asked one of my own teenagers once what they thought I could change about my parenting, they replied, "don't think about parenting so much!"

When you reflect on your own thoughts and feelings in your relationship with your teenager, you are not only setting the tone for a more balanced and connected interaction with them, but you are also helping your teenager gain a different self-perspective. By mentalizing yourself first, before mentalizing your teenager, you are establishing an environment in which feelings can be managed and don't feel so overwhelming. You are also helping your teenager to feel understood and that their point of view and experiences are valid. Ultimately, as well as improving your own relationship with them, this also enhances their relationships with others and supports their mental health.

The next chapter is devoted to the Parent MAP and the importance of understanding your own thoughts and feelings and how this influences you in parenting your teenager - mentalizing yourself as a parent. Starting with yourself and learning how to manage your own state of mind is the crucial first step to supporting your teenager to become more resilient and feel a greater sense of security as they go through adolescence.

PAUSE AND REFLECT: REFLECTIVE PARENTING

In a nutshell ...

Reflective parenting is a model of mentalization-based parenting, developed to help you use the theory of mentalizing in everyday life with your teenagers. Reflective parenting with teenagers in mind is an adaptation of the original model set out in the first Reflective parenting book, designed to keep a close connection with your teenager. Using this approach also facilitates the development of your teenager's independence.

How reflective parenting helps you ...

Becoming a reflective parent helps you to untangle the thoughts and feelings you have about yourself and your teenager from their perspective. Using the tools of the reflective parenting model: reflecting on yourself, and using an emotional thermometer, helps you to regulate your own emotions so you can be more available to your teenager. By being a reflective parent, you can model a way of managing your emotions without resorting to authoritarian (enforced boundaries without discussion) or permissive (a lack of boundaries) parenting styles, as outlined in Chapter 2. This teaches your teenager how to conduct their own relationships.

How reflective parenting helps your teenager by ...

When you embody being a reflective parent, your teenager experiences you as interested in them and validating of their experiences and feelings. They feel you respect their perspective and this creates a space for them to regulate their own feelings, particularly at times when they feel overwhelmed. When you listen empathically to your teenager, they feel understood, calmer and able to think of alternative courses of action.

How reflective parenting helps your relationship by ...

Using the reflective parenting tools – the parent MAP, emotional thermometer, parent APP and the "two-hands" approach – makes it less likely you will overreact, without thinking, to your teenager. This helps your relationship by keeping you connected to each other, you are more likely to have conversations where you are listening to each other and considering your different perspectives on the same situation. This in turn allows each of you to appreciate the other person and not get too stuck in a difficult emotion.

Keep in mind ...

- Use the tools of the reflective parenting approach to weigh up when it is best to intervene and when you should hold back.
- When you are more aware of your own feelings – by self-mentalizing – you are able to see your teenager's mind more clearly, as independent from yours.
- Being a reflective parent helps your teenager to understand their thoughts and feelings.
- Building a parent MAP makes you more aware of the influences on your parenting and therefore helps you understand the importance of separating out your own feelings from your teenager's.
- Teaching your teenager the skills of reflective parenting (through them observing the way you conduct your relationships) teaches them how to develop and maintain secure and connected relationships with peers and future partners.

2

REFLECTING ON YOURSELF AS A PARENT

"What's going on in your mind right now, and why?"

Reflecting on your experience as a parent is key to your relationship with your teenager. Tuning into your own thoughts and feelings about your parenting before thinking about what your child is thinking and feeling may feel like an odd place to start considering how to support your teenager. However, taking this approach can help you think about what might be influencing you in certain situations and causing you to feel a certain way, and to notice any particular triggers for your thoughts, feelings and reactions. These influences will be different for all of you, and will depend on a number of factors which we will explore in this chapter (Figure 2.1).

First, ask yourself, "When do I parent at my best?" as considered when thinking about reflective parenting in Chapter 1. I asked a group of parents this question in a focus group, I was initially struck by how surprised they were by the question. "It's not something I've ever thought about", said one dad; one mum commented, "I don't think about what I do well, only about the worries I have and what I could have done differently". When we explored their feelings about parenting a bit more, they started to say things like, "When things are all okay with me I think I'm a better parent; when I'm not feeling so stressed out." Another parent commented, "When I'm not distracted by work or a long 'to do' and I can just think about them, that's when I think I parent how I want to; you know, when I actually like myself as a parent".

 DOI: 10.4324/9780429459245-3

Figure 2.1

When you think about this question, what specific thoughts and feelings come to mind? Parents with very young children will often say they feel they parent best when they've had a decent sleep, or when their child goes to bed without any problems. The defining moments of parenting well when you have teenagers obviously look different. Parents of adolescents often talk about parenting at their best when, for example, they have listened to their teenager without overreacting or passing judgment on their behaviour. Or it might be when they have validated a feeling their teenager has, even when they don't personally agree with this perspective. Many of us find it easier to dwell on our shortcomings and what we consider our failures than to notice what we're doing well.

Let's start with a common parental behaviour – shouting. Why do you sometimes shout? Is it because you know that when you shout your teenager will jump up and listen to you, changing their behaviour to accommodate your thoughts and feelings? Did you jump up and respond when your parents shouted at you and you've carried this behaviour forward from your own family background? We can find ourselves shouting, for example, when we struggle to manage strong feelings, or when we feel a pile of pressures weighing down on us such as the cost of living, doing a job we don't enjoy, or having elderly parents who need an increasing amount of care. You might feel that shouting will get the response you need from your teenager. Or perhaps, more likely, you haven't even thought about what shouting actually achieves, rather it just erupts at times of heightened stress and feels beyond your control, or the only thing you've got at your disposal to elicit a response.

Simply getting a response might be what you want, or even expect. For the most part, though, parents shout out of frustration, and often because in shouting they release some of the tension building up inside themselves. So, in fact, shouting makes *them* feel better, or different, temporarily, rather than having any great impact on what their teenager might think, feel or do. Hitting, grabbing, or shaking have the same effect. These actions rarely have any impact on the behaviour of adolescents, although they invariably increase and/or escalate the conflict or aggression that you might have originally been trying to stop.

The theory behind parental mentalizing

In the past 20 years, our understanding of a parent's ability to comprehend their child's state of mind, referred to as "reflective functioning" has developed. This construct emerged from the ground-breaking research carried out in 1991 by Peter Fonagy and his colleagues, Miriam and Howard Steele, known as the London Parent-Child Project (1). Their findings showed that there was a high level of concordance between a parent's and a child's patterns of attachment. So, for example, where a parent experienced a secure attachment with their primary carer as a child, their child was likely to enjoy a similar degree of attachment with them. Or, conversely, where a parent's childhood attachment was poor, this pattern was more likely to be repeated with their own child. Reading this, you might be feeling worried if your own attachment history wasn't as secure as you would have liked, that you are destined to pass this same pattern on to your child and teenager. We now know that it is possible to change these patterns of attachment transmission by developing a more reflective – mentalizing – style with our own children. It is never too late to introduce an environment of thoughtful reflectiveness when it comes to your own and other people's states of mind, and this is the whole point of bringing this model to your parenting.

Attachment theory

When I'm teaching students about attachment theory, I often start by asking them this question: "If you had a problem with your course and you were seriously worried about whether you were going to pass your exams, what would you do?" I get a range of answers from, "I'd ring my mum, or talk to one of my friends" or, "I'd panic, get really anxious and not know what to do", to "I'd usually just work it out of my head and make a plan of how I was going to tackle each subject." Each of these responses tells us something about their attachment styles and what kind of, what Bowlby called, "internal working model" lies at the heart of their expectations about relationships and other people in the world. Some of them feel immediately that they would reach out and ask for help, believing that other people in their lives are helpful and available and there to support them (we call this pattern of attachment "secure"). Others feel it's up to them to work out a solution and they feel quite comfortable in this pragmatic, self-reliant approach (avoidant), while another group gets quite agitated, asks for lots of help in a loud and panicky way, not sure they will get it and unable to control how they feel. When they get help, it takes them a while to calm down (insecure). These different attachment styles manifest in everyday, mundane scenarios, and stem from the first few years (or 1001 days) of life. If, when you were a baby, your needs were consistently met, and you had a close attachment relationship to your main carer, you are likely to be called secure, in attachment terms. If, when you were a baby, your needs were inconsistently met; say when you cried in distress or discomfort (like when your nappy was wet, or you couldn't sleep), your main attachment carer sometimes responded with comfort to meet your needs, but sometimes didn't come to your aid, then you will have learned that to get your parent to notice and respond to you, you had to make a lot of noise. This is called insecure attachment, and it will leave you unsure if people in the world can be trusted to meet your needs. It will also leave you with a sense that you might not always *deserve* to have your needs met. Another type of attachment is called avoidant. If, as a baby, your parent sent you a message that if you were upset, distressed, angry, etc. then you were left to settle yourself, you will have learned to express less emotion, because the message you got was that you needed to sort yourself out; that if you're in distress then try to keep a grip on it because there isn't anyone there to help you, you need to be self-reliant. Growing up, you will learn that if you're experiencing difficulties, then you can't rely on others to help you, but you can look after yourself well. You might find that you don't lean much on other people and that you don't show your vulnerabilities as much as other people you know.

Whenever I talk to students about these attachment patterns, they tend to start worrying if they don't fit the secure pattern; as if somehow anything less than secure means they are doomed in life and in their relationships. This is simply not true. We now know that attachment is more fluid and that other influences and relationships in later life, particularly in adolescence, mean we can acquire features of security throughout our life when we have good experiences with available, supportive and trusting adults. If you reflect on your own childhood, I imagine you can identify with one of these patterns. There is a fourth category, called disorganised attachment, and this is less commonly found but results from a childhood where your parent or carer was particularly hard to understand in terms of their response to you. The other three categories I've just described are quite predictable strategies on the part of the parent, where an infant quickly learns what the likely response will be from their parent (even if it's the intermittently responsive one of the insecure type). In a disorganised attachment relationship, the parent might reflect back to the child something that is so incongruous with how they feel, it leaves a baby feeling confused about what it is they really feel. For example, imagine a baby is gurgling at his mother and, wide-eyed with curiosity, moves his head from side to side, smiling at her. Instead of smiling back, the mother scowls at the baby and says "don't you shake your head at me! I'm not in the mood for being told no!" This would be very confusing for a baby and if this continued throughout childhood and later on, would leave a young person extremely confused, both about how they felt and how other people feel and behave. Where there isn't a good fit, or where there is an absence of what we call marked mirroring – where the parent/carer mirrors how they think the baby feels – it leads to a very poor understanding of the self and of other people.

Secure attachment underpins the development of good mentalization and so each time you try to mentalize yourself and your teenager – by reflecting on what's going on in your mind and trying to understand theirs – you are giving your teenager an experience of a secure, connected attachment relationship with you. Of course, it's not possible to be reflective all of the time, and this wouldn't be normal, but bringing this approach into your relationship will have a positive impact on how closely connected you feel to each other.

The theory of how attachment styles relate to our reflective capacities

Fonagy and his colleagues hypothesised that the concordance between a parent's attachment style and the attachment pattern of their own child was related to a parent's capacity to see their child as a separate psychological entity with a mental experience – thoughts and feelings – of their own. In addition, the parent's capacity to be able to not only perceive but also to reflect back their child's mental state and respond accordingly was seen as strongly linked to how securely attached they were as a child to their own primary caregiver. In other words, if you are able to think about your child's states of mind and show them you understand something of how they are thinking and feeling, this is likely a skill you developed from having had a parent who did the same to you when you were younger.

This understanding led Fonagy and his colleagues to develop a measure called the "reflective-self function scale" and subsequently the "reflective functioning scale (RFS)" which measured a parent's capacity to understand their own mental state. The RFS was initially applied to the Adult Attachment Interview, (2) a measure of a parent's own attachment to their own parent as a child based on an interview where the parent reflected on their early childhood experiences. This led to the identification of markers that were seen as evidence of reflective functioning. These markers related not only to a parent's awareness of their own mental state, but also to how well they were able to reflect on their own childhood experiences and how these affected their parenting in the here and now. The research indicated that the ability of a parent to understand and reflect on their own as well as others' mental states originates from a parent–child relationship in their own early history in which they experienced a caregiver (usually their mother) as someone able to recognise and respond to their mental states.

Let's think about how this theory relates to how you parent your teenager now. If, as a baby and young child, your parent seemed to be able to put words and feelings to what you were experiencing, then this increases the likelihood that, as an adult, you can understand both how you are feeling and how your teenager feels. Taking a concrete example, imagine that as a young child, you were at the park and you noticed your older brother getting ice cream from your mum and felt cross and a bit jealous that you didn't get one. Imagine you stuck your lip out, narrowing your eyes at your parent, thinking to yourself "It's not fair." Then your mum noticed your face and, mirroring your expression, she stuck her lip out too and said, "Aww, I'm sorry, did you miss out on the ice cream while you were busy on the climbing frame? That's not a nice feeling, is it? Wait a minute and I'll see if the ice cream lady has a mini-milk for you. You like those don't you?" The experience you have in this scenario is of a parent who can interpret your behaviour and put meaning to it. The parent, by mirroring your face, is telling you that they can see how you feel. Then they put some words to it, like, "not a nice feeling". This everyday scenario is an example of a parent being able to understand a child's mental state, and it's this type of interaction that lays down the building blocks of a secure attachment. We can see how the parent is mentalizing the child by putting some meaning to their behaviour. The other part of this type of interaction involves the child learning how to understand other people as well as feel understood himself. The ability to have a "reflective self" in the context of parenting is a careful interplay between a parent reflecting on their state of mind as a parent and turning this reflective capacity onto their child's state of mind. This important balance is key to the model of reflective parenting I've developed, which helps parents increase their capacity to mentalize. With a young child, in this type of scenario, when the parent is already well-regulated in their emotions, they don't always need to mentalize themselves first because they are already in the right "emotional range." Once your child becomes a teenager, thinking about your own state of mind before reflecting on your teenager's becomes ever more important, as you are more likely to be experiencing "spikes" in your emotional temperature more frequently.

In Chapter 1, we looked at how research (3) reveals that your ability to reflect on your own mind is even more important to your relationship and interaction with your child than your ability to reflect on them and other people, and becomes increasingly so as they reach adolescence. Learning to be more reflective on your own mind might not always feel easy, and we all struggle to do this under stress, of course, but it will be hugely beneficial to all your relationships, as well as to your own state of mind, if you can learn to do this over time.

Putting the theory into practice

All of this research tells us that when we stop and reflect on ourselves – especially on our thoughts and feelings, where they come from and how they affect us, moment to moment – we can go on to have many more positive interactions with our children. In contrast, if we just focus on trying to understand our teenagers, without first getting to grips with our own state of mind, we are less likely to connect with them meaningfully. This might sound very basic, but it's surprising how little attention we pay to our own states of mind when we are parenting and how focused we are instead on the rest of the family.

Self-mentalizing plays a key role in reflective parenting and is the first step for parents who wish to follow this approach. The practical step-by-step guide explained later in this chapter will help you put this theory into practice in your own parenting.

Mind Check

To begin the process of self-mentalizing, it's useful to practice a technique called a "mind check." A "mind check" is a quick check-in with yourself; a tuning in to what's on your mind right now. It's different from thinking back to everything that's happened that day, week or even over the course of your childhood or recent life. For example, if you stop to do a mind check now, you might notice/observe that your mind isn't completely focused on what you're reading but is wandering onto other thoughts, perhaps your child's school trip – whether they remembered to pack everything they needed and how the weather might affect the trip; or whether you need to go to the shops for groceries, and so on. You may notice that your mind is pretty crowded with lots of chatter that you will need to tune out of if you're going to focus just on reading.

How about you? What's going on in your mind right now? What are you thinking and feeling? To practice doing a mind check, take a couple of minutes to notice and write down what's going on in your mind at this particular moment. Are you fully focused on the task at hand or perhaps half thinking about something you need to do later? Or are you starting to get deeper into thinking about yourself as a parent of a teenager and all the things that brings up for you? Chances are, your mind doesn't have just one thing going on.

You might find you are focused on more practical thoughts than having emotional feelings depending on your current circumstances, including where you are, who you're with, what time of day it is, what's just happened and what's happening later. There are a limitless number of influences on you at any given point and they all affect your current state of mind.

The parent "MAP"

The parent "MAP" stands for **M**entalizing **A**dolescent **P**arenting – that is, thinking about the influences on your own parenting of your teenager. This "map" is something you can start to construct, like a route through your parenting journey, either literally by jotting down notes on paper or a device, or just in your own head (Figure 2.2). Of all the tools I'm going to talk you through in this book, your parent MAP is probably the most important one. Certainly, it's the one you will need to think

Figure 2.2

about first before you start to use a reflective parenting approach on your teenager. Throughout this book, you will be prompted to stop and mentalize. At these points, the first thing to do is to think, "What's going on in my mind right now, and why?" This will involve thinking about what's happening with your parent "MAP." Let's take the example of 18-year-old Rashid, who leaves his dishes in the sink after he's had his breakfast. His dad gets so frustrated with him doing this, day after day that, sick of nagging him, he starts sending him messages via the family chat group about the state of the kitchen. This aggravates Rashid and he feels sick of his dad pointing out his mistakes (he made his own breakfast after all), so he ignores all the messages. If we were to ask Rashid's dad what he's thinking and feeling at this time, and where those thoughts and feelings come from, he might say something like, "I feel it's a small thing to ask him to do, so I feel irritated that I have to repeat myself, and I don't feel he takes me that seriously when I ask him. It's as if he doesn't respect me, or this house, and how hard I've had to work to get us a house like this."

Reading his words, we can see that his irritation at Rashid is not simply a matter of him wanting his son to do what he says, but the feeling has strong associations with his own work ethic and all the hard work he feels he had to put in to buy a home for his family. While I imagine most parents want their teenagers not to take advantage and leave their mess around, this dad's particular sensitivity to the issue of value and respect might mean that he has a stronger-than-average reaction to Rashid leaving his dishes in the sink, which probably leads to tension between them and a bad residual feeling.

When you use a reflective parenting approach, you begin to see how your own state of mind can be highly influenced by your child's emotional state, and that developing a greater calibration of your own emotions in your relationship with your teenager leads to a greater connection between you and them.

What influences your parenting?

Where do you imagine your ideas about parenting come from? Nobody actually *taught* you how to parent your child, but somehow you've got this far; although if you're anything like me, you may still have the feeling that you haven't quite nailed it. Are there things you continue to find yourself at a loss on how to handle? I am thinking back to the onset of the Covid-19 pandemic and the completely unexpected challenges to parenting. For example, exams were cancelled, end-of-school-life proms and celebrations were off and milestone teenage birthdays couldn't be celebrated as planned. Thinking back to this time, now over two years ago, we can recognise that a major challenge to parenting young people through this period was trying to regulate emotions to a degree that it enables parents to be available to help them. Not easy when you feel there is an actual threat of death hanging over you! There has probably not been an equivalent time in our recent history when there has been such a universally felt experience of anxiety and fear. What mentalizing our own parenting – using the parent "MAP" – helps us to understand is that these feelings we experience as parents have a huge impact on how we deal with our children on a day-to-day basis.

What are your thoughts about parenting teenagers?

A common theme that comes up in my clinical work with parents, including carers and adoptive parents, is their negative expectations about the adolescent years. Often, parents are able to be reflective and empathic towards their children, thinking through the dynamics of their relationship and talking through situations where they find their behaviour challenging, such as family meal times, where they would fight with each other. I recall a number of parents where, when we mapped out the road ahead, imagining what would be the potential bumps in their parenting journey, they stopped at adolescence and on one occasion drew a head with devil horns on it to represent what they imagined this period of their boys' lives would be like and how they would feel about them. When you reflect on your thoughts about parenting a teenager, do you think that you looked forward to this stage of your child's life – or if your child is pre-teen, that this is a stage you think you'll embrace? Going back to your thoughts about parenting a teenager, do you think that you looked forward to this stage of your child's life? Or do you feel highly anxious about, say, their friendships, because you remember feeling out of place at school when you were a 15-year-old, and you hadn't yet found your tribe?

The influence of your attachment history

Whatever your thoughts about parenting teenagers, they are extremely important to *how* you parent your own teenager. Their formative years with you will have been shaped heavily by your own approach to parenting and the attachment style shaped by your parenting. For example, if this was a secure one, where you were able to give your child a sense of safety and trust in people, and a complementary view of themselves as someone who was worthy of help and love, would have had a strong influence on how they feel about themselves and others when they reach adolescence. Sometimes circumstances can mean that we can't meet our child's needs consistently. This can be the case, for example, when a parent is suffering from depression, struggling financially, or looking after an unwell parent of their own. In these situations, a child can grow up unsure about how available, trustworthy and responsive other people are. They might also then have a complementary view of themselves as not always worthy and deserving of help from others. Their experience may have taught them that, as the response they need isn't always available, they are unsure about how and when to ask for help or rely on others.

Fortunately, history is not necessarily destiny, even if a child's attachment model wasn't' ideal, it's possible to develop and acquire feelings of security throughout our lives. If you don't feel your child had the optimal sense of security you would have liked to have given them when they were younger, it's certainly not too late to offer a more secure and available attachment relationship to them in their teenage years.

Different parenting styles

A commonly expressed sentiment from parents of teenagers is, "They don't respect my authority." This usually implies that there has been an attempt on the part of the parent to set down some rules, or possibly demands, and the teenager has pushed back or completely refused to do what is asked of them. This can leave us all wondering, what's the line between setting rules and boundaries and having some authority, and becoming a tyrant who is constantly berating their teenager for things they have or haven't done. The psychologist Diana Baumrind first developed the idea of different parenting styles and these were later expanded on by psychologists Eleanor Maccoby and John Martin (4). They categorised the following four distinct parenting styles.

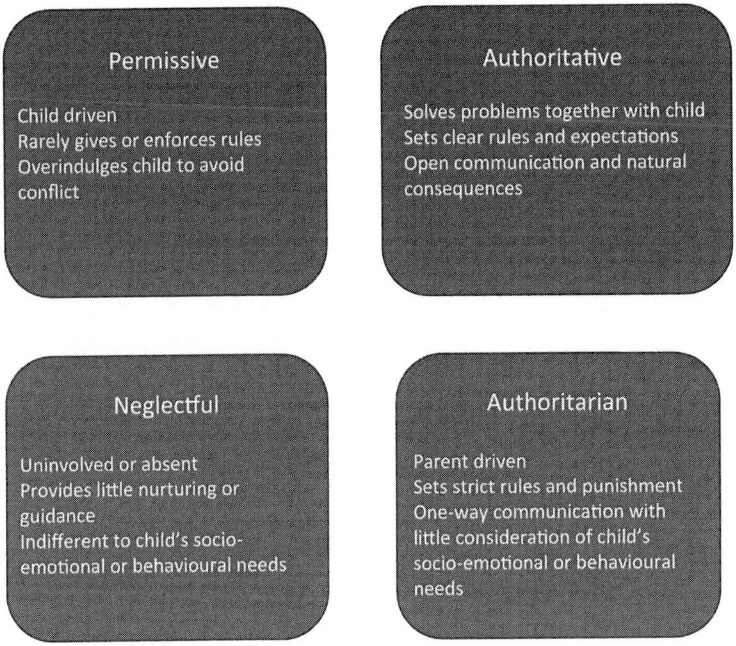

Figure 2.3

Parenting styles are categorised based on two dimensions of parenting behaviour – demanding and responsive. A demanding parenting style refers to how parents control their child's behaviour or demand maturity. Responsiveness refers to how much parents are accepting and sensitive to their children's emotional and developmental needs.

Looking at these different styles, I wonder if you recognise one from your own childhood? If you focus on the authoritative parenting style, you might see that this is the one that fits within a reflective parenting approach. Being an authoritative parent means you hold high expectations for achievement and maturity, but you are also warm and responsive. Being authoritative also involves setting rules and enforcing boundaries by monitoring – for example, by using the "two-hands" approach – having open discussions and providing guidance. Authoritative parents also provide reasoning and an explanation for their actions, which give children a sense of awareness and teach them about values, morals and goals. Authoritative parents are assertive but not intrusive or restrictive. Their disciplinary styles are supportive rather than punitive. They respect their children's autonomy, provide them with a lot of freedom and encourage independence.

Exercise

Take a moment to reflect on your own experiences as a child. Write down what you remember from your childhood experiences of how you were parented. Which parenting category does your own experience most closely connect with? Maybe it's more than one.

Now think about a recent difficult interaction with your teenager and reflect on which parenting style you used in this interaction. If it was an authoritative approach, it's likely you were responsive and warm to your teenager, but you still set down a boundary or expectation around their behaviour and actions. You might have explained the consequences to them of what they were doing.

If you took a different approach to the authoritative one, think about what worked and didn't work with this approach. Perhaps you took an authoritarian approach, setting out a strict rule or laying down a punishment. Perhaps in using this approach, you didn't just criticise your teenager's behaviour, but also criticised them, labelling them in some way, for example, as being "lazy" or "disrespectful." Perhaps if you used this approach you exploded with anger or punished them by withdrawing your help and affection. Did you and your teenager feel closely connected at the end of this interaction, or were you perhaps driven further apart? Perhaps you felt bad afterwards and/or your teenager was left feeling angry, upset or even ashamed?

As you go through this book, maybe dipping in and out of different scenarios, try to hold in mind the type of parenting approach you want to take. Reflect on what works best in your current style, and what you could work on a bit more to bring about a greater warmth and connection in your relationship with your teenager.

The impact of your relationship with your teenager's other parent

An argument with a partner, close friend or family member inevitably impacts how we feel and, without being aware of it, we bring the feelings from these negative interactions into our parenting in ways that can interfere with the individual needs of our teenagers. The relationship with your teenager's other parent plays an important role, not just in how you parent your teenager, but also influences other areas of their development. In Chapter 5, we think about how your relationship with your partner influences how they learn to conduct other relationships, and in Chapter 10, on the longer-term impact of your relationships on their adult life. For now, if you simply start to reflect on what your relationship with their other parent is like, this is a good start. You might be in a relationship where there is a general level of agreement between you on parenting, or you might have very different styles – partly as a result of your different childhoods, current influences, culture, etc. – and in either case, it will be helpful to make a mental note of how these affect your teenager. When there are high levels of conflict in the parent relationship, it's undoubted that this has a profound negative effect on children and teenagers. Research on families where there are high levels of conflict (5) shows us that children can become triangulated. There are different forms of this, but in essence, they all involve children becoming involved in adult disputes and forming problematic alliances with one of their parents over another. For example, in one form of triangulation (known as "pathological triangulation"), one parent uses the child as a confidant and excludes and demeans the other parent. Some parents may not make negative comments about the other parent, but because they hold strong feelings of distress and/or anger towards that parent, they find it easier simply not to talk about that parent. While this might seem on the surface preferable to a parent who is constantly bad-mouthing their teenager's other parent, it still has the same impact of not supporting the teenager's relationship with the distanced parent. It also makes it harder for the teenager to access positive memories of this parent. You should always aim for your teenager to have a "good enough" relationship with both of their parents, whatever your own feelings.

On the other hand, having just one or two supportive relationships, whether with a partner or friend, can be a positive influence on your parenting. A supportive partner or friend, who validates how you think and feel and who validates some of the highs and lows of parenting adolescents, will put you in a frame of mind where it is easier to separate out your own state of mind from that of your teenagers'. If you are a single parent, or with a partner but struggling with life's difficulties and having problems with your teenagers, then there is often nothing more helpful than to talk with other parents in the same position as you. Sharing the failures as well as successes of parenting is so important, and can be a really helpful way to improve family relationships in the future. Parenting can often feel competitive and sharing your failures is usually a better way to get closer to other parents than signaling all your successes.

When miscommunication and misunderstanding build between you and your teenager, you can think of these as times where your mentalizing may have gone "off-line"; in other words, where the strength or dominance of your own thoughts and feelings got in the way of being able to think reflectively about your teenager. By first constructing your "MAP," as explained below, and putting in the time to reflect on the factors that go into making you the parent you are to your teenagers, you can start to validate some of the current ways you think, feel and act, recognising that you are probably doing your utmost best most of the time. You can also start to gently challenge and make shifts in your thinking in a way that promotes mentalizing and enables you to take some responsibility for lapses in mentalizing by considering what influenced your thoughts, feelings, and responses in specific parenting situations. If Rashid's dad was able to do this, instead of nagging him and sending messages to the family group chat, he might calmly explain to Rashid why, to him, taking care of their house feels hugely important. When Rashid doesn't look after it, even though he doesn't mean to annoy him, it makes him feel that his hard work was wasted. If Rashid sees that his dad's strong reaction is partly to do with his dad and not him, he can perhaps feel more inclined to do what his dad wants, and it feels less of a personal attack on him.

When you give yourself the time and space to reflect on your own state of mind – for example, what made you so snappy with your teenager at breakfast, or react so strongly, you will find that you're in a much better state of preparedness for thinking about your teenager in a reflective way. In other words, once you've started to manage your own feelings and got those under what feels like a sense of control, or that you have an understanding of them, you will be in a much better position to think about what's going on in your teenager's mind.

Building your parent "MAP"

Managing your own emotions in the face of some strong ones from your teenager is a really tough job. At times you may find yourself being pushed to the absolute brink of what you feel you can, and even should have to, take from your teenager. Engaging your emotional thermometer, as discussed in Chapter 1, is useful in these moments. When your teenager says or does something that causes you to feel anxious, angry or upset, your "temperature" on the emotional thermometer will be too high to think in any clear way. The trick in these moments is to find a way to bring your temperature back down into a normal, or middle, range, so you can then think more clearly or reflectively.

Thinking back to the list of themes in Chapter 1 parents spoke about in the focus groups, one of the most common was a lack of thoughtfulness or a lack of respect for other people. Teenagers will almost certainly vent strong feelings and often what feels like ill-considered random thoughts around you a lot of the time. It can be hard, not to say near impossible at times, to keep your cool and know what the best response is in these moments. Don't panic though, this is exactly what developing a parent MAP, outlined in the steps below, will be good for.

Step one – **Use the emotional thermometer.** Engage your emotional thermometer to notice where your emotional temperature is right now. If it's too hot or too cold, then you are not in the right place to be able to work things out with your teenager. You won't be able to think reflectively about yourself or them in any useful way. Do whatever helps you to bring your temperature down, or up, whether that's taking a pause and waiting, walking away from the situation, speaking to someone else not directly involved in the situation, or doing something calming and distracting, such as listening to music.

Step two – **Check in on your current state of mind.** Do a mind check, if you haven't already done this. Ask yourself, "How am I feeling right now? What's made me feel this way?" For example, you might realise that you are feeling anxious. When you start to be curious about what that anxiety is about you might trace it to one main thing, say a worry you've got about your health, or to a number of factors. That anxiety is *yours* and recognising that this is *your* feeling about you, separate from your teenager, is the first important step in starting to mentalize yourself.

Now try to notice what it is that you're thinking. This might feel harder than noticing your feelings and it's a somewhat unnatural or unfamiliar experience as we don't go around with a conscious awareness of our thoughts. Even doing this exercise in a deliberate way might feel difficult at first. You might not be able to observe your thoughts initially, but when you practice a bit and start to note them down, or talk to a partner or friend about your thoughts and feelings, you will increase your awareness of what's going on in your own mind. This will be extremely useful to you the next time you start to mentalize your teenager as explored in Chapter 3. For example, if you have a phone call you need to make, you might notice that you're thinking, "I've got to get on with work, but I've forgotten I was meant to ring the GP back this morning." Becoming aware of this thought helps me to connect it with the feeling of anxiety and to own these thoughts and feelings as my own. If then your teenager wants your attention, you can manage to hold on to your own mind without it interfering with the dynamic between you and your teenager, but you have to make a conscious effort, particularly when they start to ask about something which will make a demand on your time. You will then need to really work hard to regulate yourself because of your underlying state of mind.

Step three – **Thinking about your cultural, social and personal identity**

Thinking about your cultural, racial, social and personal identity is a crucial aspect of reflecting on your own mind and on your parenting style. I am a white, British, middle-aged, heterosexual, married woman. I was born in the East Midlands in a mining town and witnessed the miners' strike during my teenage years, which fired up some strong feelings about social justice during my mid to late teens. The area was very working class, but my family were half middle class (my mum) and half working class (my dad) and I was raised in a house with easy access to books, film, and culture. I attended a comprehensive school and the majority of my friends were from working-class, mining families. These are *all* important cultural factors in my ability to mentalize my parenting – to form my own MAP – that feature in how I think about myself, conduct my relationships and parent my own teenagers.

When you build your own parent "MAP," it's important to reflect on your own identity and how this has shaped you and your parenting. Some influences will feel more important and relevant than others. For example, I was raised as a Methodist and my mum had a strong faith, but I have not raised my own children with any particular religious beliefs. On the other hand, I feel strongly about social justice and have spoken a great deal about the class system to my children over the years. One important value to me is that they understand that people can be at the bottom of the pile through absolutely no fault of their own.

What are the important aspects of your identity that you would place on your MAP? How much are they currently influencing your parenting, in both positive and negative ways?

Step four – **Think about your family history, past experiences and relationships**

It's almost a cliché for a psychologist to be asking, "What about your early history with your own parents?" and it would be overly simplistic to imply that your current parenting is a straightforward reflection of your own early family experiences. However, it is undeniable that many of our parenting practices have been imprinted on us from an early age from our only experience of parenting – the one in our own birth families, for better or worse. We have one dominant template for how to parent, and that's the one we've observed in our own family. The process of reflecting on past family experiences and relationships may be an easy or uncomfortable one, or often a mixture of both. You may have had a very unhappy or disturbing experience in your own childhood, or seen your parents behave in ways that you don't want to repeat (I definitely don't want my children to grow up with bickering parents, understanding something personally of the damage this does). Please note that becoming a reflective parent to your teenager doesn't involve personal psychotherapy or a very deep dive into your history. It is more about starting to tune in to those aspects of your parenting that have echoes from your own past history on which aspects from your own history are more or less helpful to your current parent-adolescent relationship. This can feel like quite an empowering and satisfying experience as you sort out the "sock drawer" of your own history of being parented; working out which ones to throw away because they don't fit, don't suit your particular needs or are just worn out, from the ones that you find comfortable, reliable and useful.

Reflecting on my own family history, past experiences and relationships, I would note that my parents were both only children and had no experience of having a sibling. I have a brother, two years older than me who was a bully towards me growing up, and my parents didn't know how to manage this dynamic at all. My dad's parents raised him not to express too much emotion, whereas my mum's family expressed more emotion and were warm and loving. My mum spent the first few years of my life as a stay-at-home housewife and then, having left school at 16, went back to college and then university, before becoming a teacher. My dad's family were farm and factory workers, but he studied to become an architect. I had a close relationship with both sets of grandparents and used to spend many weekends at my maternal grandparent's house, which was in the countryside with a large garden where I could explore. My parents used to argue a lot and divorced when I was 12 years old. I stayed with my mum and brother while my dad moved out. I could go on, but hopefully, you can see how I'm drawing out a picture of my past family culture and experiences to understand how these formative years have influenced me as a parent. For example, I would describe my own parents as quite permissive, and as a consequence I have set firmer boundaries and rules with my own children into adolescence. My personal reflection is that this permissiveness left me confused at times as to who was in authority and as a consequence I took on more responsibility than I felt equipped to handle. Having tuned into this aspect of my personal family history, I have used this experience to inform a different style of parenting, where limits and responsibilities are clear. On the other hand, I have tried to bring my mother's sense of optimism and hopefulness into my parenting in the way that I try to encourage my teenagers to think that they can achieve anything if they put their minds to it.

One mum I worked with, Mary, told me her parents were very close to each other, almost to the exclusion of her and her brother. Although she said it was lovely to have parents who were so in love, it made her feel that she would never mean as much to them as they did to each other. As a parent herself to two young people – one 18-year-old son and a 23-year-old daughter, she realised when thinking about her parent MAP that she had always prioritised her children before her husband and that this created a problematic dynamic in her family. Her husband has done the same, for different reasons. As a result, they are both extremely anxious about the prospect of one day their two children leaving home as, having focused their whole parenting lives on putting the children ahead of their relationship, they have become unsure of what they have in common as a couple. Being aware of this – through self-reflection – they can notice how their emotional temperatures rise during conversations about their children leaving home.

Mapping out your influences should be done in a non-judgmental way. In other words, you are not criticising yourself for how you parent, but simply becoming increasingly aware of the influence of these past experiences and relationships on yourself in your current parenting. This might feel hard at times as it can be painful to recall upsetting family dynamics, particularly if you have had a traumatic childhood or a few very negative or abusive experiences. Try not to fall into a pattern of thinking that your past determines your present in a negative way, but more that by becoming *aware* of your experiences, you are working out a coherent narrative about what happened to you. The more clear or coherent this story of your own life experiences is, the more you will be able to gain control over your own emotions, separate these out from your teenager's and be available to them to stay connected through the ups and downs of their lives.

Step five – **Explore current influences and relationships**

This point on the parent MAP concerns all the current relationships that influence your state of mind at this moment. These can include partners, friends, extended family, work colleagues, teachers, social workers, mental and physical health professionals, sports coaches, and so on. Just as our past family relationships have an impact on how we think and feel day to day, so do our current relationships, possibly more so. We are certainly likely to be more aware of our current relationships than of the influence of past ones. If I continue to plot out my own parent MAP I would include things like having lost both my parents recently, having a job as a child and adolescent clinical psychologist, the colleagues I work with, my husband and my friends.

Let's look at the following scenario of a typical parent-teenager conflict and consider how the steps to building a parent MAP could be used by this parent.

> Jade's 13-year-old daughter, Amy, comes in from school on Friday and is walking around the house with her phone tightly clutched in one hand. With the other hand, she takes a biscuit out of the cupboard, drops her bag by the front door and kicks off her school shoes using the one remaining hand, which land in a haphazard pile in the middle of the sitting room. Jade, watching her daughter trail around the house like this, glued to the screen she's holding in one hand, which seems to be showing repeat episodes of the show *Friends*, starts berating her; "Amy, can't you put that phone down, put your bag and shoes away properly in your room, and while you're up there, tidy up your bedroom, you didn't even straighten your duvet this morning before you left, and don't eat a biscuit the minute you come home from school, I'm about to start making something for dinner. And why are you even on that phone so much of the time? I'd like you to please put it down, and pick up a book instead. Why don't you read anymore? You used to read all the time. How many episodes of Friends can you even watch anyway? It took me years to watch it all the way through, you seem to have managed the entire series in just a few weeks. Amy! Amy! Are you even listening to me?" Jade's voice is getting louder and louder until she is shouting at the top of her voice about her need for Amy to read more books. Amy eventually looks up from her phone screen at her mum and says, "Mum, this is my free time now." She goes into her bedroom and slams the door firmly behind her.

What is your reaction to this scenario? What are you thinking and feeling as you read this? Try to tune in, particularly to how you would feel if you were Jade, the parent, in this situation.

Jade told me this story about the interaction with her teenage daughter, whom she has a generally great relationship with, and so

I asked her how and why she found herself shouting so much. Jade replied, "I just had to let it out." When we went on to unpack what it was about this situation that got to Jade, she explained that it wasn't just the fact that Amy was making a mess as she walked into the house, but there were several things going on. One of these is Jade's feeling that Amy is rejecting her and gradually moving away from her and she sees her lack of interaction with her straight after school as a sign that she is unimportant to her. She keeps thinking about how close they used to be. This worry about teenagers becoming more independent is one I hear many times from parents, along with the worries about their mental health. The other important trigger for Jade is that her general use of the phone bothers her because, some of the time, Amy videos what's going on in her house and then shows it to her friends, causing the mum of one of Amy's friends, who knows their family well, to comment to Jade, "I see you were in your dressing gown this morning", which Jade feels is an invasion of the private world she has tried to create and protect in her own home with her family, and which she feels is now being encroached on by other people seeing the most mundane, and often quite banal, detail of their everyday lives. Finally, she reflects that the other issue that was somewhere in the back of her mind was a growing feeling of dread that as Amy grows up, she's going to get more and more drawn towards influences from outside the family and less concerned with what her mum thinks about her.

There are other things, of course, at work in this interaction between Jade and Amy. Jade wants her daughter to respect her, keep her belongings tidy, and eat regular food and not biscuits before her dinner. For example, she feels a strong emotional reaction to the line "Mum, this is my free time", as if somehow Jade is seen as intruding on time Amy feels entitled to. This entitled feeling gets Jade's back up, particularly as she has been working all day and doesn't get her own "free time" until she's made a family dinner, tidied away and sorted out something for her younger child for their sports day the next day.

Reflecting on the parent – putting the MAP into action

Let's mentalize Jade now. How might we help Jade use her Parent MAP to identify which part of her strong feelings and thoughts about her daughter are more connected to her own mind and life than her daughter's? When practicing reflecting parenting, the Parent MAP exercise is always done first and sometimes might be the only tool needed to avoid conflict and bring about a closer connection with your teenager. This is because if you can understand something of where your own reaction comes from in the context of your relationship with your teenagers, it will help you to manage your response, regulate your emotions and get into a more connected and constructive dialogue and interaction with your teenager.

Thinking about Jade's Parent MAP would need to involve more information about her past history and current circumstances, but with what I know of her I can start to help her plot these points on her MAP.

Step one – **Use the emotional thermometer**

The first step is for Jade to become aware of where she is on the emotional thermometer. When Amy first came in from school, was she already a bit overheated by a busy day? As she starts to name all the things that are getting to her, and which she's anxious about, her emotional temperature is going up, making it almost impossible for her to mentalize herself. Going over this incident later will help Jade use her emotional thermometer to first get herself into the right temperature or mentalizing range.

Step two – **Check in on your current state of mind.**

Jade is currently having a very stressful time at work. She works in a large insurance company where she doesn't feel she's been able to progress much since she started working there three years ago. She has missed out on many opportunities for promotion and feels her manager takes her for granted – rarely praising her work. Her partner has a higher-paid job than her and is much happier in his work. This has caused some tension between them recently as it's caused Jade to reflect more on how dissatisfied she is in her own job. Using a Parent MAP doesn't mean that she can change anything about this current situation or state of mind but, by bringing it into her awareness, Jade can start to see that part of her reaction to Amy is related to her own raised level of stress.

Step three – **Thinking about your cultural, social and personal identity**

Jade is from a white, working-class background and there were no books in her house as a child. Her partner's family are middle class, and he was university-educated when they met. Both families were warm and loving, and Jade's dad would always make a special occasion of dinner on Friday nights as he finished his long day at his office. She becomes aware that her daughter, Amy's attitude, has already made her feel tense about the prospect of a difficult Friday evening. She becomes more aware of the fact that her upbringing is different from her daughter's and becomes more anxious about how different the two of them are.

Step four – **Think about your family history, past experiences and relationships**

Jade can identify that an important part of her Parent MAP with regard to her family history is her relationship with her own mother, which was particularly close throughout her life, but two years ago, as Jade turned 45, her mother died. She has been proud of the similarly close relationship she has with Amy and has put all her energies into having a close relationship with her daughter. The thought that her relationship with Amy is possibly becoming less close, together with her relatively recent bereavement, makes her feel anxious and upset. Small rejections feel huge to her. Jade is conscious of not having had the same education as her husband and feels very anxious that her daughter is turning away from books and education and is more concerned with her phone.

Step five – **Explore current influences and relationships**

Jade's husband has a laid-back attitude to their two teenagers and this is helpful at times, but she finds it hard to talk about her increasing feeling that her teenage daughter is moving away from her with him, as his response is that this is normal and to be encouraged. Without her mother in her life, she feels a bit lost as to who she can really talk to about these feelings.

Thinking together

We started with mentalizing Jade, now let us try to mentalize the situation together. It is completely understandable that Jade should feel frustrated and angry about Amy's apparent lack of respect for her mum when she asks her to put her phone and things away. However, these are not the things that lead her to shout and lose control around her daughter. Instead, the strong emotions she feels, which build up inside her, are a result of deeper feelings about a sense of loss and lack of relevance in her daughter's life, which she fears may ultimately lead to her moving away from her completely. She has been thinking for some time that Amy is starting to move away from her to a more autonomous stage of development, where her friends' views of her are more important than her mum's. In addition, the current influences of her work situation, her husband's contrasting attitude to their daughter's independence and her lack of support in the absence of her mother make the feelings stronger than they might be in a different situation.

Reflecting on Amy

Amy is glued to the episodes of *Friends* because this is one of the major topics for discussion among her own peer group and it's important that she keeps up with them. Even though she knows her mum has watched the whole collection of series of this show, her mum's opinion on the show isn't the one she wants to hear about, and it makes her cringe a bit to think that her mum likes the same show as her friends. To Amy, the most important thing is to feel close to her friends, and not quite so close to her mum. She hears her mum shouting and it feels like a pressure to pay attention to her when all she wants to do is connect with her friends on social media/the groupchat later that evening and talk through the final episode. Her mum's shouting is just making her feel bad after a long day at school when she was looking forward to having a bit of time to herself to wind down from a day of intense dynamics with her friends, which often leave her a bit confused about her place in the group.

Why is reflecting on your own mind important when it's your teenager who needs to change?

You would imagine that if your teenager is being difficult and acting out and causing you a great deal of stress and anxiety, the answer would be to try to find a fix for their behaviour or attitude and all would be well again in your relationship. The research mentioned earlier (6) suggests that the most helpful thing for your relationship is to reflect on yourself and focus on how you manage your own emotional life. This is one of the biggest factors in improving the quality of your relationship and everyday interactions with your teenager.

When you feel unable to help your teenager on your own

When worried parents feel unable to help their troubled teenager, they may turn to mental health services to help them, or at least enable them to gain an understanding of the problem. Problems can not only seem overwhelming at times to parents, but can also feel out of their reach or level of understanding, so reaching out to another person for help is a natural thing to do. After all, if your son or daughter had a physical illness, presumably you would take them to their GP, not try to heal them yourself. Especially if you thought the problem was serious.

Of course, there are times when getting another perspective and recruiting help are necessary, which is discussed in Chapter 8. This is often the case when the difficulties feel so overwhelming and serious that parents feel the best way of keeping their adolescent safe is to seek outside help. However, when the problems your teenager experiences are less serious, it is not always helpful to your relationship with your teenager to step back from them and their difficulties and hand them over to someone else. When you're equipped with the right tools, you can become the expert on your teenager and learn to tackle problems without the need for outside help. Although this might feel a bit intimidating at first, the best people to help young people navigate their way through life's difficulties and steer them in the right direction, are their parents or carers. If I can leave you feeling better equipped to do this by the end of the book, I will feel I've done a good job!

There are many reasons why we as parents seek outside professional help for our teenager's mental health:

- Because our child is older now, we want to give them space to talk to someone else about their worries to show them we respect their need for space and autonomy.
- We worry that trying to talk to teenagers about how they feel and why might cause an even greater rupture to a perhaps already fragile relationship.
- We worry about risk and whether we are missing something. What if our teenager does something so risky it could put their life in danger? Can we manage this?
- Our very presence and relationship with them is sometimes seen as the cause of their difficulties, or certainly a trigger for them, so how can we possibly be the best people to help them?

- We're too old to "get it." How could anyone over the age of 21 possibly know what it's like to be a teenager? We feel we are too far removed from their immediate experiences to empathise with what they feel like.

All these parental worries, coupled with teenagers' expressed views that we are not always welcome inside their world, lead to a gradually growing distance between parents and adolescents that can actually increase their risk of deteriorating mental health. Instead, working on your own state of mind, as we've discussed throughout this chapter, can be just as helpful, if not more so to your relationship with your teenager than just focusing on your teenager's state of mind.

As we go through the book, we will keep referring to the need to first mentalize yourself as a parent – to be curious about what's going on in your own mind, what triggered your thoughts and feelings and how you can learn to manage these feelings or get support for yourself. You will soon discover that mentalizing yourself is an extremely useful tool that changes and shapes your future relationship with your teenager in a positive way and also starts to impact their developing mental health.

PAUSE AND REFLECT: MENTALIZING YOURSELF

In a nutshell ...

Secure attachment underpins the development of good mentalization and so each time you try to mentalize yourself and your teenager, you are giving your teenager an experience of a secure, connected attachment relationship with you. Mentalizing yourself helps you to regulate your emotional temperature and makes it easier to reflect afterwards on what's going on with your teenager.

Mentalizing yourself helps you by ...

The Parent MAP stands for mentalizing adolescent parenting and is a way of thinking about yourself and your thoughts and feelings (mentalizing yourself).

It is a method for sorting out the things that influence you in your parenting: past family history and experiences, culture and identity, and your current influences and circumstances.

Mentalizing yourself helps your teenager by ...

The Parent MAP helps you to separate out those feelings that belong to you and those that belong to your teenager. If you separate your mind from your teenager's, then you are less likely to come into conflict and they are less likely to feel misunderstood or misinterpreted.

Mentalizing yourself – using a parent MAP – helps your relationship by …

Using this new awareness of the thoughts and feelings that influence your parenting in particular interactions can help you be a bit better prepared the next time. For example, you might know that you are going to be snappy with your teenager after a busy day at work or when they do something that seems to signal that they don't need you as much anymore. Becoming aware of these times when your feelings are stronger can help you to manage them better the next time, knowing that they are yours and understanding where they come from.

Keep in mind …

- Practice a mind check. This is a quick check with yourself; a tuning in to what's on your mind right now. Don't go over everything from the past week, but just see if you can notice what you are thinking and feeling right now. Note it down.
- Try to start a parent MAP. Think about a recent difficult interaction you had with your teenager. What was happening? Where were you both situated? What was the difficulty about? Try to remember the things you said and what you were thinking and feeling at the time.
- Now think about what the influences might have been in your own life – on your parent MAP – that contributed to that difficult exchange between you. Perhaps you'd had a stressful day at work? Maybe someone else in your family had said something upsetting or rejecting? Perhaps you were just exhausted. Think about what some of your possible triggers are to getting into a heated interaction with your teenager.
- Check your own "temperature" using the emotional thermometer before you tackle a difficult situation with your teenager. If you're too hot to have a reflective conversation, do something first to feel calmer and then return to your teenager when you are in the "warm" range on the thermometer. You will be able to mentalize better and your teenager will be more open to talking and listening.
- Practice noticing times when there are links between experiences in your past and how your react to your teenager now.

3

REFLECTING ON YOUR TEENAGER

The parent APP

> *"We don't want you to be like Sherlock Holmes ... just be interested."*

Teenagers often say that they don't feel their parents really "get it." What does this mean, though? I see it as teenagers feeling that their parents are unable to relate to things they do, or that they feel misunderstood or misinterpreted by their parents. It might also be interpreted as teenagers feeling that parents are driven by their own agendas, or need for authority or control, which makes them unable to tune in to the needs of their teenagers. I asked a 20-year-old recently to reflect back on the most helpful and most annoying aspects of being parented during his late teens. How would he have liked his parents to respond to him, say, after staying out late on a night out? "When I've been out at a club for a big night and the next day, I'm all tired and hungover, don't make a thing out of me having a hangover, or somehow make me feel that I've done something wrong. And don't ask me loads of questions about who was there and where I went, you know, just questions that are for your information but not at all relevant to me. Ask me if I've had a brilliant time and lots of fun and tell me that you are happy I've had a really great night out. That's what I need – and then maybe ask me if I'd like a big fry-up for breakfast. Then leave it at that."

I think this example highlights the teenager's need to experience the feeling of his parents stepping into his shoes momentarily to imagine what the experience was like for him; to validate his experience and then to show curiosity about it. It also shows how comments that impose a parent's logic or perspective on the teenager's experience are unwelcome. Looking back, this young

DOI: 10.4324/9780429459245-4

person could articulate his need as a teenager to be separate from his parents, while also expressing his need for their non-judgemental support and interest. Despite his independent experience, he also still wanted some nurturing from his parent – hence the fry-up!

This feeling was reiterated by a 16-year-old boy in a focus group, this particular one for teenage boys, who said, "We don't want parents to be like Sherlock Holmes." The others in the group agreed with him and said how annoying it felt to be asked lots of questions that "seem to be for their information only." Another young person in the same group spoke about his experience of a lack of active listening on the part of his parents. He said he felt as though he was talking to his parents, but they weren't really engaged in what he was saying as his interests didn't interest them. Young people often tell me that their parents just "hear what they want to hear, and tell me what they think I've said," and that this is often an inaccurate interpretation. This might seem at odds with a reflective parenting approach, with its stance of attention and curiosity. However, these teenagers are referring to a parent's tendency to ask questions that are in *their* interests – offering them reassurance or perhaps a sense of intimacy with their teenager, or even a feeling of control. Whereas being a reflective parent is about using your curiosity to step into your teenager's shoes and get a better insight into *their* needs.

Why it can be harder reflective parenting your teenager

The complex mix of brain changes during adolescence, described in chapter one, means your teenager struggles to plan, prioritise and make good decisions, and the importance of acceptance among the peer group at this age makes this a particularly tricky period for young people. Adolescents deserve our empathy, understanding and, where appropriate, guidance. Reflective parenting becomes more complex with adolescents because, while younger children seem to appreciate and benefit from feeling that their parents want to understand them, help them, and reflect to them how they are feeling, adolescents can find this kind of parenting extremely intrusive. When our children are younger, they benefit enormously from us putting their feelings into words. For example, if a young child seems upset that his older sibling is getting to stay up later than him, his parent might say something like, "It feels unfair when you're the younger one and you have to go to bed earlier, doesn't it?" While this reflection is age-appropriate for a younger child, it's much more uncomfortable for an adolescent – to hear their parent put their feelings into words – as they need to express what an experience feels like for *them*. Your reflections on their feelings might leave them feeling you've invaded their privacy. Equally, the need for autonomy (discussed in the next two chapters) might mean they don't want to feel so intimately connected to you at times. This chapter will look at how to adapt your approach when mentalizing your teenager so that it feels comfortable for them and enables a connection between you.

When Laura's youngest son was ten, she had invited a couple of his mates around to play and she made three jellies for them, knowing this was one of their favourite foods. She stuck them in the fridge for later as they played Nerf gun fights in the garden and ran around the house.

One of her twins, who was nearly 17 then, was hanging around the kitchen while his younger brother was tearing up the house with his mates. He started muttering about how irritating they were and how, "He'd better stay out of my room", playing the sophisticated older brother's role. The conversation turned to a party he was going to later that evening and Laura asked a few questions about where it was, who was going and how was he getting there. The more questions she asked, the more she could feel his irritation rising, until he snapped, "What's the need to know, Mum? That detail just isn't relevant. I'm not a little kid anymore!" before adding, "I'm starving, what is there to eat?"

He opened the fridge door and exclaimed with delight, "Jelly!"

How confusing must it be to carry these contradictory feelings of needing independence, autonomy, and separation from your parents, while still feeling at times like a young child who experiences child-like excitement? Striving, on the one hand, to be so different and separate from parents and your younger self, and at the same time craving comfort and reassurance and security, but only when they indicate that they want to access it.

Reflecting on your teenager

Chapter Two explored why self-mentalizing can be such a useful tool for parents. It allows you to start to be curious about yourself and other people, instead of striving for certainty. It helps you to make sense of what's going on in your mind and how your mental state affects your reaction to your teenager.

Part of being a parent is experiencing a strong urge to make everything work out well for our children. We are frequently called on to fix things and have answers to difficult questions or dilemmas when our children are younger. We need to make sure our child stays alive, is fed nutritional food, gets enough sleep, develops some friendships, does well at school and then has healthy relationships and good physical and mental health in older life. When our children get into difficulties, we want to be able to fix that too, after all, this is another part of our job isn't it? Parents are also often required to have the right answers to life's difficult problems and dilemmas, and feel they need to provide certainty. It is possible, however, to sit with uncertainty safely and even to learn to appreciate this as a useful and helpful approach to how you can get closer to your teenager and help them with this, often difficult, stage of their life. The key to using a reflective parenting, mentalizing, stance with your teenager is to find a balance between your natural curiosity and your "need to know and fix", and the importance of understanding the strong feelings articulated by many adolescents that being questioned feels unhelpful and intrusive and, at worst, judgemental. Achieving this balance means you can show curiosity and interest in your teenager's perspective in a way that feels supportive and connecting for them, while also managing your own emotional response to some of their behaviours or things they might tell you that threaten to unbalance your emotions. As a result, you provide your teenager with a positive and useful model of reflectiveness.

Mentalizing your teenager involves curiosity and interest in the motives, feelings, thoughts, and intentions behind their behaviour. To help you do this, you can use the parent APP. The purpose of the parent "APP" – standing for **Attention and curiosity; Perspective taking and providing Empathy** – is to help to turn your mind explicitly toward your teenager's mind instead of focusing solely on their behaviour. For example, if your teenager doesn't want to leave the house, or make any plans with their friends, instead of trying to fix this by suggesting things they could do and places to go, you turn your attention and curiosity to why they are feeling so reluctant/anxious/avoidant about in-person meet-ups. This enables you to connect with the real experience of your teenager and in turn helps them to feel understood, supported and close to you.

The core principle of mentalizing your teenager is to pay specific and active attention to them and to try to see their perspective. By paying active attention and being curious about your teenager, you begin to step into their shoes and understand their experience as they want you to see it, setting aside your own opinion momentarily to connect with their world (Figure 3.1).

Figure 3.1

Being curious and reflective in your relationship with your teenager is quite an active process, so it can be helpful to practice it in situations where you might normally take a more directive approach. Thinking about how you might mentalize the teenager in the following example can help you practise this technique.

Dhillon is 17 and lives with his mum, dad and younger sister, Cara. He spends a lot of time in his room when he's not at school, playing on his game console and listening to music on his headphones. He comes out of his room for a meal with his family in the evening but then goes straight back up afterwards. Once in his room, his parents mostly leave him alone, thinking he prefers not to have them interfere too much.

One evening, just before she's about to go to bed, Dhillon's mum asks him how he's doing as they pass each other coming in and out of the bathroom. Dhillon shrugs and says, "I dunno. I guess I'm pretty low. There's nothing to say though. It is what it is."

Taken aback by this statement, Dhillon's mum says, "Want to have a chat, love?" Dhillon says, "Sure, but there's nothing you can do about it." They sit down on the edge of Dhillon's mum's bed, and she asks, "So, what's going on? What's made you feel 'low'"? Dhillon replies, "I dunno. It just happens." He doesn't appear to want to say anymore and goes quiet as he struggles to think what to say next.

The parent APP can be used in any sequence, so you might for example start with empathy by saying, "I'm so sorry to hear that" or you could start with attention and curiosity by asking some more about the feelings Dhillon has or any thoughts running through his head.

Using the principles of the parent APP – attention and curiosity, perspective taking and empathy – how should Dhillon's mum respond to his statement that he feels "low" and what could she say and do to help him feel understood and supported?

Reflecting on yourself and Dhillon's mum

First, consider your response to this scenario. Do you have any strong feelings, either about Dhillon or about his mum? Perhaps you can relate to his mum being taken aback, and maybe it evokes a familiar feeling of anxiety if you think about your own teenager. Or you might think you would have reacted to Dhillon in a different way.

Understand and manage your own feelings first

Taking a reflective parenting approach would involve Dhillon's mum first having to manage her own feelings – that is, to self-mentalize, as explored in chapter two with the parent MAP. She might be feeling anxious and desperate to ask lots of questions and leap to a quick-fix approach. We can imagine she might want to try to do or say something to immediately make him feel better. Another possibility is that she might say something that invalidates his feelings, makes her feel better, and distracts him from his negative thoughts and emotions, for example by saying, "You seem to be doing OK most of the time when I see you, love." Or she might try to "Ted Talk" him out of it by telling him this is "all part of being a teenager. It's just a phase."

None of these approaches is likely to help Dhillon think that his mum wants to understand what it feels like to be him. The aim of mentalizing your teenager – by paying attention and being curious, thinking about perspective and providing empathy – is to maintain a connection between you both. It may be that you feel you've lost this and you want to convey that you would like to understand them better. Mentalizing your teenager conveys that you can help them to find their own way to either come to a solution on their own, or get any help they might need from friends, family, or others in their network. It's important to keep in mind that they need you, while at the same time recognising that they want to be able to find their own solutions; to feel that they have a sense of control. Your urge to fix things instantly must be modified to focus instead on maintaining a connection with them by validating their perspective and feelings.

Use attention and curiosity

Thinking further about this scenario, Dhillon's mum could tentatively ask some more questions about what he thinks is making him feel so low. However, it seems that Dhillon is lost for words and perhaps confused about why he feels this way. However, as it seems that Dhillon is lost for words and perhaps confused about why he feels this way, this might not be helpful for him. His mum could say, "You don't have to tell me why you feel low, love, and you might not even know. I'm just glad you feel you can tell me."

Use perspective-taking, empathy and validation

She might also want to offer a sense of safety, security and perspective by saying something like, "It's very normal to feel low from time to time. We all do. I'm here for you, to help in any way I can, whenever you need me." Sometimes, simply being empathic can be a powerful way of responding to your teenager's feelings, without any further questions or offer of solutions; for example, Dhillon's mum might say, "It's hard when you don't know why you feel the way you do. Feeling low is tough."

When you mentalize your teenager successfully, you achieve the aim of increasing your connection. Your curiosity and attention shouldn't be about what you want to know for your own information. Questions such as "what did you do with your day?", while completely normal, don't help you to connect with your teenager on an emotional level. Asking instead, "What was it like for you yesterday when you saw some of your friends?" shows your teenager that you want to know about their experience and that you care about it. Your teenager will know that you are genuinely interested in how they feel; that you care about them without judgement and that you can manage their strong feelings without being overwhelmed by them yourself. In the example with Dhillon, we explored mentalizing a teenager. To be able to do this clearly, it's vital your feelings don't get tangled up with your teenager's as this will confuse them and make their feelings harder to manage. This means using both your self-mentalizing skills *and* your tools for mentalizing your teenager – your parent APP skills – at the same time. The following example looks at how to combine these two concepts in practice.

Combining the parent MAP with the parent APP

Thinking back to the definition of mentalizing in the introduction, it was defined as, "the ability to read other people and attribute thoughts and feelings to them." When you begin to mentalize your teenager, using attention and curiosity, perspective-taking and providing empathy, it's important you make a clear distinction between what *you* think and feel and what's going on in your teenager's mind. For example, one of my sons was nearly 16 and wanted to get the bus into town to go to a party, I wanted to drive him and his friends but it was clear this was the last thing he wanted, so I started to ask all sorts of questions, which only made him become more evasive about the plans. What I *should* have said was something about my own feelings and how these were obviously different to his. I might have said something like, "I know you are ready to get the bus to a party with your friends, it's just that I'm not quite as ready as you are. I feel anxious about the things that could happen to you and that's my worry; it doesn't mean I don't think you are perfectly capable of getting there and back safely. So, just bear with me because I've got to get used to the fact that you're older now and can do a lot of things responsibly without needing my help for everything."

By saying something like this – mentalizing myself first, then mentalizing his feelings – I'm still making it clear that there is a boundary in my mind and that I am concerned with the safety of public transport at night. Despite my son's reaction to me to back off, this offers some reassurance to him that his parent is still concerned for his safety, and my offering an insight into what is going on in my mind allows him to consider another perspective to his. It doesn't change his behaviour significantly, but it does plant another perspective in his mind so that when he gets on the bus, he isn't oblivious to the risks of travelling at night. As a result, he may, perhaps unconsciously, behave with greater awareness of the potential dangers, while also feeling a sense of autonomy and connection to his friends which is all-important. The other purpose of making a statement along these lines is to keep a connection with your teenager. Simply banning activities with strict rules, without any explanation of your thinking, will likely lead to them being broken, possibly behind your back.

In the next scenario, Sherine is struggling to mentalize herself and finds it hard not to project her own thoughts and feelings – all the things on her parent MAP – onto her son Anthony.

Sherine is a parent to one 14-year-old teenager, Anthony, and two younger daughters (aged seven and nine). They are a close family and while Sherine and her partner, Des, have jobs, they both enjoy spending a lot of time with the children. Sherine loves cooking and takes a lot of pride in preparing meals for the family.

Recently, Anthony has been spending more time with his friends, both at his house and hanging out with them at their houses. Every evening after dinner, he rushes up to his room to speak to his friends on the phone or online while gaming with them. At weekends, where previously he had gone out with his family to parks and visited family friends, Anthony makes plans to see his friends and politely declines his parents' invitations to do things with them. One Saturday, Sherine tells Anthony that they are planning a day trip to a town by the coast, a couple of hours' drive away. She tells him they will be having his favourite food (fish and chips) with her sister (his aunt) and her children, who live on the coast. She says, "It'll be great. You can see your cousins." Anthony replies, "I hardly know my cousins, mum. They like different stuff to me. Is it OK if I stay home and have my friends over instead? You go. I'm happy staying here."

Sherine gets upset saying, "You need to have a relationship with your family, Anthony. You can see your friends anytime. This will be a fun day out for all of us. Please don't make a fuss about it. We're leaving at 9.30 on Saturday." Anthony looks downcast and says, "I'll come if I really *have* to, but I'm telling you now, I won't enjoy it and I don't want to go." He goes up to his room and stays there for the rest of the evening, messaging his friends on his phone.

Reflecting on Sherine

What is your reaction to this scenario? If you start by mentalizing Sherine first, what do you imagine is going on in her mind? Can you relate to this, and can you identify any strong feelings or thoughts that come up for you when you think about her relationship with Anthony? We know she is feeling upset and we might imagine this is related to her concern that her family life is changing and that the sense of closeness she previously felt with Anthony has become more fragmented with his wish to have greater independence. She might also feel strongly that the little time she spends with her family outside of work is being cut short. This will cause her emotional arousal to rise even higher and make it harder to step into Anthony's shoes.

Reflecting on Anthony

If we were to help Sherine mentalize Anthony, how might she turn her attention and curiosity towards his mind to understand

and connect with his current experience? It is clear Anthony wants to spend a lot of time with his friends and that they have become a hugely important part of his life. His need for closeness and security with his family hasn't disappeared, but it's not as obvious from his behaviour and this is hurtful, particularly to his mum. Sherine needs to try to manage her feelings, that she has been abandoned by her oldest son in favour of his friends, and to try to mentalize him. What would it feel like for Anthony to get cut off from his friends at this time in his life? He is putting all his energies into his peer group to find a sense of social connection that is different from his family connection (which he can trust and rely on). Perhaps he can't yet trust that his peer group is a stable one, and Sherine might try to connect with this uncertain or insecure feeling that Anthony is experiencing. She could try saying something like, "Your friends are much more important to you than your cousins right now. I can see why you wouldn't want to go." When Anthony experiences his mum's understanding of his perspective, he is likely to be more able to understand why the trip is important to his mum. Sherine might then say, "I know it's quite a boring day out for you, but it means a lot to me to keep us all connected to each other as a big family. I hope you understand."

Using the parent APP alongside your emotional thermometer

Thinking about the principles of the parent APP – attention and curiosity, perspective taking and providing empathy – can be particularly useful if you feel the temperature on your emotional thermometer rising. In this case, Sherine is getting upset at the thought that Anthony no longer prioritises being with her and the family as much as he used to. As she gets upset and her emotional temperature rises, she finds it harder to mentalize both herself and Anthony. This causes her to say, "You need to have a relationship with your family, Anthony. You can see your friends anytime", which shows that her own strong emotions are getting in the way of her ability to mentalize his current feelings. She is struggling to regulate her emotions, and this leads her to fail to see Anthony's perspective (even if she might not agree with it). At the same time, she might express her concern that she's leaving 14-year-old Anthony on his own for the whole day. If Sherine can notice her emotional arousal rising, she can take steps to bring it down.

For example, she might speak to her partner to cool off, or to another parent. When her emotional arousal has come down and she's in a more reflective state of mind, she can tune in to Anthony's thoughts and feelings more easily.

Our tendency as parents to want to fix things, which feels almost written into the job description, needs to be modified when our children reach adolescence. Aside from them not wanting us to fix things for them, it's also not ideal for their development. One of the ways that our job changes when they get older is that we need to teach them how to fix these things for themselves.

Michael, a parent of two teenage girls, one of whom experiences difficulties with her mental health (a mixture of low mood and anxiety), was asked how he approached parenting his teenagers. He said that he avoids using the same approach he would have done when they were younger, which might have involved taking them for pizza and putting on some music in the car. Instead, he tries to create an environment where his daughter can find a way to make herself happy. I was curious about what he meant by this as it seemed to fit with a reflective parenting stance. What Michael does is try to mentalize his daughter's need to feel differently but without complete reliance on her parents. He also shares some of his own experiences at their age to help bring in a new perspective, while validating his daughter's. His mentalizing involves helping his daughter to develop problem-solving skills. It's a gradual process that starts with helping her to think a little bit about different perspectives on her situation. Doing this helps her to think of alternative ways to view situations that make her feel anxious. She can then start to manage her difficult feelings, and this gradually builds her resourcefulness and resilience. It is important to note that this all started with having her dad empathise with how dreadful she was feeling and share a bit of some of the feelings he had when he was her age, when the world felt confusing. After taking an empathic approach, Michael started to encourage his daughter to think (together with his support) about how she might solve certain particularly challenging situations.

Reflecting on Michael

What do you think about Michael's approach? Would you have done something similar, or do you think your own teenager's low mood and anxiety would have led you to do something different? Let's imagine that Michael hadn't encouraged problem-solving skills or any independence or resilience-building in his daughter. Imagine that Michael sees his principal role as making his daughters feel better when they face life's difficulties. He might like the sense of achievement and satisfaction he gets when he fixes their problems. Michael might have spent his whole parenting life to date driving his children around and sorting their lives out for them; getting things when they needed them. What will this approach feel like for his children when they're 17 or 18, in terms of how they get to places on their own or how they work out a problem for themselves? Does this approach show an understanding of their perspective?

Michael has instead tried to mentalize how his daughters might need different things from him now they are teenagers. He has thought about their developmental needs, particularly in terms of how he could support them towards greater independence and a sense of autonomy. By doing this, he is still making himself available to them while at the same time giving the message that he understands it might not always be helpful to them for him to step in straight away. He has also communicated something about *his* changing role, from the dad who did things *for* them, to the dad who can help facilitate them in coming up with their own solutions.

How teenagers respond to attention and curiosity

The first principle of mentalizing your teenager – attention and curiosity – is a tricky one to get right. We've already thought about how much teenagers hate lots of questions, so how do you show curiosity without creating tension and animosity? It is by using curiosity in a different way with your teenager; that is, to be interested in how things seem from their point of view, and not to be overly interested in all the details, as though on a fact-finding mission. Think back to Chapter One and the teenager who said "We don't want you to be like Sherlock Holmes" and instead, try being interested, curious and attentive to the experience of your teenager – to the feelings that they are experiencing and the kind of mood that they might be in. This approach shows that you're not just bringing your own thoughts, feelings and agenda to situations, but that you're truly interested in what your teenager's experience is like and how the world looks through their eyes.

One of the difficulties you might experience if you adopt this stance of curiosity is that often it can be difficult for an adolescent to explain to you what they feel like, as the example of Dhillon illustrated, through considering changes in the brain that are going on. It's not as straightforward for teenagers as saying, "I feel anxious", "I feel depressed", "I feel worried" or "I'm excited". Those emotional states might have been easier to name when they were younger, but it is much more difficult and complex to work out internal states when they are going through adolescence. The changes taking place in the brain during this time, such as the slower development of the prefrontal cortex, which helps us to weigh up risks and make informed decisions, help us understand that it's much harder to regulate these emotions and that impulsivity will be much stronger. We understand that stopping and thinking before doing something doesn't necessarily come naturally to adolescents and impulsive behaviour is part of the norm during this time. It means you will have to accept a certain amount of uncertainty if your teenager says, "I don't know" when you ask how they're feeling, and uncertainty can be anxiety-provoking for many parents. Try to accept that it's fine not to know and offer to listen when they are ready to talk.

How teenagers respond to perspective-taking

The second principle of the parent "APP" – perspective-taking – is important when trying to work out what might lie behind your teenager's behaviour or their apparent state of mind. The core principle here is to not assume you know, even though you might be desperate to point out that you really do know how they're feeling (because you feel you know them inside out). You need to stick to your curious stance and try to understand and appreciate that you and your teenager will have a very different perspective on things. Sometimes naming these different perspectives explicitly is helpful for your teenager, even if this might seem a little bit clunky or awkward. For example, you might try saying, "I know that for you this may not be such a big deal, but it is for me, and I'm struggling a bit, you know. I'm finding it a little hard that you don't need me so much" or, "I'm finding it a bit hard that you don't want to tell me everything or that sometimes I can't fix your mood, but I do really want to listen and try to understand." Making this distinction between you and them is at the core of mentalizing and reflective parenting and can be extremely helpful for your teenager – helping them to feel both understood and close to you, and permitted to have their own independent thoughts and feelings.

How teenagers respond to empathy and validation

The final part of the parent APP is the empathy and validation principle. First, let's look at the difference between these two things. Empathy is when you share some of the feelings with another person, for example, your friend tells you that their beloved dog has died and they have tears in their eyes as they are telling you. You can see and feel their sadness and you might give them a hug and say how sorry you are, or how much you know they loved their dog. This has the impact of connecting the two of you, of your friend feeling understood and it might make the feeling of sadness even a bit stronger in that moment, because you are sharing it together. When we validate someone, this is a less emotional experience and has the impact of allowing someone to tell you something and feel heard and understood, without increasing the feeling they are experiencing. When we validate someone, we are helping them to manage or even control the feeling. Validating can be useful to practice with your teenager if they are getting very upset about something and you want to help them not get overwhelmed by the feeling. For example, if your teenager is getting extremely anxious and upset about a forthcoming party and what they are going to say to people they don't know, you can say something like, "I can see it's all quite daunting to think of a room full of people you don't know. I think if we plan some things you might say and what time you will arrive and leave the party, that might help." There is less emotion in your voice when you validate, and it helps your teenager to move on from an overwhelming feeling and use the thinking rather than feeling part of their brain.

Most of us like to feel that we are empathic towards the people we love, but this can sometimes feel like a struggle, especially if you strongly disagree or even disapprove of the way your teenager is behaving. You might be worried that in showing empathy for how they feel, you are showing approval for their behaviour, but these are two different things. Mickey, a parent I spoke to, told me that she finds it easiest to parent her teenage girls when they *want* to tell her things. Whatever your point of view on your teenager's behaviour, it is important that if they have taken the big decision to share their feelings with you, you show an empathic response that feels authentic. Teenagers are very astute and can easily detect a patronising or inauthentic tone of voice, and quite rightly so, if we try to show that we understand but we're not really feeling it. Empathy is a really powerful tool, and we can underestimate the importance of it in situations where we perhaps have nothing particularly insightful to say or no immediate solution to the difficulties that teenagers are going through. What we can see is their pain and their struggle; just telling them this, reflecting back how difficult we can see things are for them, is really important on its own. It is unhelpful in these sorts of situations to focus too much on trying to make your teenager happy by giving a 'theoretical' interpretation, or by placing your adult logic onto an adolescent perspective. Rather, the important factor here is to just mirror how your teenager is feeling and, for example, if they're telling you that life is really bad, then you need to validate this. Let's say your teenager has been locked down during the pandemic, they've missed seeing their friends and life feels a bit rubbish all-round; to stay connected with your teenager, the best thing you can say in this situation is an empathic, "Yeah, it does seem really bad for you. It's not fair, it is hard for you. I really wish I could say something to change things, but I'm glad you told me and I'm sorry that I can't change what's happened. Is there anything that would help you right now?"

Empathy is also incredibly helpful in letting your teenager know that even when they feel like they can't do anything to change a situation, you care. A large part of feeling connected, which is such a crucial part of reflective parenting, is feeling seen and heard. This is an important part of using the principles of the parent APP, to help validate your teenager. When your teenager is feeling alone; confused and unsure of what to do, and perhaps anxious a lot of the time, it's hard for them to imagine that anybody else can help them or understands what it really feels like to be them. Just the simple act of listening empathically and being attentive to teenagers in itself makes a difference. Staying connected to your teenager reflects their sense of security and attachment to you. The mentalizing stance helps your teenager to experience a feeling that you are there, even if just in the background; sometimes, being attentive in a hands-off but curious way shows them that you're holding them in mind.

Letting your teenager know they can still reach you

Imagine that you have long arms and are still giving your teenager the message that you are within reach, but just not holding them as closely. For example, if your teenager is out with their friends and you want to allow them the freedom to enjoy their friendships but not get completely cut off from you, you might ask them to keep in touch by messaging you. They won't want to feel you are being too intrusive or over-protective, but neither should you completely retreat and be out of sight and mind. If you remember from the introduction, adolescents still need to feel their attachment relationships are secure and available when they want and need them. Being listened to and held in mind creates a sense of safety and security that is important in all family relationships. The experience of being listened to empathically communicates to your teenager not only that you are available to them, but also that they are deserving of that help and understanding. This latter point shouldn't be underestimated as it's extremely easy during adolescence for a young person to question their self-worth and to lose their self-esteem. As a result, they can easily lose their way and become unsure about the extent to which other people are interested in them or want to help them. They can often feel overly scrutinised and observed by others in a way that feels critical, undermining or, at worst, even shaming. Giving a consistent message that they have a secure base with you is just as important at this time of their life as when they were younger.

Expressing a different opinion

Mentalizing your teenager – explicitly showing that you are interested in their perspective – does not mean you have to let go of your own perspective or not have a difference of opinion. For your teenager, having an experience of you reflecting on their inner world – being mentalized by you – will help them feel more closely connected to you and have a greater sense that you want to understand them. You may still disagree with their way of doing things or of their behaviour; mentalizing is not about having to agree with another person's perspective, but rather to show that you are interested in trying to *understand* it.

When it's difficult to manage your own feelings

Before getting into a conversation or tackling a difficult situation with your teenager, first try noticing what it is *you* are thinking and feeling, and work on regulating yourself and managing your own feelings – essentially, go over the principles of the parent MAP. You take this self-reflective step first, then you can give your full attention and curiosity to your teenager's perspective, and they will experience you as somebody steady, consistent and trustworthy. This can be extremely hard for parents as we worry a lot about our teenagers and regulating emotions is difficult sometimes. One parent of a 17-year-old who had been suffering quite severely with his mental health talked about the need to prepare herself for difficult conversations with him. She reflected that, often, leaping in too quickly, driven by her own anxiety and desire to fix things, resulted in situations escalating, which then created a greater distance between her and her teenager. On the other hand, when she was able to prepare herself for a big conversation and take steps to reflect on and work on her own state of mind (which might involve talking it through with her partner, or taking a step back and waiting a bit longer), she then managed the conversation differently. She mentalized herself this way – by reflecting with her partner's help on her thoughts and feelings – and then, feeling more regulated, she showed, first, curiosity and attention, then listened to her son's perspective on things, and then empathised. She was able to acknowledge to herself, with her partner's support, how difficult it is for her to have an ongoing situation where her teenager is suffering so much, and recognising this in turn helped the conversation to go differently. I noted how when she did this her son then came back to her later for a conversation, and how he thanked her for considering her feelings, he took a step to check in that she was OK and thanked her for trying to help him. I was struck by how much he appreciated her owning her feelings as distinct, separate and different from his. Her ability to mentalize herself helped her *and* her son.

Keshia is 16 and has just finished her exams at secondary school. Year 11 was a hard year for her as she struggled with her friendships, preferring to stay outside a circle of girls her age. She doesn't enjoy the type of conversations her peers have about makeup and relationships, and she often feels uncomfortable and unsure of what to say in these groups. She doesn't feel she has anything interesting to post on social media, which her friends seem to use a lot. Despite this, she wants to be part of the friend group, so when they all say they're going to go to a festival after the exams, Keshia is keen to join them and gets herself invited along.

At the festival, while they get their tents set up, Keshia feels awkward and unsure about how to start the "right" conversation about the festival. She becomes self-conscious and awkward and finds it hard to be her real self in the group. Her three friends say they're going to go out and get some more water, and they'll see her later. Over three hours later, the girls still haven't returned, and Keshia spends the time alone in her tent, feeling really upset and wondering why they lied to her about going to get water when they clearly didn't want to spend time with her. She brave-faces it when they come back and spends the rest of the festival sometimes enjoying seeing bands on her own and other times just being with them but feeling on the outside. When she gets home, she tells her parents what had happened. Her mum feels incredibly upset for Keisha and her immediate reaction is to burst into tears. Her dad wants to talk to the other girls' parents about how they treated his daughter; he is livid.

Reflecting on Keshia using the parent APP

What are your immediate thoughts and feelings about what Keshia is going through? Do you think she's upset about the festival or are there other things that are bothering her? Is she right to feel upset or do you think that maybe something else is going on for Keisha that she hasn't explained or that hasn't been fully understood by either her or her parents perhaps? If this was your teenager, would you react like her mum and be upset, or angry like her dad? Maybe you would have a different reaction, or be a mixture of them both?

Using the reflective parenting tools to help Keisha

If Keshia's mum and dad mentalized their daughter, using the principles of the parent APP – attention and curiosity, perspective-taking and providing empathy – first, they would wonder about what happened at the festival. They might then start to feel that there's a lot more behind the events of the evening in the tent than just one incident and begin to be curious about how the whole thing had been set up.

How can they be curious about her friendships without leaving Keshia feeling that there's something wrong with her, or feeling that her parents are against her friend group? The principles of the APP don't have to *all* be used and they don't need to be used in any order – it depends on the context. In this situation, they might realise that first and foremost they need to show empathy and validation. Her parents could start by empathising with Keshia's experience at the festival. They might say something like, "It sounds horrible and lonely, and you must have felt quite confused and lost in that situation, maybe even a bit frightened?" Note that the language is a bit tentative because the parents can't assume they *know* what their daughter is feeling. They might be tempted to express their opinion that the other girls were mean to Keshia, however, because at this point they don't know if this connects with Keisha's view of the situation, they could hold this thought back until Keisha has expressed it herself. They need to hold on to their own feelings about what's happened to her and try instead to connect with what *she* feels.

It's possible that Keisha doesn't want to acknowledge that her friends were mean, but they could follow her lead and check to see what she's feeling and how far she wants to go in talking about her feelings before they leap to her defence. They might offer their own perspective by saying something like, "In that situation, I know I would feel a bit let down/abandoned/upset by my friends." Keshia needs her parents to be on her side, but not to make her feel worse about herself, and at the start of the conversation they don't know what she is feeling about herself or about her friends. While she needs her parents' support and to not feel alone, it's equally likely that she wants to feel part of the group and not different. If her parents fail to mentalize this, based on what they already know about the difficult year she has had, they are likely to leave her feeling more disconnected.

Keshia's mum's immediate reaction is to become upset, which is understandable but not helpful to Keisha, as it leaves her worried that her parents are so concerned about her (or by her) that she might be left with a sense of guilt or responsibility for her mum's feelings.

What might Keisha's parents do differently to show that they might start to think about the kind of support Keshia needs, either from them or from other people in her network? They could reflect on what feels like a comfortable level of interaction with friends from Keshia's perspective, and how this might differ from their own experiences at school and with friends now. We sense, reading this scenario, that Keisha possibly has some more general problems with friendships, and it would help Keisha for her parents to be curious and interested in this, to give her the assurance that they can help her understand this problem and figure it out. They could also be curious about any difficulties Keisha has more generally in her friendships. It would be helpful for her parents to bear in mind that this is the time in Keisha's life when the most important thing is getting approval from her peers, while also being the time when she is most vulnerable to being rejected by peers. This means that it's likely her everyday life is fraught with possible opportunities for her own mentalizing to break down, which can mean she becomes separated from her social world. When teenagers become separated from their peers and their social world, they lose contact with what's most important to them in the world. If Keshia had already been experiencing some problems in her relationships with her friends, and perhaps with her mental health, then she would be even more vulnerable to feeling rejected by them at the festival. It's important, therefore, for her parents to be vigilant that she doesn't then turn this feeling of rejection on herself and perhaps find unhelpful (even harmful) ways of trying to manage some of these more difficult emotions.

How a teenager's emotional temperature affects how they feel about others

So, when we mentalize by reflecting on the thoughts, feelings and intentions of ourselves and others, we can appreciate how quickly and frequently anxiety levels can escalate during adolescence, a time when teenagers are hypersensitive to how their peers respond to them and have high levels of anxiety about being rejected, mocked or judged. We have already thought about the emotional thermometer; how when anxiety increases, arousal levels increase and the capacity to reflect on ourselves and others goes down. The ability of a teenager to make sense of themselves and others in their social world naturally goes down and then that capacity to mentalize is lost. This in turn means they're unable to make sense of social relationships and may suddenly feel overwhelmed by their feelings. Given the difficulty adolescents have with controlling their strong feelings some of the time, it's not surprising that mentalizing becomes harder for them.

The consequences of losing mentalizing capacity

Losing our capacity to mentalize has other knock-on effects. When we lose our reflective skills, because we are too stressed, anxious, confused or full of self-doubt like Keisha, we can get into "ineffective mentalizing" (described in the introduction) and return to one of our earlier pre-mentalizing modes. For example, often, what happens is that *thoughts* become **facts** (the pre-mentalizing, psychic equivalence mode). So, for Keisha, one of her thoughts might be that her friends don't care about her and they've left her because of something about her. In her mind, this becomes more than a thought, it actually becomes a fact. As a result, Keisha loses her ability to be compassionate about herself; she starts to judge herself and this might lead her to experience negative feelings, for example, that she's bad or worthless. Subsequently, not only does she start to feel this about herself, but she also loses her ability to mentalize her friends. She becomes increasingly certain that they also feel negative about her, and this leads her to experience unbearable and overwhelming feelings of rejection. In her mind, any kind of action that helps her to escape these unbearable feelings can feel like a solution. The worst-case scenario explains the rush to self-harm, discussed in chapter seven, experienced by so many young people who are struggling to process and manage intolerable and overwhelming feelings. It might sound contradictory, but for the young person in a predicament like this, sometimes an action such as self-harm provides some form of short-term relief as it eases them of an intolerable or unbearable state of mind and leads to something actually being done – the healing of a wound. We look at this in detail in chapter seven.

In this scenario, the helpful response from Keisha's parents would be to try to understand her experience and be supportive, empathic and validating. By doing this, they will help her to reduce the amount of strongly negative thoughts and feelings she has and instead help her to feel calm. As a result, she can start to restore some of her mentalizing capacity so that she becomes a little more reflective about what actually happened (possibly seeing a new perspective) and moves away from turning the situation in on herself. So, to get alongside teenagers, taking a curious, empathic interest in their perspective – using the parent APP – parents have to show enough interest and curiosity into what it actually feels like to be them that leads to them feeling the way they do.

Slowing down and rewinding

Another helpful strategy for parents is to try to slow things down. Try to help your teenager pause, go back – or rewind – and think a little bit about what was in their mind before the incident that made them feel so bad. Often, rewinding back to the moment before they started to feel unable to manage their feelings can help them uncover unhelpful and judgmental thoughts about themselves, which you can then explore together. Just by adopting a curious, listening, not-knowing stance – by being a reflective, mentalizing parent – you can start to ask more open questions, such as "What happened before your friends left you in the tent on your own?" Your teenager might say, "I just felt terrible about myself" or, "I was thinking 'I bet they wish they hadn't invited me'" or they might say, "Nothing happened before I felt like that", but by taking this approach, you are modelling that you don't necessarily know best, but you are keen to understand how an experience was for your teenager. This is extremely effective. After this, you might say, "Can you tell me a little bit more about what was happening before then?" The message then to your teenager is, "I really want to know what you experienced. Can you take me back there so we can look at it together?" Your teenager's feelings then usually start to unfold themselves. If you and your teenager can pinpoint the moment where the emotional arousal changed, it is very helpful to reflect on this moment. For Keisha, the important feeling to reflect on might be the sense that she isn't wanted by her friends. This can then open up a pathway to more mentalizing – reflecting on thoughts, such as "I'm not interesting", "I'm different", or "I always get rejected." If she is able to mentalize herself this way, by being helped to rewind to the moment when her emotional temperature rose, it's likely that this will lead to a greater understanding of herself and ultimately of other people.

Importantly, always try to ensure you focus not on what your teenager actually did, i.e. their behaviour, but rather on what was going on in their mind, then how they are feeling in the here and now. For example, if a teenager expresses how incredibly upset they feel after splitting from a partner, it is probably not helpful to think about things in the past and how they have contributed to the break up as this will mean that you are detached from how they are feeling right now. Revisiting the past in this way is quite likely to feel invalidating to your teenager of what they're going through now, and more like a parent "fact-finding mission". It's possible that your teenager might end up feeling misunderstood, so the most important thing to focus on is how your teenager is feeling here and now and how you can help them make sense of those feelings. In Keshia's case, her parents would do well not to focus excessively on what happened in the tent and what she did next, but more on what was going on in her head so that she feels really understood by them. In this way, they will stay connected. Over time, this change of perspective will hopefully allow a bigger conversation to open up from a position of trust and security. At this point, her parents can really help her resolve what it is that's really going on in her friendships. For example, they help her to question whether she is aligning herself with friends who don't share her interests and are too different from her. This type of conversation will support Keisha in learning how to mentalize herself, which will then lead to her being able to regulate her emotions better and understand the kind of friends and social situations she feels comfortable with.

From all these scenarios, it's clear that mentalizing your teenager involves achieving the right balance between helping them feel understood, while not intruding too much in their lives as they try to become independent. The following chapter explores how to navigate your teenager's need to push away from you and be autonomous while also maintaining your connection.

PAUSE AND REFLECT: MENTALIZING YOUR TEENAGER

In a nutshell ...

Mentalizing your teenager involves curiosity and interest in the motives, feelings, thoughts, and intentions behind their behaviour. The parent APP stands for **Attention and curiosity; Perspective-taking and providing Empathy.** The core principle of mentalizing your teenager is to pay specific and active attention to them and to try to see their perspective.

Mentalizing your teenager helps you by ...

By paying active attention and being curious about your teenager, you begin to step into their shoes and understand their experience as they want you to see it, setting aside your own opinion momentarily to connect with their world. This helps you to shift your focus to what's going on *inside* your teenager's mind, rather than getting fixed on their behaviour or attitude. It helps you to separate out their perspective from yours and other people's. Mentalizing your teenager helps you to understand that their thoughts and feelings are entirely separate from yours.

Mentalizing your teenager helps them by …

Each time you mentalize your teenager – using the principles of the parent APP – you are helping them to see you as someone who will listen, see their perspective and understand. This helps your teenager to feel more connected to you and more likely to trust you. It also models a reflective mind, which will support the development of your teenager's capacity for reflecting on thoughts and feelings. This will help your teenager to make and maintain stronger relationships with others.

Mentalizing your teenager – using a parent APP – helps your relationship by …

As you seek to understand your teenager's thoughts and feelings, and validate and empathise with their perspective on the world, they will feel a greater emotional connection with you and an increased understanding of themselves. This is particularly important during adolescence when brain changes make it harder to understand the intentions of others and harder to manage their own emotions. You will have better and more emotionally attuned conversations and feel a sense of increased security in your relationship.

Keep in mind …

- Be actively attentive to what your teenager is thinking and feeling and try to listen more than you talk.
- Pause and reflect before you jump in to offer your opinion, and take time to first understand what their perspective is. Pay particular attention to what feels important to them, no matter what your opinion of this is.
- It's fine not to understand or know what your teenager thinks and feels and why. It's important not to pretend you understand, or to offer an opinion when you don't understand their perspective. It's okay to be unsure about what to say or to struggle to understand how they feel, but show that you are keen to understand.

- First, regulate your own feelings – by using the emotional thermometer to check how you're feeling – then choose a moment when you're calm to mentalize your teenager more effectively.
- Practice doing a mind check to notice what's in your mind. Then when you've done this, start to notice and be curious about what might be in your teenager's mind, but don't be too intrusive.
- Respect your teenager's need to have some autonomy. When you express curiosity about what they are thinking and feeling, gauge when it's the right time, and allow them some private thoughts that are theirs alone.
- Be aware of your tone and facial expression. Teenagers are sensitive to voices that sound patronising or judgemental. Speak to your teenager as you would want to be spoken to.
- Help your teenager to problem-solve, knowing that this can be difficult during adolescence when the brain acts more impulsively.

4

AUTONOMY

Your teenager's need to separate

> *"Can I have a bit of privacy here? You're stepping on my rug!"*

Recently, it was my youngest son's 14th birthday. I wanted us to do something special with him as a family so asked around a group of my friends with similar-aged kids for ideas on somewhere fun to take him for a meal. Settling on a place where you could sit at the counter and watch the cooks make the food – dishes flaming and high-energy action in the kitchen in front of us – I thought I was on to a winner. I presented this to my nearly 14-year-old son who said, quite politely, "Thanks Mum, but I think that kind of place would be much more fun with my friends." I was a bit crushed.

This chapter will look at your teenager's need for autonomy within the family, alongside the growing importance of their friendships. One of the main reasons adolescents push for greater autonomy in this period of their lives is because they need to form strong relationships with their peer group as part of their transition into adulthood. The pull and push of your teenager – on the one hand wanting security and stability and on the other, pushing you away to go their own way – is a common experience for most parents and carers that can often lead to conflict. As parents, we can struggle to let go when our teenagers want us to and at other times we miss their cues that they need us to hold on. The internal battle between this push-pull creates a degree of turmoil for both parents and teenagers. How do you help your teenager to develop a sense of autonomy and support the development of healthy and supportive relationships with peers, while also staying connected to them? We could worry that our teenagers' focus on and desire to be with their peers is a negative influence on them. Taking a

 DOI: 10.4324/9780429459245-5

mentalizing approach can help you with this daily dilemma. We will look at the importance of peers in chapter five.

Young children tend to act out their feelings via their behaviour when they feel that their needs are frustrated. Often, adolescents do the same; for example, by slamming the bedroom door in your face when you are trying to reason with them. An adolescent's need for privacy as well as autonomy can often leave parents feeling shut out of their teenager's life. When parents feel shut out, this often increases their anxiety about their teenager, or conversely, it can breed an atmosphere of complacency, where teenagers are left unmonitored to – and *on* – their own devices. All of this is often compounded by the fact that as children get older, they also learn to lie. Adolescents will use their skills to lie because they want to do things without your knowledge, without your interference and without risking you not granting your permission.

When teenagers lie

The ability to lie arises initially around the age of four when children develop something called a "theory of mind". This theory describes the ability to appreciate that someone can hold a false belief or a belief that is different from your own. When I carried out my own research in this area, the findings demonstrated that children who were more securely attached – who had an early experience with a parent who was available, mirrored their feelings and responded to their needs – passed this test much earlier than children who had insecure patterns of attachment (1). In other words, the ability to appreciate that other people could hold beliefs that were different from their own was related to the security of attachment a child had with their parent. This makes sense because the way in which we learn to understand minds (both our own and other people's) is through the attachment relationship, where parents and carers reflect to the baby what they think the baby is thinking and feeling. My fascination with these findings fuelled my later interest in mentalizing as a therapeutic tool.

Your teenager's need for privacy

How is this understanding relevant to adolescence and your relationship with your teenager now? Your teenager wants to have a part of themselves that is entirely private and separate from you, and sometimes this involves them lying about what they're doing and who they're with – both to protect you from worrying, but also to protect their own privacy and individual identity. This adolescent need for privacy is often an uncomfortable feeling for parents, but accepting this is a very important stage of your development as a parent, just as seeking privacy and autonomy is an important part of your teenager's development. When your teenager lies to you about a party they are going to, it isn't because they want to hurt you or consciously deceive you, but often because they increasingly need to keep parts of their lives private from you so they can forge their own identity, and so they can feel close to their friends – the group that is becoming part of their own "tribe". Taking a mentalizing stance towards yourself and your teenager will allow you to be curious about *why* they needed to lie and to start to be curious about yourself and why *you* felt so keen to know what they were really doing. Naturally, part of your strong feelings will stem from your wish to keep them safe, but another part might be related to other factors in your relationship and thoughts about your role as a parent. Learning to be a reflective parent will help you to validate both sets of feelings and to stay connected to your teenager, as opposed to trying to correct their behaviour, further alienating them from you.

There are, of course, many other reasons why adolescents lie; for example, they might lie to avoid being punished, restricted or shamed. As parents we know that some of the things teenagers want to do are illegal, maintaining authority is a constant challenge as they seek to set boundaries while also struggling to manage their own fears and anxieties and keep a connection alive with their teenagers.

Connection not correction

So much of the literature around parenting and the programmes available to parents, online and in person, are about trying to change a child or teenager's behaviour. How much of your own attempts so far to correct your teenager's behaviour has strengthened your relationship with them? When a teenager is actively seeking to be more autonomous and distinguish themselves from you, how do you stay connected to them? When you take time to look at what is happening in the relationship between the two of you, instead of focusing on what they are doing and trying to correct a problem that seems to you to lie within them, this will give your teenager what they need from you the most. Adolescents need a sense of a secure, loving and accepting relationship just as much as a young child does.

They also need you to speak to them in a way you would hope they can connect with and respond to. So, if you speak to your teenager in a way that expresses an angry feeling such as "Why on earth did you do THAT? No wonder your friend didn't message you", followed by a criticism of your teenager, then they are likely to respond in a similarly aggressive, critical way. On the other hand, if you speak in a way that connects with how you think they want to be seen, say as mature, thoughtful, and/or interesting, then you will get a thoughtful and mature response. For example, you might say, "I'm interested in what happened to you yesterday. What are your thoughts about why your friend didn't message you?".

Feeling judged, disapproved of, rejected and/or criticised will not help to keep you connected, but is more likely to create a rupture in your relationship. It can be such a struggle when your teenager is busy forming their own identity, as both their character and response to you can change dramatically. What was once a loving, affectionate child, can suddenly feel like a rejecting, hurtful, openly critical, and unkind young person, which is very hard for any parent to take. The good news is that, once your teenager feels more secure in their own identity as a near-adult with their own set of friends, college or work commitments and status, their need to state their own separateness from you so strenuously will diminish and your loving, affectionate offspring will return. To get through this period, you will need to work on keeping the connection with them going in your relationship, while they learn to achieve the autonomy they desire without causing you to feel rejected. This is where mentalizing yourself (perhaps with the help of your parent MAP) becomes essential to both you and your relationship with your teenager. Work on your own mind first.

The push/pull of teenagers

What are your own feelings about your teenager becoming more independent and separate from you? Does it feel like an exciting stage in their life, or does it fill you with fear and sadness, and a sense of loss, rejection, or envy? You might be the parent of a teenager who is not striving for autonomy, who you feel is too dependent on you. For many parents, a common worry is that their teenager lacks social networks and feels lonely, bullied or socially anxious and isolated. The place of the parent is to step in when needed, when the social network fails. You are relegated to the bench rather than playing for the first team. Parenting is an art rather than a science because there is no precise formula for knowing when to go forward and when to pull back. If you are worried that, by pulling away from you, your teenager is getting into danger, you need to be able to judge when the danger is real and when it's in your imagination. Equally, if your teenager experiments with becoming independent and autonomous but is disappointed if this doesn't quite work out, be mindful that a warm and fuzzy response from you could be misconstrued as laughing at their efforts, which is likely to feel shameful to them and damage their ego. Instead, try being more curious and attentive to their motives and the thoughts behind their actions, so that you can get a better understanding of what's in their mind. They may have a feeling that you are laughing at them rather than empathising with them because your teenager isn't interested in the wisdom of your insights into adolescence, even if you feel these are well-grounded in your own experiences.

Depending on many factors in your own life, both past and present, you will have strong feelings from time to time about your teenager's need for autonomy or dependency. For example, your own past experiences when you were an adolescent, and your feelings about moving to a new stage of your family life, without young children dependent on you, will influence your feelings. To get to the root of these feelings, it's important to look at what autonomy versus dependency means for both you and your teenager. In the following scenario, we can explore Dad Lenny's parenting dilemmas.

Lenny is a single dad to two boys. His youngest, Mason, is 11 years old and his oldest, Isaac, is 16 years old. Isaac has come in from school on Friday evening and gone straight up to his bedroom where he's making a fair bit of noise, moving things around, opening up his wardrobe and cupboard doors and slamming them shut, so Lenny goes up to see what's going on. He walks into Isaac's bedroom and Isaac says, "Knock?" as his dad hasn't knocked on the door before entering.

Lenny:	"What's all the noise?"
Isaac:	"Just putting some stuff together. I'm heading out with some mates later."
Lenny:	"Which friends?" "Where are you

	going?" "I've just started making some dinner."
Isaac:	"Just mates. It's not relevant, Dad"
Lenny (raising his voice):	"It's relevant to me! Who are you meeting up with and what are you putting in the bag?"
Isaac:	"Just stuff. There's a meetup at Shane's house. It's not that deep. Just a few of us. Have you seen my controller?"
Lenny:	"Are you eating with us first then, or what? You look like you're in a hurry! Shall I give you a lift there? It's already dark."
Isaac:	"No thanks, Luke's picking me up in a minute. Dad, can you get out of my room please?"
Lenny:	"Don't talk to me like that, I'm your dad!"
Isaac (moving towards the door to hold it open and gesturing to his dad to leave):	"Can I have a bit of privacy here? You're stepping on my rug!" Lenny leaves the room feeling angry, hurt and a bit confused.

Isaac slams the door after him.

Reflecting on the scenario

What is your reaction to this scenario? What are you thinking and feeling as you read this? Try to tune in to how you would feel if you were Lenny in this situation. Then tune in to what you think Isaac is thinking and feeling.

When we take a reflective parenting stance, we always start with our feelings first. To untangle the feelings we have as parents about what is going on with Isaac, we need to mentalize the parent first – to step into Lenny's shoes and reflect on his thoughts and feelings – before reflecting on what might be going on in Isaac's mind.

Reflecting on Lenny – If we imagine some of the thoughts and feelings Lenny is experiencing, we might think his first thought is "Where is Isaac going and with whom? Why can't I know some details, such as which friends he's meeting up with?" We might imagine that Lenny is feeling worried, anxious, angry, disrespected and/or used as a father – possibly also overlooked and undermined. His emotional arousal level is going up quickly as his son doesn't give him the information he's looking for. Thinking back to the emotional thermometer in Chapter One, when our emotional temperature increases, our ability to mentalize decreases, simply meaning that it's harder to think reflectively when we are in a heightened state of emotion (and equally hard when we are in a switched off state, when we have a low level of emotional arousal). If we think about Lenny, we could start to be curious about where these thoughts and feelings come from and what is influencing them. We could ask questions about Lenny's own family history and whether his parents were protective or allowed him a lot of freedom. Did he confide in his parents and tell them what he was doing, or did he have a private life from them? What was the family culture he grew up in? We could also start to be curious about the current influences on Lenny's state of mind. He seems to be very worried about what is in Isaac's bag. Is he worried about the sort of clothes he might have in there or something worse, such as whether he has alcohol or drugs? What are his values about these things? If I added some detail and told you that Lenny was raised in a culture where strict parenting was the norm and his parents had a strict upbringing which Lenny has questioned in his own parenting of his two boys – what would you think then might be going on for him? I could add that his wife died three years ago and, since this time, Lenny has been raising the boys on his own whilst working long hours in a local school where he is the Deputy Head. Using these details, we can start to build up a map – following the steps of the parent MAP in Chapter Two – of Lenny's parenting and consider all the different things influencing his thoughts and feelings at this moment with his son. If Lenny were to reflect on this himself, he would start to regulate his emotions a little – figuring out whether he had reacted too strongly, perhaps because of his own state of mind – or if his reaction was appropriate to the situation.

Most of the time we are unaware of how our personal context affects our behaviour and reactions in the moment. Here, Lenny is unlikely to be thinking about the influences that are behind his behaviour. When we are in situations like this and our emotional temperature has risen, we are unlikely to be able to reflect on where our thoughts and feelings come from. Going back over stressful situations afterwards can be helpful for regulating your feelings and understanding what might be influencing them. For Lenny, doing this would mean that in his next encounter with Isaac, he can be more aware of the strong influences there are on his own parenting that affect him in the moment. In the next encounter with Isaac, Lenny might notice that he has some strong influences on his own parent MAP which are affecting him in the moment. For example, his conscious attempts to try to not be as strict as his own parents might be preventing him from setting a boundary. Once he has insight and understanding of these, this will help him to separate out his own strong feelings from anything going on with his son. If he can mentalize himself, he will be more likely to not project onto Isaac the full strength of his own feelings.

Reflecting on Isaac – Isaac has gone straight from school up to his room to pack his bag, so we might imagine he's excited and that he is in a hurry to meet up with his friends. His mind is on what he's going to be doing when he gets together with his friends – gaming, his favourite pastime. He values the private space of his own room and is perhaps feeling agitated by his dad's presence, which is ruining his flow as he tries to think about what he wants to take to his friend's house. This agitation causes him to lose track of where he's put his controller, which he needs to be able to game with his friends. He feels irritated by his dad's intrusion into his bedroom without knocking, and so when his dad asks him questions, these feel even more intrusive than usual and he overlooks the offer of a lift or dinner, too irritated and annoyed to be able to mentalize his dad. He might be thinking, "Why does he need to know all these details?" Something he was looking forward to doing independently has been made into something bad or secret and he feels angry that his mood has shifted because of his dad. What else might be going on for Isaac that is less visible? Knowing he lost his mum three years before, when he had just turned thirteen, we can begin to imagine some of the powerful feelings he has been trying to manage and the importance of his friendships. We can also start to be curious about his feelings towards his dad; perhaps he feels protective of him and doesn't want to give him any more worries, or perhaps he feels angry that no one could save his mum. He might even have a sense of responsibility himself because when we experience death and loss at a very young age it is much harder to understand them. He might also have a sense of his dad's struggle to find a balance between his own strict upbringing and how he is trying to raise his own boys. He might feel a sense of responsibility for his dad, which he finds overwhelming or burdensome at times. Perhaps he is scared of his dad's reaction if he tells him what he's doing with his friends, or is he simply being a typical adolescent, wanting a bit of space and privacy away from his dad and brother?

What might be going on? – Thinking about this scenario, we can imagine Lenny's annoyance and share in his feeling of being overlooked, after all, as a very basic, doesn't a parent need to know if their teenager is going to be eating dinner with the family? At the same time, when a young person is being asked lots of questions, their immediate default is to shut down. What difference does it make if his dad knows the names of the people he's gaming with? What this scenario says is that there's a great deal of parental anxiety around Lenny wanting to know the details of his son's Friday evening, without any clear rationale for *why* he wants to know. What is the anxiety and frustration about? Is it possible that Lenny, as a single parent, feels that *his* evening has been ruined and a meal that he was looking forward to with his sons at the end of the week has been sabotaged or rejected? Lenny feels it is his *right* to know the details of his son's activities, but is it? Would you agree or disagree with this feeling? Or is there something else happening inside Lenny's mind? Perhaps, having lost his wife, he is deeply anxious and protective of his sons, feeling the weight both of his loss and of the sole responsibility he has for his sons. There are many more things that you can probably start to imagine or relate to but, as with every parent–teenager relationship, these will be individual to Lenny and Isaac's dynamic.

Thinking together

We are likely to have some clear initial thoughts when we think over this brief scenario. First might be that the way Isaac speaks to his dad seems rude to us, as adults. Second, that it's frustrating, potentially upsetting and even a waste of money to cook food for someone who isn't around to eat it. If we really mentalize both dad and teenager in this scenario, we might start to understand that for Lenny, the factors that affect his behaviour and responses – that he's likely to uncover when going through the steps of his parent MAP – mean there is something that's being triggered. We might also be curious about what Lenny feels about his oldest child moving away from him and towards his friends. Is his anger and upset part of a bigger worry that Isaac doesn't need him as much now as he used to? Is Lenny missing the fact his teenager has to have things that are just *his* experiences? Perhaps, like a lot of teenagers, he doesn't feel he needs to relate every detail. We might reflect further on how a parent's need to talk might not tally with when their teenager feels ready to. The timing of these conversations can be hard to get right but is critical to keeping a connection with your teenager, because picking the wrong time (as Lenny did) can lead to total shutdown.

Balancing authoritative parenting with reflection – using the two-hands approach

The two-hands approach, outlined in Chapter One is a useful tool for understanding your teenager's behaviour while at the same time responding to it, for example, by setting in place a boundary or a consequence. In Lenny's case, adopting this approach with Isaac would help him to feel that he still has authority as a

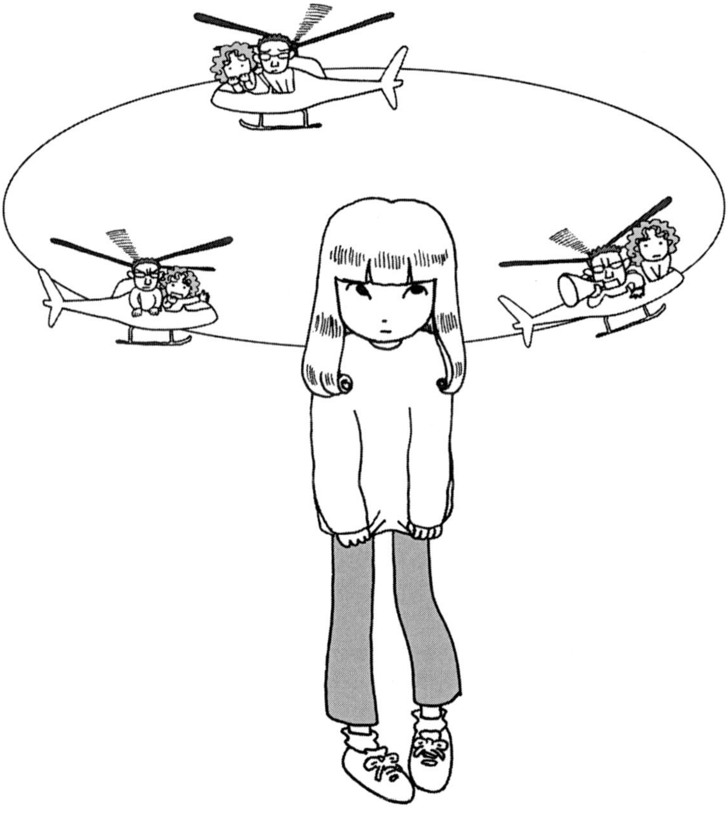

Figure 4.1

parent. For example, Lenny might use the one "hand" to take a mentalizing stance of curiosity and empathy for Isaac's need to be a bit independent from him – spending time with his friends and wanting a bit of privacy – while at the same time using the other "hand" to agree on a limit about the time Isaac needs to come home, or he might have said, "Let's eat together first as the food is ready." The trick is to try to deploy both "hands" at the same time so that your teenager feels you have some authority, but at the same time, they still experience you as warm and understanding of their perspective. This keeps them feeling safe and secure.

Let's look at the reflections of a mother to three teenagers.

Anna is a mum to three teenagers: two boys and one girl. She has found it particularly stormy parenting her teenage girl, Cassie, who is now 19.

Anna described Cassie as a "risk taker". Cassie hit puberty at 11 and Anna felt she didn't manage this at all well as Cassie seemed to suddenly push all the boundaries she had put in place. Anna's way of dealing with her daughter's pushback was to become strict about the things she couldn't do and she developed a list of rules of what was not allowed – "not in my house" became her mantra for a while.

The first thing Anna noticed change in Cassie was her attitude; her previously polite and biddable daughter became defiant and challenging. At school, she got into a gang culture. Anna was shocked to see that Cassie was attracted to this gang. She discovered that Cassie was looking at social media a lot and that her friends were starting to smoke weed when they were 11 to 12 years old. Anna found that the stricter she was, the more wilful Cassie became.

When one day, Cassie told her mum that a friend of hers had had sex at the age of 12, Anna started to worry seriously that she needed to take a different approach with her daughter. She had been setting down boundaries and rules, but she could see that all this was doing was pushing Cassie away, and now she really started to panic that her daughter was going to start copying the behaviour of the friends she was hanging around with. She had to question whether laying down the law was at all effective and decided to take a different tack.

She reflected that she was walking a fine line at this point between not lecturing her, giving her boundaries as a parent, and giving her autonomy. She couldn't believe she was having to swallow a whole new set of rules, and it made her extremely anxious whenever she allowed Cassie any autonomy, as immediately Anna's mind would jump to a potentially risky situation. There were times when they would go out together, just the two of them and Anna's intention would be to just be curious. To Anna's surprise, she found that Cassie would open up during those outings; she would not assure Anna but would tell her what she wanted for herself. She also told her mum that she had found the situation with her friend and boyfriend scary. As Anna became more open and curious to find out how Cassie would feel, rather than putting down the rules first, her daughter started to confide more in her. Cassie said she could see that the girl loved the boy and, rather than wanting to copy her friend, she told her mum that she was worried for her friend as she thought that he didn't love her and wanted sex rather than a loving relationship.

When at 16 she told her mum she wanted to leave school and not take her exams, it became clear that she didn't want to do anything Anna suggested. Anna decided to not live with the fear of what might happen to her daughter and instead adopted an approach in which she validated Cassie's wish to take a different course, so she supported her starting an apprenticeship and Cassie felt extremely relieved not to have to take A levels. As the pressure of her mum's expectations lifted, Cassie became closer to her mum and more confident of her future.

Reflecting on Anna's parenting

Anna initially adopted an approach many of us would do if we felt our teenager was going down a road that seemed risky to us. She started putting hard rules and boundaries in place about things that were and were not allowed in her house. We can understand this as Anna's fear about her daughter's safety, and also her fear about losing control over her daughter as she pushed Anna away. Her emotional temperature probably suddenly escalated when Cassie old her about what her friends were doing, and we can imagine shet-suddenly panicked and stopped being able to think clearly. When our emotions go up, we tend to jump to taking action or setting a strict rule without thinking it through. Our brains simply aren't able to reflect at these times. We could start to be curious about where Anna's beliefs came from: was her own mother a rule-setter? Or perhaps she was the opposite and Anna felt she needed to be more boundaried than her own parents. Once she adopted a mentalizing approach of open curiosity and not knowing, we can see there was a shift in their relationship. She decided to have faith in her daughter finding her own direction. We can see that she tried to mentalize Cassie – using some of the principles of the parent APP and took a stance of open curiosity and not knowing. This set the scene for enabling Cassie to talk about her real feelings.

Anna had a lot of anxiety about school and how Cassie was going to manage without doing her exams, particularly knowing she was mixing with a risk-taking group outside of school. It must have been extremely hard for her to let go of her initial approach of "not in my house", but she could see this wasn't working and that Cassie was closing down when she took this stance. She tried at first to put more pressure on her to behave herself, but found that what made the most difference was when she pushed back against the school who wanted her to take her exams, and showed Cassie she was taking her corner, seeing that Cassie was clearly suffering in that environment. Cassie went on to leave school, get a job she loved in the local veterinary surgery and kept up a strong friendship group.

I wonder if you agree with Anna's approach or if it makes you feel anxious. You might feel you would take a very different approach and, of course, you will have a different background and current circumstances that will influence your parenting. Anna was curious to see how taking a risk in her parenting approach might work, as she could see that her first approach wasn't helping her stay connected to her daughter. The risk for Anna was that if she held on to her initial stance, she would lose the connection with Cassie and, in doing so, possibly put her daughter at greater risk. Anna's decision to change her approach paid off for her and Cassie. For others, taking this approach would feel uncomfortable and possibly too permissive. Our parenting approach doesn't have to stay static, and reflecting on what type of parenting approach is working or isn't working is helpful to both you and your teenager. You may have started out quite permissive, but become more authoritative as your teenager gets older, or vice versa like Anna.

Peer relationships and autonomy in adolescence.

There is an extensive history of social psychology research into adolescent peer relationships and the significance and importance of these relationships. Research shows that as they get older, adolescents spend an increasing amount of time with their peers proportional to the amount of time they spend with their family. These findings are culturally specific and much of the research is carried out on white, western cultures (predominately in the United States). In some other countries, for example, South Korea, India and Japan, adolescents spend equal amounts of time with their families as they did when they were children. Interestingly, the results from Western studies show some gender differences, with adolescent girls spending a greater amount of time with their friendship group than boys, whereas boys tended to spend more time alone, the same amount of time as girls with friends and less time with their parents. These are trends and, of course, are not true for all teenagers. Your teenager may prefer to be on their own than with their friends for most of the time, or they might prefer being with friends over being alone. However your teenager spends their time, they are biologically driven to need greater autonomy and it is part of our responsibility as parents to help them achieve this.

The risks of overprotection

Despite our instincts to protect our children, there can be risks in over-protective parenting, and in not supporting our teenagers to achieve some autonomy. For example, if we look at risk-taking, discussed in more detail in chapter six, there is a continuum and at the lower end of this scale are adolescents who don't take any risks at all. These teenagers tend to have greater difficulties with their mental health than the adolescents in the middle of the scale, who take more calculated risks (such as sometimes drinking too much at a party, or playing a dangerous sport). So where over-protective parenting means there is an absence of risk-taking, this can mean that teenagers fail to achieve autonomy, which leads to a far greater threat to mental health in later adolescence and adulthood. We will look in more detail in Chapter Six at the difficulties for adolescents if they don't take risks, but in terms of their need for autonomy, there are serious consequences if this is not facilitated by parents. Say, for example, your teenager wants to take a trip into town with their friends and

Figure 4.2

it would be the first time you allowed them to go anywhere without you, what would be the consequence of you insisting on driving them there, or accompanying them on the trip? It would certainly stifle their need for independence, but it would also compromise any developing problem-solving skills as you would be at hand, providing all the solutions for them. This in turn leaves your teenager more vulnerable than if you were to give them some advice on public transport routes and ask them to message you when they arrive at their destination. In Chapter Six, where we look at risk, we see that in fact, teenagers today are striving *less* for autonomy and independence than in previous generations, and that this brings with it its own risks.

Autonomy and parenting teenagers with ASD

If you are parenting a teenage boy with ASD, there is a different set of issues relating to their need for autonomy and independence. We have already thought a bit about how teenage boys tend to increase the amount of time they spend on their own, away from their parents. Teenage boys with ASD, while struggling as much with their identity as teenage girls, can often retreat more into their bedrooms and into their special interests and world, away from others in a bid for autonomy. While at times it will be important for them to have a safe space where they can feel calm and more regulated in their emotions, it is equally important to try to stay connected to your teenager and to coax them out of their room and into a more social world. It is easier to feel more disconnected from your teenager with ASD, compared with a neurotypical teenager. Parents can experience a profound lack of emotional connectedness to children with ASD, whether or not this has been diagnosed, that feels qualitatively different from the experience of being with a teenager without ASD. I was working with one family where the mum of a teenage boy with ASD felt extremely sad that he didn't appear to need her company or express any strong emotions towards her. It left her feeling very lonely and a little redundant as a parent. In this situation, it is helpful to mentalize yourself and understand that what you are experiencing is a normal reaction and that the degree of intimacy you wish for in your relationship with them is sometimes different from what they desire. That is not to say that teenagers with ASD don't want connection or loving relationships, but that the need for autonomy and space can sometimes be incompatible with their parents' need for closeness. It can be extremely hard accepting this, but important to acknowledge that this is not a reflection of how much your teenager loves you or needs you, but more likely related to their need to have more time where they feel in control of the situation and their feelings, and this can often mean more time alone.

When autonomy leads to conflict with parents

In some instances, an adolescent's need for autonomy can lead to protracted conflict between them and their parents.

Research tells us that adolescents learn more by reward than punishment and are also more likely to respond to immediate rewards than longer-term ones (2). This helps us to understand that your teenager is unlikely to engage in a task where the reward for it is far off; for example, "If you revise for your exams now, you are more likely to get a better job later" is less likely to be effective than, "If you revise for your exams this evening, I'll get us a take-out afterwards." Research on adolescents also tells us that punishing behaviour is unlikely to yield the behaviour changes we might hope for. For example, "You didn't do any revision last night, so I'm taking your phone off you tonight so you can revise more."

The problem is that when your emotional temperature is high because *you* are feeling anxious or stressed about, say, the longer-term outcomes for your teenager if they don't study hard, you are more likely to struggle to mentalize yourself and understand that this is *your* worry. You are in turn also more likely to project your stress onto your teenager, in an attempt to get them as worried as you are. When we are in this mode, we go back to the *pre-mentalizing* modes described in the introduction, such as labelling our teenagers or taking rapid action (such as dishing out a punishment) without thinking through its impact. We often get into this mode when we feel our teenagers are on the attack, and unfortunately, it only escalates the conflict.

Almost every parent I've known has been hurt by the hostility their teenager has aimed at them at some point in their relationship. Adolescents express the type of strong feelings you might usually associate with a toddler. Usually, this comes and goes, but in some instances, the hostility and opposition to normal parental authority can become so strong that a sort of stand-off emerges, where parent and teenager are on opposite sides of what feels like a battlefield. In chapter one, we looked at the changes to the brain occurring during adolescence, so we can understand that some of this hostility comes from a difficulty at this stage of development where the thinking, rational part of the brain, in the frontal cortex, is lagging behind in its development, compared with the emotional part of the brain. So, we can see that it's likely your teenager will react emotionally first and, as a result, think much later. As their parent, you also have a part to play. There are often very negative preconceptions about what being a teenager means. For many parents, even the word "teenager" is synonymous with being difficult or unreasonable, or wilfully trying to push your buttons. It's almost as if they can't do anything right if they don't live up to their parents' expectations. This criticism can lead teenagers to feel repressed and often very angry. If you go into your child's teenage years with these negative expectations, you are likely to be met with a hostile and "unreasonable" adolescent. The more entrenched difficulties between parents and teenagers – where there is chronic miscommunication, lack of connection and open hostility – are often in families where the parents have failed to validate their teenager's experience of things and simultaneously struggled to manage their own emotional response to their teenager's strongly expressed feelings about things.

Teenagers have a strong sense of injustice and will push back if you appear to be blaming or criticising them for something they don't feel they've done. It is important to try to stay calm so you can attempt to mentalize yourself and regulate your emotions, even when your teenager seems to be out of control. It's natural to get angry or upset when your teenager is raging at you or shutting you out of their life, but reacting this way will lead to a cycle of negativity and hostility between you and your teenager, and ultimately will break the connection you want to have with them. If you mentalize yourself as well as your teenager, instead of getting upset and angry, you can try saying something like, "I don't like it when you get angry at me, but I do understand why. I love you no matter what."

What you can do at times of conflict with your teenager

We know that heightened emotions lead to a breakdown in mentalizing capacity – the ability to reflect on thoughts and feelings – so appealing to your teenager's emotional brain, as opposed to their logical, thinking brain, will be more effective during times of conflict. So, thinking back to the parent APP in Chapter Three, where you mentalize your teenager, it would be more effective when your teenager is angry to actively listen (A), show interest in their perspective (P) and provide empathy (P). This can be very difficult to do when you're angry and upset, so the second-best thing to do if you're not in the right emotional temperature to empathise or tune in to your teenager's emotions is simply to describe how you think they're feeling. You might say something like:

> "You feel it's unfair that I won't let you stay out late with your friends."
>
> "You're annoyed that your brother took your jacket without asking."
>
> "It feels really boring to have to revise after you've been at school all day."

You can then turn to your mentalizing tool and show more curiosity in what they are thinking and feeling, by just listening and asking if they can tell you more about how they feel. If they can't describe the feeling, don't push, simply show very clearly that you are curious and care about whatever it is they're feeling. You can still hold some parental authority by saying that you felt hurt by them shouting at you, being rude, or whatever it was, but at the same time show an interest and understanding in how they feel – this uses a Two-Hands approach. Try to keep the focus on what they feel and what is important to them. By talking more about these feelings and shifting the focus away from the person or thing that made them angry in the first place, you are helping your teenager to mentalize themselves, and ultimately, this will help them to regulate their feelings.

When it comes to conflict, if you have a teenager with ASD, there will be additional difficulties for them, as they are likely to find recognising and managing conflict difficult (certainly compared with non-autistic teenagers) and this will impact their ability to repair and maintain friendships. Although, as we've described, being on the receiving end of your teenager's hostility is always hard, there is an important task in working through conflict with a teenager with ASD, which involves some explicit teaching of perspective-taking. Chapter Five looks at the closely linked topic of socialisation and ASD.

Let's look at a scenario where a teenager has been in protracted and prolonged conflict with his parents over his desire for more freedom, where he feels his parents are being over-protective.

Josh is 15 and in year 10, building up to his first major exams. He lives with his mum, dad and younger sister, Carly. He has recently formed a new friendship group – a mix of boys and girls – who he wants to spend most of the weekend seeing. In Year 9, he was mostly interested in playing and watching football, and his dad used to take him to play in his local team, and on weekends they would go to Nottingham Forest to watch the match. His dad had been a lifelong season ticket holder and was delighted Josh was into it as much as him. After a school trip, Josh's mum and dad noticed he seemed different and wanted to see more of his friends, which, at first, they were pleased about. Gradually, Josh started telling them, rather than asking them, that he was going round to a friend's house and his dad started stating the rules in a way that he found really annoying.

Dad:	"I'm going to walk round to meet you from Gav's house because it's dangerous walking home after dark."
Josh:	"I don't need you to walk me home, that's a bit extra. It's just a couple of streets away. I'll make my own way home."
Dad:	"I'm not going to argue with you about it. There was a kid stabbed in Nottingham last week, I'm not having you walking around at night. You're only 15."
Josh:	"It's Gav's birthday on Saturday and there's a group of us going. You don't need to get me. I'll walk with the others. It's only a few streets away."
Dad:	"I'd like the address please and can you give me Gavin's mum or dad's number please?"
Josh (getting agitated):	"I don't know if we'll be at Gav's place the whole evening, we might go to another mate's house. There's a few different things going on the same night."
Dad (getting angry):	"Like what things? I need to know who you're with and what you're doing."
Josh:	"What does it matter? It's just a few mates. Why do you need to know so much?"
Dad:	"Because I'm your DAD and I need to make sure you're safe!"
Josh:	"I'm going upstairs for a bit."

Josh goes upstairs, slams his bedroom door, swearing under his breath about his dad, and starts to message his friend, Gav, and others in the group about the plans for the weekend. He decides he won't give his dad any more information and starts to work out a cover story for what he's doing. His dad bursts into his room without knocking and starts shouting at Josh, who shouts back about what an "annoying and over-protective parent" he is and how he's "not a baby like Carly anymore", before screaming at his dad, "just get out of my room!"

Reflecting on the parent

In this scenario, we can see that Josh and his dad are at opposite ends of the scale with regard to their views about how risky his actions are. While his dad is aware of the dangers of walking the streets, Josh is preoccupied with his new friends. Dad has enjoyed a close relationship with Josh until recently, so it must come as a shock to see his son retreat from him into a different world. He possibly feels sad about the loss of the closeness he felt with Josh when they went to football together, and he might even be feeling a bit jealous of Josh's new life with his friends. Equally, he might be very anxious about losing him permanently if he leaves him to walk around the streets at night. He's particularly aware of a recent violent incident not far away.

Reflecting on the teenager

From Josh's perspective, we can imagine that he experienced a new feeling of independence when he went on the school trip and that since then he has been enjoying a new friendship group. The group is mixed and we might be curious about whether Josh is becoming interested in the girls in the group (or in the boys, we don't know about his preference). For Josh, part of the excitement of this new part of his life is that it is separate from the family activities he used to do, and he likely wants this to be his experience alone and something he can keep private. He is annoyed at his dad wanting to be involved, even if it's just walking him home. He feels that this could spoil his flow on the evening and maybe even embarrass him in front of his friends.

Thinking together

We can see both perspectives and you might find yourself empathising more with Josh's dad than with Josh if you have experienced something similar or are starting to fear your teenager's growing interest in being away from you, where you don't know if they are safe or not. If we think about the reflective parenting model and how it can help repair the rupture between Josh and his dad, we will start with helping his dad to mentalize himself first. He could start to recognise that he's too worried about Josh's safety to empathise fully right now with what his son wants, plus he's angry that Josh is being so rude and dismissive of him. Instead, he could begin to name some of what Josh is feeling, for example, by saying something like, "I can understand that you are happy being with your friends, although I don't like you being rude to me. I still love you and am happy you have a group of friends you really like." This would show Josh that he understands the importance of the relationships. It's also more likely to open up a conversation between the two of them, rather than force a situation where Josh gives even less information to his dad. If his dad can mentalize himself first, he can start to manage his feelings a bit better and become more curious about how strongly Josh feels about seeing his friends, and how keen he is to gain some independence and autonomy from his parents.

PAUSE AND REFLECT: AUTONOMY

In a nutshell ...

Typically, adolescents want autonomy before their parents are ready to grant it. Being a reflective parent, particularly using an authoritative parenting stance, has been found to be most beneficial to supporting a teenager's autonomy.

Being a reflective parent helps you by ...

As a reminder, this is the type of parenting where there is warmth but boundary-setting in the relationship. Being a reflective parent helps you to understand your own reaction and, in stepping back, to realise that you have a different perspective from your teenager. This can help you to remain calm, particularly when you feel you are being pushed away by your teenager's need for autonomy.

Being a reflective parent helps your teenager's autonomy by ...

Your teenager needs to feel that they are allowed to forge their own identity without being judged or criticised by you. They can easily feel shamed if you don't show curiosity about and appreciation of their perspective. Where there are no limits or boundaries, teenagers are left without containment, even when adolescents want to push those limits and challenge the rules.

Being a reflective parent helps your relationship by ...

When you are parenting a teenager who needs autonomy, or a teenager with ASD, they find it hard to understand and control their own emotions some of the time. They also find it hard to understand other people's minds at times. You and your teenager will gain a better connection and understanding of each other if you use a reflective parenting approach – mentalizing yourself first and then your teenager.

Keep in mind ...

- Be aware of your teenager's need to forge an identity that is separate and distinct from you – particularly of the importance of this for their survival in the social network of peers.
- Try using the "two-hands" concept, which involves both warmth and curiosity about the meaning of your teenager's behaviour as well as a boundary-setting approach. For example, be curious about your teenager's need to have their separate life and allow them the privacy they want, while at the same time setting some limits to what you expect from them, such as being home at a certain time, eating meals together, and doing school revision.
- With teenagers with ASD, always make your intentions clear – it is not always self-evident to your teenager why you do things, or what they mean. Mentalize yourself and then explain to your teenager what's going on in your mind so they are clear about your thinking.
- Make a clear distinction between what you are thinking and feeling and what's going on in your teenager's mind. If you project too much of your own emotions onto your teenager, they will become easily confused and find it hard to figure out what they feel and want.

5

AUTONOMY

Your teenager's social world

Being in this sort of friendship group also gives you anxieties about things like how you look.

Alongside an adolescent's need for autonomy, explored in Chapter 4, is the critical importance of their relationships with peers and other influences outside of the family. In this chapter, we explore your teenager's peer relationships, the role of social media in their lives, and how to support teenagers with ASD with their friendships. Every child and teenager is part of a system, which includes their extended family and peers as well as their school, online, social and sports clubs. How do you feel about the current influences in your teenager's life? How do you respond when you feel that these influences – whether friends, social media, or school teenage culture – are beyond your control and have a negative or coercive impact on your teenager? In this chapter, we will look at the significance of peer relationships on your teenager's development and sense of security and belonging. We will then explore how a reflective parenting approach can help you to understand and work through any worries you may have about the influences on your teenager and open up conversations between you.

In addition to influences outside of the family, we will also look at the impact of your other relationships on your teenager, particularly the one you have with your teenager's other parent, whether or not they live with you. How you and your teenager's other parent each manage conflict with your teenager and how you manage your own relationship has a big impact on your teenager's understanding of relationships.

DOI: 10.4324/9780429459245-6

Parental relationships

In Chapter 2, we thought about your and your partner's parenting style. Here, we are going to turn to thinking about the influence your relationship with your teenager's other parent has on your teenager's relationship with other people in their social world.

You are the template for your teenager's relationships; from their infancy onwards, they have been watching how you relate to your partner, your friends, extended family and people in your community. Out of all your relationships, the one you have with your partner (if you have one) or your child's other parent, will be the one that has the biggest influence on your teenager. Moreover, *how* you get on with them will have a huge impact on your child's well-being and mental health. It doesn't matter what type of family you live in; parents might be same-sex couples, single parents, living with grandparents, older parents, or young parents – it makes no difference. The research tells us clearly that it's the quality of that relationship that matters most; when teenagers and parents were asked about whether parents getting on well with each other is important to raising happy children, an overwhelming 70% of teenagers agreed. Interestingly, only 33% of parents agreed. If I reflect on my own childhood experience, I don't think my parents had much idea of just how significant their arguments were to my day-to-day happiness. Until your teenager starts talking to you about their friendships or relationships, it's unlikely you have spoken explicitly to them about relationships, but they have been observing yours for years. Perhaps you have volatile relationships with people you are close to; full of highs and lows, with laughter, but also disagreements and rows. Perhaps you have a relationship with your partner where you barely ever row, preferring to keep your feelings to yourselves, and the level of emotion expressed in your household is quite low. You might be openly loving and demonstrative, or very reserved and private in your relationship. Whatever form your relationship takes though, you can be assured that your teenager has picked up some of their skills of relating to others from how you behave in your own relationships. This section looks at how important it is to reflect on your own relationships and the example these set for your teenager and also how to support your teenager in their social relationships.

Conflict between parents

Arguing with your partner is not bad or wrong, per se; it's *how* you argue and, more importantly, how you make up afterwards and understand and work through what's happened. Clearly, if you are in a state of perpetual conflict with your partner and there is the constant threat of one person abandoning the other, this will have a hugely negative impact on your teenager, who will become anxious in the family atmosphere of the threat of separation. In therapeutic work, the concepts of rupture and repair are important for understanding relationships. It's neither healthy nor realistic to think that people in relationships will never disagree with each other. In fact, mentalizing actively encourages curiosity in someone else's view, and different perspectives, but that's very different from criticising someone for having a different view in the first place, which is where conflict can arise. Let's look at an everyday example.

Jim comes home from a long day at work and his partner, Anya, has been working at home all day. She's been on calls and hasn't had a moment to leave the house. Anya texted Jim before he left work to ask if he would pick up some milk from the shop on his way back from the train station. Jim walks into the house, shouting a tired, "Hi" to Anya and the teenagers (who are both upstairs in their rooms). "Hi," says Anya, "Did you get the milk?" Jim says, "No, I didn't see your message until I was nearly home, then I was too shattered to go back to the shop. Haven't you been here all day, couldn't you have popped out?" Anya feels immediately cross and defensive, "I have actually been working, even though I've been at home. I haven't managed to get off the screen all day."

A row erupts about who has had the hardest day and Jim and Anya both end up shouting loudly as they defend themselves. It culminates in Anya shouting, "You don't take my work seriously enough! Why didn't you check your messages earlier? You're always so wrapped up in your own stuff!"

Upstairs, the two teenagers hear the shouting. One puts on his headphones to tune out the noise and listen to music while the other turns up the volume on his device where he's watching a movie. They both decide not to come downstairs for a while.

In the heat of the moment – when the emotional thermometer discussed in Chapter 1 is red hot – it's too hard for either Jim or Anya to mentalize themselves or each other. Neither of them is regulated enough in their emotions to even be curious about the other person's day. Anya can't appreciate Jim's day or why he forgot to get the milk for her and is on the defensive following his accusation that it would have been an easier task for her. To tackle this, both parents need to calm down first and lower their emotional temperature. Rarely do you hear an argument where one person is shouting and the other person has said, "Yes, I see your point of view!" We can't possibly take anyone else's perspective when our emotions are running high. However, there is an opportunity afterwards to be curious about each other's perspectives and to validate and respect them.

The impact of this argument or rupture on the teenagers is self-evident. In the moment, it threatens their sense of security so they both stay in their rooms, preferring to withdraw. The family then becomes momentarily fragmented and everyone inhabits a separate space in the house. If this happens repeatedly, it creates a constant state of uncertainty and insecurity within the family. What's critical to the repair part of this rupture scenario is to understand what went wrong and why each partner felt misunderstood. For Anya and Tim, this can involve mentalizing themselves. For example, Jim might say, "I'm sorry I didn't go back to get the milk when I saw your text. I've had such a crappy day, I just wanted to get home to see you. I would have gone out later. I guess I was in quite a wound-up mood already." Or, Anya could have said, "I feel so frustrated about being at home on the screen all day. I get so tired and grumpy when I'm in front of the screen for a long time, so I was on quite a short fuse and annoyed that my job means I can't even get enough of a break to pop out in the lunch hour."

These types of statements, where you are reflecting on yourself and starting your sentence with "I" rather than "you," are useful because they are a helpful prompt to self-reflect (or self-mentalize) before considering the other person's view. Arguments are usually about levelling accusations at another person, and reflections and repairs can go well if they start with self-reflection, for example, "I did this because I was feeling this way." We tend to mentalize the other person inaccurately when we come out with accusatory statements such as, "You don't take my work seriously enough! You're always so wrapped up in your own stuff!" These types of statements are almost always jarring because they imply that you think you know someone else's mind better than they know it themselves. Of course, most of us pass judgement on other people in our lives; sometimes with humour, sometimes out of anger or frustration. However, when this happens within parent and family relationships, it sends out a communication that there is a lack of curiosity in someone else's perspective and experiences. This usually ends with arguments, shouting, avoiding and withdrawing; it fuels disruption and fracture rather than connection and repair. This isn't to say that you have to take on the other person's position, but you do at least have to be curious about it, and validate it, if you are to model something positive to your teenager about functional relationships. On the other hand, if you can model in your own relationships, a mature, reflective and understanding approach during disagreements – followed by a repair or compatible resolution at the end – your teenager will learn some incredibly helpful ways of conducting their own social relationships.

Your teenager's social world of friendships

Issues related to friendships are the most commonly cited by teenagers. Whether the focus is on difficulties in forming friendships, feeling left out by friends, getting into conflict with close friends, anxieties about being part of a group or a lack of a sense of belonging, the preoccupation is clear and very real for adolescents. At worst, young people can be brutally bullied for their hair colour, size, personality, special interests, race, or sexual and gender identity. And of course, some young people are the perpetrators with their own underlying issues. All of these issues raise understandable concern on the part of parents about their teenager's friendships. It is vital to understand, though, that at this time of their lives, your teenager will put you on the sidelines while their friends become centre-stage. As much as you might understand this intellectually, it's difficult not to feel hurt at times when your teenager needs to connect with your friends in preference to you. However, your acceptance of this is crucial to maintaining your long-term connection with your teenager.

When you model reflective parenting, you can develop a greater curiosity in your teenager's friendship group and support their relationships with peers as a vital part of their development. Interestingly, a body of research shows us that, while peer relationships predict future resilience, the quality of the relationship with parents, particularly too much proximity to parents, actually diminishes resilience, making adolescents too dependent and keeping them stagnated. One of the many important functions of peer relationships is to help your teenager become more resilient in life; letting them go a little helps them build this resilience.

Why are friendships so important to your teenager?

Peers are literally essential for your teenagers' survival. Without a group of friends, who will your teenager depend on when they leave home? It's no wonder then that they are the main focus for the vast majority of adolescents.

When one of my teenage sons was 17, he was going through the process of applying to universities, which involved going to a bunch of away days. When it came to the visit to Leeds, I was busy organising our train fares when my son said, "I think I'll give the Leeds visit a miss, Mum. There's a party for Josh and he's getting a limo for us all to ride around in with drinks before the party." I remonstrated with him about the importance of the university visit before giving in. After the limo ride, he sent me a phone video of himself beaming in the back of the limo, his girlfriend at his side. I could hear the sound of his friends laughing as they drove through town with music playing in the back of the limo. Leeds or the limo? It was an easy choice for him! Of course, the limo was more fun, but it was also the importance of being with his friends and not missing out on a bonding opportunity. If I mentalize myself in this situation, I realise that my fantasy is that if he sees Leeds he will start working furiously for his exams and he will get into the university. I'm fantasising that it will be pivotal in his decision-making. He feels bad about me spending the money on the train fare and disappointing me, so he doesn't feel shame, he feels guilt. This is an important distinction as shame is feeling bad about oneself and guilt is feeling bad about one's behaviour. Guilt is the healthier emotion. It is so important not to shame your teenager because shame has a high level of toxicity for adolescents, whereas a bit of guilt can actually be helpful, so it's important to avoid shaming your teenager. It's fine to say, "I can understand you wanting to do this, but it's hurting me a bit."

Your teenager's early attachment relationship with you is still relevant, however, evidence from attachment researchers, such as

John Allen (1), shows that a secure early attachment relationship as a young infant carries forward, so the good relationship between you and your child early on affords your teenager a level of security. Studies by psychologist Dante Ciccetti (2) and his colleagues show that teenagers who had good enough early attachment relationships may still engage in risky behaviour, afterwards, they will return to the relationship that provided the secure attachment. Your relationship with your teenager doesn't therefore necessarily decrease the likelihood of them engaging in risky behaviour as we will see in Chapter 6, but it does mean the attachment relationship is important for their security and longer-term well-being. In short, a secure early attachment relationship between you and your teenager doesn't necessarily predict good outcomes, but it does predict resilience. This, in itself, can improve outcomes and mean that your teenager will be better able to cope with adversity in life.

What helps your teenager build friendships?

Many factors are at play in your teenager's success in building friendships. First, the neural networks in their brain to develop relationships with other teenagers and the areas of the brain responsible for these – the prefrontal cortex predominantly – are not fully developed until we are in our mid to late twenties. Given this limitation, you need to display more confidence in your teenager's ability to build relationships with peers. All of your teenager's mentalizing skills are being used for establishing their social network, which means they don't always have much left for you. What this means in everyday life is that you should always take seriously your teenager's concerns about their friendship group and the details of their experience and expectations for their group of friends. For example, try not to be dismissive of them by saying things like, "typical teens" if they seem to be hanging around the house aimlessly. Instead ask, "what are you guys interested in watching/eating?" Validate your teenager's group and their shared interests and your teenager will feel understood and closer to you.

The preference for peers over parents can be seen as an important part of the process of developing a separate identity from parents – a process of individuation – and it is a parent's job to help facilitate this, while also maintaining a strong attachment and being a reliable presence in their lives. It's not an *either/or* process of parents or peers, but more, how does being a reflective parent help you and your teenager stay connected, while *at the same time* facilitating the development of healthy peer relationships outside of the family? First, being an authoritative, reflective parent helps you to maintain a position where you can help and advise while trying to understand more about your teenager's perspective. If they are worried about a dynamic in their group or feel unsure about how popular they are for instance, you can take an attentive curiosity to what their particular worries are, helping your teenager to manage some difficult feelings, through your empathy. After this, they are more likely to want to ask you questions about what *you* think they might do. That is, when you've mentalized your teenager, they will be in a clearer, more regulated, state of mind which allows them to listen to your or another person's perspective on the situation. They will also feel more secure and this links to their ability to develop and maintain friendships. In a study I carried out in the mid-90s, I found that children who were more securely attached to their parents and good at mentalizing other people (I tested out their theory of mind skills) were also more popular in their peer group (3).

In the girls' focus group, we talked about experiences of friendship groups and one young person, aged 17, said the following:

> I used to be in a friendship group where we partied every weekend and the girls all felt like they were there to get the right picture on social media, and had to be friends with the coolest person. I was a bit embarrassed being in that group. At the beginning, I was best friends with a very cool girl in the group who talks to everyone. Then I started to notice little things like girls talking 'shit' behind their backs when they were not listening, even about their mutual friends, and I was shocked. I think it's really hard being in this sort of group. You have to be in 100 percent and if you're not, you get dropped and have no friends suddenly. Being in this sort of friendship group also gives you anxieties about things like how you look.

I wondered how Michelle got out of this group. She replied, "I suddenly realised I didn't want to be with such a superficial group. I had a better group of friends at school who were more welcoming and accepting and I'd never felt the type of negative dynamic with them that I felt with the other group. They give to others rather than take. We felt more like family and supported each other – I'm very comfortable to be around this group all the time."

> A couple of friends from that first group had their 'nudes' leaked and they were circulated across the school, with one of their boyfriends putting it on chat groups so lots of people could see it. She adopted a mind-set of 'I don't care', so it was dropped quite quickly because she didn't seem bothered. It was on Instagram for a while, though.

In this example, imagine you are Michelle's parent. What is your reaction? Would you feel pleased that Michelle knew herself well enough to get out of one social group and into another? Are you wondering about the "nudes" that went around on the phones? Did it trigger any worries you have about your own daughter or son and how they use Instagram or other apps? Does your teenager confide in you about what goes on in their friendship group or are you mostly kept in the dark?

In speaking with Michelle, I was impressed that she had figured out for herself what she wanted from her friendships, but also struck by her nonchalant way of speaking about the images that had gone around of one of the girls. Michelle told me that she feels able to speak openly to her parents and that they don't judge her. She had told them about the nudes. She said that the older she gets, the more she appreciates how supportive they have been and accepting of her need to socialise a lot with her friends.

Different experiences for boys and girls

In the separate focus groups I carried out for boys and girls, I was struck by the difference between the two groups, with the complex dynamics of the girls' group and the more straightforward, but less sociable, nature of the boys' one. After discussing parental worries about teenagers going astray and staying out too late, or in unknown places, we moved on to whether parents also worried about teenagers not going out *enough*.

The boys acknowledged that there was a certain safety in not going out. It took off the pressure of having to look a certain way, have the right clothes, speak to the right people, and that staying home was a "lot more relaxed." In their view, not wanting to socialise face to face as much as the girls was not a problem for them and didn't reflect a lack of friendships as a lot of their social interactions took place online in gaming forums. I asked if there was something lacking in playing online as opposed to being with friends in person. One of the boys, Atti, said he didn't think the two things were comparable. "We went to the city centre once, a group of us, and it was really good fun. But I might be on my games console with one of my friends, and I'm still having the same amount of fun. What I do to socialise is spend time with a group of friends at one of our houses, and for me, that's just as fulfilling as going to a party is for someone else." Another young person, Joe, when asked the same question about gaming with friends versus hanging out in person with them said, "Emotionally, no it's not as fulfilling, but it's just as much fun." Another boy in the group said, "When I play video games, it's not like you get less fun from it, it's just completely different. When you're walking around with your friends, moving, or exercising, your whole mood feels different, better, you know, movement releases good vibes or something doesn't it? Dopamine. It is different, the feeling, to when you're just sitting in your room not moving."

Although this particular group of teenage boys didn't see the problem of spending a lot of their time at home, I have sometimes seen this become a risk of withdrawal from face-to-face contact with friends, due to increased social anxiety. This was particularly problematic during the pandemic and, while it is perfectly normal to have a combination of home and outside-world socialising, the balance for some tips too far into a socially anxious withdrawal. Let's look at the example of Zack, who's become withdrawn from his friends and family during the lockdown of 2020.

Zack is 13 and lives with his older sister, Loren (17) and his mum Georgie. Zack had been having a few issues at school before the Covid-19 pandemic broke out in March 2020. He found it hard to keep up with the banter of his peer group, often feeling his friends were poking fun at him rather than joking with each other. He sometimes told his mum that he felt ill in the morning, preferring to stay in bed rather than go to school. Academically, he was doing okay but found himself feeling less interested lately in schoolwork and more interested in playing his favourite game online.

When he was sent home from school, along with everyone else, on March 23rd and told his lessons would be online for the foreseeable future, Zack felt a massive sense of relief. His sister, Loren was in the middle of her final exams, so felt anxious at first and then a bit relieved that she would have her grades predicted. She was upset though that she probably wasn't going to have her school prom, and the end-of-term show she had been involved in was most likely now going to be cancelled. She spent a lot of time talking with her friends and messaging them in a group chat. Meanwhile, Zack stayed up in his room seemingly happy gaming with other people, until one evening, on her way to the bathroom, Georgie decided to pop her head around his bedroom door and found Zack lying on his bed staring up at his ceiling.

Georgie: "Everything ok, love?"
Zack: "Yeah. Calm, mum."
Georgie: "I've not seen you much this week, it's been mad trying to do my job online. It's back-to-back meetings. I bet you're the same with your lessons, hey?"
Zack: "Kind of."
Georgie: "Shall I leave you, then? You happy just hanging out in your room so much? I suppose everyone is the same now, aren't they?"
Zack: "Yeah, I guess so. It's fine, mum. I'm just chilling."

Georgie suddenly remembers she hasn't replied to an email, so quickly says, "Love you" to Zack and goes back to her laptop downstairs. It's only after she's answered the email, that she realises that Zack hasn't met anyone at all, even socially distanced, since the first day of lockdown. It's now nearly June.

Reflecting on Georgie

Zack's mum's head seems to be full of work but we might imagine she is also struggling, like everyone else, to adapt to the transition from in-person working to an online job. She seems curious to find out what's happening with Zack, but only when she happens to pass his room, and we might wonder why he hasn't been on her mind a bit more. Perhaps she's been busy worrying about her older child's exams as she's at the end of her school life. We could also imagine that Zack tends to tell her he is okay, and she takes this at face value. While she asks the question is Zack happy hanging out in his room, she doesn't wait for a reply before adding, "I suppose everyone is the same now," making it hard for Zack to say what he's really feeling. It's only when Georgie has answered the email that she has space in her mind to reflect on the fact that it's now nearly three months since Zack was first sent home from school, and we might imagine in this moment she could begin to feel terribly anxious that he hasn't been on her mind as much as he might normally be. Perhaps the impact and shock of the pandemic have made it extremely hard for Georgie to mentalize herself or anyone else. After all, many people have said that they lost their ability to focus and concentrate when they were preoccupied with health fears during this time.

Reflecting on Zack

If we step into Zack's shoes, we might imagine he's experiencing a mixture of relief and anxiety about the global pandemic (Figure 5.1). On the one hand, it gets him out of school and the daily anxiety about his friendship group. On the other hand, without the daily challenge of navigating this social world, he has retreated into his room and there don't seem to be any signs of him having connected with anyone. He may possibly have discovered a social world through his online gaming, but the fact that he is lying on the bed, staring up at the ceiling, should make us question what's going on underneath his "chilling" appearance.

Thinking together

If Georgie were to take a mentalizing approach, she might be able to recognise that her mind has been so crowded with anxious "chatter" about the pandemic and how she is going to do her job online, on top of her worry about Loren's final exams, that she has lost sight of Zack temporarily. If she can tune into her current thoughts and feelings, she might then be able to recognise that it's been increasingly hard to manage her emotional temperature, and for much of the time she's been at the hot end of the thermometer. Other times, when it all felt overwhelming, she switched off and tried not to engage with the daily news about the pandemic. This has also meant that she hasn't been able to mentalize. Imagine that

Figure 5.1

she did a quick mind check and became aware of her busy mind, she might then go back to Zack's room and say something like, "I've noticed you've been up here a lot in your room and I wondered if you were up here because you want to be, or if you were feeling too worried to leave it?" or "I know it was sometimes hard going to school, perhaps you're a bit relieved about being home?" and "I'm pretty worried about how long the lockdown will last and whether we'll all find it weird to meet up with people in real life again, what about you?" She might just sit on the edge of his bed and have a general chat, resolving to pop in more often and invite Zack down to spend time with her and Loren, rather than leaving him alone, assuming he's okay.

Teenage girls and friendship groups

One of the most concerning trends in the past ten years has been the significant rise in the number of teenage girls experiencing anxiety and depression, particularly in relation to their peer group and the constant comparison with others. According to NHS England data from 2021, the figure for mental health disorders in children is 1 in 6, rising to 1 in 4 for adolescent girls aged between 17 and 19, and an even higher number of younger adolescent girls. While in children aged up to 18, boys have a significantly higher incidence of mental health disorders. More recent data suggests that this trend has increased further since the Covid-19 pandemic, with an even steeper increase in mental health problems for adolescent girls; anxiety particularly has been on the rise. In the next chapter, we look at this in more depth when we think about risk.

There is a complexity about female friendship groups and the ostracising of girls within a group is a common occurrence compared with a more all-inclusive feel of male friendship groups. This starts even before adolescence, as girls develop a more sophisticated understanding of the emotions of other people ahead of boys. I can recall a conversation about birthday parties when my older boys were at primary school; they must have been around nine or ten years old. My friend was telling me about her daughter's dilemma about who to invite and not invite to her party. When I asked my son who he would invite to his party, his response was, "All the boys in my class, Mum." It hadn't occurred to him that there might be some he wouldn't want to come.

The role of social media and the online world in your teen's life

Today, everyone is dependent on their phones and it's rare for both adults and teenagers alike to be without a phone by their side. For adolescents, it is an almost constant companion; you will be familiar with your teenager having a phone in hand, in pocket, or on the table next to them, wherever they are. You might be the same yourself, or you might have taken a stance to limit your own phone and social media use. In the UK, 95 percent of the population was using the internet in 2020 and 79 million mobile phone subscriptions were registered, which is astonishing given the current UK population is estimated at just over 68 million. The average daily phone usage for a UK teenager is six and a half hours. This excludes time spent on the phone for homework, listening to music or reading books, which makes the time jump by another couple of hours. When you think that adolescents are in school for six hours out of every day, it means that for the remaining six hours of the day, they must be almost exclusively on their phones. The mobile phone has become their almost constant companion, but it can also feel like their enemy when there are difficulties, particularly with friends (Figure 5.2).

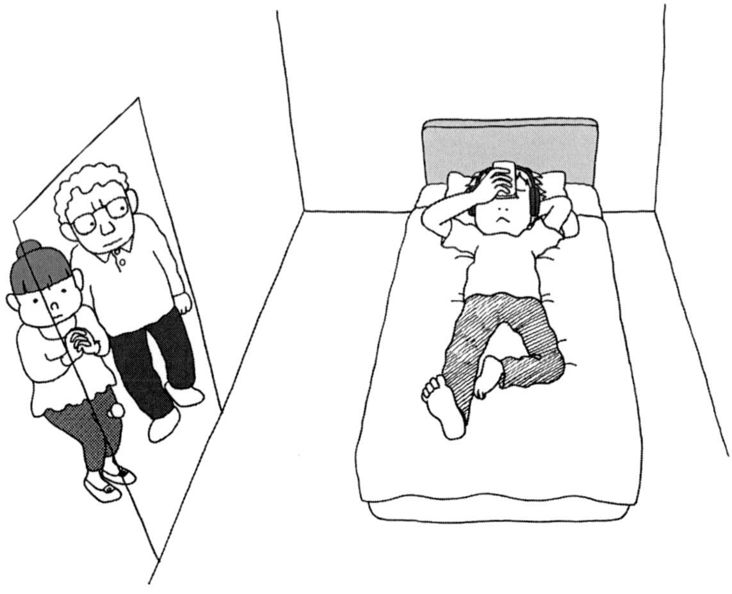

Figure 5.2

The conversation around social media use can easily become polarised – adolescents think it's good for them and parents and carers think it's bad for them. A better way forward is to be curious about your teenager's views on social media – to be open to exploring and hearing their perspective about the role it plays in their life for good or bad, to think with them about how it helps and doesn't and to consider what kind of limits might work. Obviously, this won't work for all of you, but it might create different kinds of discussions.

I have been surprised when including adolescents in planning around what's a reasonable amount of the time that they should use social media and asking whether they would want to hand their phone in before bed, that some of them see these as positive choices they are making, rather than a rule that's imposed on them. As parents, we need to adjust our mindset about how teenagers use phones as surveys show that most teenagers use their phones to watch videos and programmes, in much the same way that we watch TV. If you are a family that watches TV until you go to bed, then criticising your teenager for being on their phone could be seen as somewhat hypocritical. There is little distinction in teenagers' minds and the videos on their phones are much more engaging from their perspective.

The impact of social media on teenagers' social world

If you want to reduce your teenager's time spent on their devices, you need to consider what social media and gaming mean for them and how they might lose out socially by reducing their usage. For example, you should acknowledge that this is their main way of staying in touch with their friendship group and the world. Before you talk to your teenager about social media, you need to accept that it is here to stay and that social media platforms are a hugely important part of their life.

That's not to say you shouldn't feel concerned of course. The reality is that screen time can become addictive, with many teenagers finding it extremely hard to be away from their screens. Whereas pre-internet, young people had huge swathes of time, our teenagers have rarely experienced boredom in their lives. There is always something entertaining for them; always a conversation between friends, an online video to watch, a constant stream of information and clips streaming on their phones. The way these apps are designed, they grab young people's attention by designing engaging and entertaining short clips, which are constantly streamed to keep our attention. We will look at the risks of the online world in more detail in the next chapter on risk.

We can't ignore the importance of social media and of screens in general in our teenager's lives, and to do so would be naïve. Limiting the amount of time spent on screens is something you can exert some control over though, which comes back to parental authority and modelling behaviour.

Some guidelines for social media use

- Accept it as part of our lives and it will become more increasingly prevalent.
- If you are unaware of what your teenager is doing on their phone and how much time they spend online, teenagers might be resistant to being told to keep track of their daily usage. Encourage them to reduce this time.
- Discuss with younger teenagers what they are up to online. A younger teenager may be more open to explaining to you what they like to watch, so ask open questions and show an interest, so that this doesn't become a private world which excludes you.
- Have conversations about the use of social media and limits and boundaries around it in advance, not in the heat of the moment when you want your teenager to come off it. This will just lead to them hiding it from you.
- Think about your own use of social media. If your teenager sees you always on your computer and you say, "Yes but I'm using this platform for work" and continue to use it around them to a high degree, how can you expect them not to use it as well?
- Make spending less time on their phone worth it for your teenager. To your teenager, social media is likely to be exciting, seductive and potentially addictive. If you want your teenager to come off it, then you must make your relationship with them also exciting and rewarding so that they want to spend time with you or with their friends in person. If they come off their phone, only to find you are staring at yours, what is in it for them?

Gaming and your teenager's social world

Gaming has been around for decades in various forms. When I was growing up in the 1970s, we would go to arcades to play games there. By the time I had reached my teens, there were game boys, consoles and computers. When my first children were born there were mobile devices in the early 2000s and now there are eSports and many advancements in video games. According to the analysis company, Newzoo, 2.8 billion people will play video games in 2021. The popularity of these games has sparked considerable debate across the world about how gaming may affect children and adolescents.

Statistics showed that *boys* from the age of 14 use video *games* up *to* five times more than *girls*, while *girls* are on social media much more. A study from 2021 (4) showed that gaming is more socially significant for boys than social media is. Gender differences in video gaming are not necessarily a problem per se, as they may reflect gender-specific motivations and interests. However, the study also finds that girls feel less encouraged than boys to play video games due to different gender-related experiences of video gaming. Despite this, more girls are becoming interested in gaming, although it remains predominantly the domain of boys.

Given the popularity of gaming, it is likely that almost everyone reading this book will know a teenager who enjoys gaming. Thinking about gaming in relation to your teenager's social world, it's important to recognise that it is an important part of how they interact with their peers. Many teenagers who game overwhelmingly report that they find it a highly enjoyable pastime, and many teenage boys say that it's the most fun they can think of having, even when they've grown out of it. Here are some of the reasons your teenager enjoys gaming as part of their social world:

- When gaming, the brain receives a rush of dopamine – the hormones secreted by the brain's reward system, released when we achieve something.
- Many online games are played by teams, so your teenager is often gaming against another team with their friends. Teenagers report feeling bonded to their friends and find it great fun to compete against other people as one team.
- It is a topic of conversation when friends meet up in real life after gaming online. Teenagers need to feel part of a group and this common interest bonds them together as they discuss the details of the game.

- Indoor activities can be limited and it can be hard to have a group of teenagers all in one place for many reasons, such as space, distance from one another, and weather preventing travelling. Being online with friends gives teenagers a greater opportunity to connect with one another.
- Similar social skills are used for online gaming as are used for in-person gatherings. A group of people who get together in person to play football or pool in their teens will sometimes have more fun than playing online, but at other times there is an equal amount of enjoyment online.
- Teenagers who are relatively shy or who find in-person group gatherings a little overwhelming can be part of a group more easily when they game. Similarly, some teenagers report feeling more at ease and able to be themselves in a gaming group chat than in person.
- Gaming can be a good distraction from boredom and is something that's easily accessible.
- Some teenage gamers who aren't considered cool by their peers will have greater access to a wider group of friends online and these friends often make plans after gaming to meet up for other activities.

When social media use isn't controlled or a teenager is unable to regulate their responses when gaming online, then this could have a detrimental effect on the mental health of some, while for others there may be problems with addiction; Chapter 6 explores these associated risks of social media. Let's hear from a young gamer to see how he reflects on his use of both social media and online gaming.

Santi is a 14-year-old boy who enjoys being on his phone and uses it for making social plans with his friends, as well as looking at the content he enjoys on various apps, from clips of kittens to football highlights. He recognises that there are some downsides to it too and spoke about the pros and cons of social media from his perspective.

"There is a risk of getting addicted, so I make sure I limit my time on my Xbox to no more than one and a half hours a day, and I don't even play every day, especially in the summer. I'm worse on my phone though – I find myself on it for hours, scrolling through apps without realising how long I've been looking at it for, and wasting time that I could be doing other things. I sometimes think, 'I could be meeting with friends, spending time with my family.' You get a feeling of not being productive."

Santi monitors his usage of some of his favourite apps, mainly TikTok, and notes it's around 20 minutes at a time and for no more than one and a half to two hours per day. He said, "The majority of my friends are on it for four hours per day." I did wonder, as he told me this, if he was aware that adults think teenagers spend too long on their phones and so he was trying to downplay it. I asked Santi how much fun he had, watching the clips and programmes on the social media apps on his phone. He said, "If I'm watching a series or programme on YouTube it has some meaning but on TikTok you instantly forget about it, so it has no long-lasting impact." I wondered if there were any other disadvantages to social media apps and he said he was aware that some large group chats could lead to cyberbullying, but he had not experienced this. He was very aware of the downside of the apps leading to excessive comparison with others, and that, "this feels negative, it makes you have unrealistic expectations about what you're doing with your life, comparing your body, looking at other friends' groups." He also felt it was easy to "get trapped in your room or in bed for too long if have your phone next to your bed. If you have an argument with someone online you feel you'd be happier without your phone, but then miss it." Santi noted that when he went on a school trip and had friends around, he felt happier without the phone because he didn't need it and so didn't miss it. I was interested in the fact that, since the weather had improved and he had started a relationship with someone his age, he said he had lost interest a bit in scrolling.

There's no doubt that we all use our phones to access information and teenagers are the same. Where we might once have had to look something up in a book, we all now have immediate access to a wealth of useful information. Santi observed, "It's great what you can find out about things like music and clothes and get an idea of what you like and what's out there." Santi felt that the major downside of not being on his phone was that, "If I didn't have it at other times, I would lose contact with (my) friendship group. I just go to the phone if I haven't got other things going on." His phone is Santi's main way of making plans and interacting with his friends. He mostly does this by gaming online with them and said, "Parents worry a lot about us wasting our time gaming, but online gaming allows you to meet more people, make more friends and have regular time with them."

Another advantage Santi spoke about was using his phone and various apps to learn new skills. He's started to cook and follows a few chefs and said he also uses his phone's apps to help him with revision; he said, "You can find out about events going on in the world, such as advertising clothing events you might otherwise not know about." For Santi and millions of other teenagers, his use of online apps allows him access to a world of information and connection with others.

We can see from the teenager's perspective how important the online world is to their social life, so what makes it so hard for many parents to accept this part of their teenager's life?

Reflecting on yourself in relation to your teenager's social media use

There is inevitably going to be a disconnect between how much time you think it's okay for them to be on their phone and how much you would prefer them to be doing other things. There is also an inevitable difference between your worries for their online safety and who they might be encountering in online groups. Using a reflective parenting stance, start with mentalizing yourself and being aware of your own beliefs and feelings about your teenager's online life. Is there a lack of understanding on your part about the apps they use and their safety or dangers? Do you find yourself disapproving because you believe that non-digital activities are inherently better than anything related to their phones or devices? For example, if you hold a very strong belief that being with friends in person – playing sports or just hanging out – is fundamentally better, then you are always going to bring this strong belief into any conversations you have with your teenager about social media and gaming. Check on your own capacity to mentalize yourself before you dive into a conflict with your teenager over their digital activity. Once you have managed to regulate yourself, then step into your teenager's shoes and start to mentalize what is going on for them; including all the advantages to them of having contact with other people and all the resources they can access online that can help them explore and forge their own identity. Then return to mentalizing yourself and your worries about some of the negative influences. Rather than plunge into a punitive phone-banning strategy, ask yourself what is going to make your teenager aware of these dangers and be responsible in their online activity. Removing their phone is only likely to increase your teenager's desire to access it once it's returned, their dependency on it and, crucially, their distance from you. At all times keep in mind – connection not correction.

Reflecting on your teenager

Santi's reflective capacity when it came to weighing up the pros and cons of social media was impressive. He was aware of the limitations and the risk of addiction, but at the same time could see great benefits in terms of his social life and access to information. It was telling that when he compared online contact with friends to real-life contact with them, he sometimes preferred the face-to-face experience. One of the points he raised is worthy of closer examination: the issue of comparison.

Comparison and social media

Since 2004 with the advent of Facebook, the steady rise of social media has meant that comparison with peers in adolescence has heightened. It's human nature to compare ourselves with other people and this is especially true of teenagers. In 1954, psychologist Leon Festinger proposed the theory of social comparison (5). This theory states that adolescents need to compare and contrast themselves with others as part of the process of forming their identity. This process helps adolescents to form their own beliefs, attitudes, and preferences in life. There is a healthy side to comparison, therefore, as it can help inspire and motivate teenagers. However, comparison has changed with the advent of social media. Before this online era, we had only limited knowledge of what our friends were doing when we weren't with them and relied on a postcard from their holiday or a conversation at school break time about a party that had happened locally to know what they were up to. We needed in-person contact, and occasionally the family landline, for information about our social networks. We were also largely oblivious to the lives of celebrities, except for the information we gathered from music magazines, which would tell us a bit about our favourite performers. So, our comparison pool was pretty small. Today, children and teenagers compare themselves not only to their social network, but also to a whole world of celebrities and online influencers. As well as there being an overwhelming number of people to compare themselves to, teenagers are also constantly exposed to perfect images of other people's lives. These images are carefully packaged and communicated in a way to show only the positive side of someone's life. What impact does the endless comparison with others online have on your teenagers' mental health?

Festinger proposed that humans have an innate drive to evaluate themselves and that they base their perceptions of their own social and personal worth on how they compare with others. Teenagers tend to focus on perceived attractiveness and social popularity when they make these comparisons. Or they might focus on sporting or academic achievements. The comparison is connected to the things that matter most to the adolescent identity. When teenagers compare themselves constantly with their peers and others, this can leave even more secure teenagers, at times, feeling at best inadequate and at worst depressed and full of self-loathing. It is so hard for teenagers to feel secure in their own identity at this particularly vulnerable stage of their development when they are working out who they are. However, supporting your teenager in figuring out what *they* think about what's happening in their world and what *they* feel about their own appearance, without comparison with others, is well worth spending time on. What is of paramount importance at this time is their sense of security and safety in the home and in their relationship with you, as this forms the backbone for them forming their own identity and helps them deal with the painful comparisons this process involves.

When your teenager struggles with friendships: social anxiety and ASD

Like adults, all young people are individual in their social skills and levels of confidence in social situations. For some teenagers, they will mix easily within a large group and feel relatively confident going to parties and events. Others will be at the opposite end of the scale, feeling acutely self-conscious, anxious about how they come across and fearful of not being accepted into the group. However, almost everyone at some point experiences a little social anxiety and during adolescence, when teenagers are much more self-focused and aware of what others are thinking about them, this anxiety is often heightened.

When we think about adolescents with ASD, it's even more likely that social anxiety and self-doubt will be even more prevalent as, by its very nature, having a social communication difficulty or developmental difference, makes it much more confusing to work out the nuances of social situations. One of the most common difficulties this group of young people experience is in understanding and regulating their emotions, particularly when they are in social groups. Because it is harder to express the full extent of how they feel, this makes adolescents with ASD much more vulnerable. It is important to their identity for a teenager with ASD to understand where their differences lie (and their strengths too, of course) and to be able to know what their particular triggers will be in social situations. Social situations are complex and your teenager's ability to read these situations will vary. As we know, when the emotional temperature rises – as it does when we're anxious – we all lose our capacity for mentalizing or reflection. So, a teenager with ASD, who already has some difficulties in understanding complex social situations, will be more anxious and less likely to mentalize themselves and others. If you are the parent or carer of one of these young people, supporting them with a mentalizing approach can be extremely helpful as it teaches them a way of understanding their emotional world and the world of social relationships. In other words, the more you reflect on your own thoughts and feelings, and make these clear and understandable for your teenager, the more you will be able to help them to develop their own emotional language for describing and understanding how they feel.

Teenage girls and ASD

In recent years, there has been an increase in referrals to mental health services for young women (usually around 15–18 years old) who have difficulties managing their emotions and their relationships with peers. The emotions commonly expressed are of feeling detached from the peer group and struggling to understand how to relate to others in the group in a way that feels authentic to them and fits in with the group. On further assessment, a fair proportion of these young women have either traits or a full diagnosis of ASD. They had learned to mask their ASD effectively for most of their primary school life, but once in secondary school, more complex peer group dynamics and the need to behave a certain way put further pressure on them to show a sophisticated set of social skills.

In girls with ASD, social behaviours and friendships are often different from other children's. ASD girls have social behaviours that look very different from both those of autistic boys and non-autistic girls. For example, girls with ASD may mimic the behaviours, interests and even speech patterns of people they are friends with in an attempt to fit in and to be accepted. They may also memorise information about their friends' interests or learn "scripts" so that they can talk to new people.

Alternatively, girls with ASD can become fixated on one person in particular and focus on making that person their best – and only – friend. This can be very intense for both people and can sometimes lead to a falling out. Then when it comes to conflict, your teenage daughter (with ASD) is likely to find recognising and managing conflict difficult (certainly compared with non-autistic girls) and this will be impacting on their ability to repair and maintain friendships. Some girls will form many casual friendships, but not stick to one group, and have no close friends with whom they spend most of their time. Girls who have just one or two very intense friendships may need help widening their circle and understanding why this can be helpful.

Naila is a 17-year-old girl who went to adolescent mental health services after her mother referred her over concerns regarding her lack of motivation and concentration, which started during lockdown with the switch to online learning. Her mum wondered if she had a generally negative view of herself that had gotten worse during the lockdown. Naila spoke about how unhappy she was with the way she looked, believing she was overweight. She had a prom coming up at the end of the school year and a holiday in France with her family, and she was feeling increasingly anxious around her friends. Naila's mum recalled how she had been on a clothes shopping trip with her and from the moment Naila started trying on clothes, things went downhill. Being in the changing rooms and not being able to wear her usual size and seeing herself in the mirror, all triggered a lot of bottled-up emotions. In her own session, Naila spoke about her past history of difficult friendships, where she described herself as always "trying to be how the other person wants me to be" and feeling at times like she was "looking down on myself, observing myself from outside, but not really taking part." She told her psychologist, "When I just go into town on my own for a day, I feel really happy. I know that sounds weird, but I feel safe and comfortable on my own." Later, when Naila was given an ASD assessment it was that she met the criteria for a diagnosis of high-functioning autism.

A month later, Naila went to her school prom where she had arranged to meet up with friends. When she arrived, she saw her friends all talking to another group she didn't know and she felt too awkward to go over to them. She couldn't think of anything to say so headed over to the table where the food was laid out and started helping herself, feeling uncomfortable about her outfit of choice. She pulled at the neckline of her dress, looking around to see if others were watching her. She started to feel so anxious as she looked at the door and wondered if anyone would notice if she ran out.

Reflecting on Naila's mum

Naila's mum seems to be predominantly worried about her daughter's eating and preoccupation with her weight and size. This is completely understandable and Naila talks a great deal about how she "hates" the way she looks and covers her legs at all times, even in the height of summer and always wears several layers of clothes. Naila's mum had an eating disorder when she was an adolescent and is strict about what she eats and comments on other people's size all the time. Naila's mum has clearly become extremely concerned about her daughter because of her own difficulties in adolescence, but she is missing the problems Naila is having with her friends. For Naila's mum, mentalizing herself first will help her to separate out her state of mind and then focus clearly on the problems Naila is expressing. It's likely that her own preoccupation with food means she is trying hard to ensure her daughter doesn't suffer in the same way she did, and this in turn has put an unhelpful focus on diet. This preoccupation with diet is also obscuring something very important going on with her daughter involving her identity, her sense of security with friends and her need to regulate the distance between herself and her friends so she can regulate her emotions when she is on her own.

Reflecting on Naila

Naila is having a horrible time with her peer group. We can imagine what she must have felt like, preparing for her prom at the end of her exams when she feels neither confident about her appearance nor her sociability around her friends. Then there is the experience at the school prom. We can understand and empathise with her anxiety and sense of awkwardness as she struggles to understand social etiquette when she gets there. Naila appears to go to the buffet table as a strategy for managing the social situation. Once there, she feels embarrassed about her dress and uncomfortable in it. Becoming more self-conscious she pulls at her neckline and we might imagine that her thoughts are going back to her weight. She doesn't feel confident enough to go over to her friends as they're talking to others she doesn't know.

Thinking together

Through taking a mentalizing approach, Naila's mum could start to be more curious about what is going on with her daughter, while encouraging her to be aware of the triggers for her own anxiety so that she can manage this better. Mentalizing had broken down in Naila's relationship with her mum, largely because of her mum's anxiety, which was getting in the way of her capacity to think about her daughter without becoming overwhelmed with emotions. When her mum started to take a curious approach with Naila about her experience with other people, Naila gradually started to talk about her difficulty in reading other people, which correlated with her subsequent ASD diagnosis. With help from the mental health professional, Naila was referred to for her diagnosis, Naila was able to think about what she thought the most comfortable level of distance or closeness was to others. Empathising with Naila about the prom allowed her to mentalize herself and recognise how anxious she feels when she has to "put on a front" for people she doesn't really get on with.

How can you support your teenage girl with ASD in her social world?

Using a Reflective Parenting stance to support your teenage daughter if she has this type of difficulty can help her to, firstly, feel understood and, secondly and most importantly, start to understand herself a bit better.

Step one – Be curious about what your daughter feels comfortable with. Would she like to expand her friendship group, or is she more comfortable having just one friend with whom she can control the amount of closeness she has? Is she actually suffering as a result of any difficulties in her social relationships or is it more your worry that she doesn't have as many friends as you would like her to? The most important thing is to help your teenage daughter understand that, even if she is different from some of her peers, feeling comfortable in her own skin and finding the level of closeness that feels right for *her* in relationships is more important than trying to fit in and be someone she isn't.

Step two – Girls with just one or two very intense friendships may need help widening their circle and understanding why this matters.

Step three – Take on board that your daughter carries an overwhelming level of unseen anxiety that builds up during the day at school. Check out your anxiety too. Offer empathy for her anxiety after you've taken time to reflect on your own feelings. Recognise that your daughter's daily minefield of worries takes up a large portion of her headspace, and the concentration required to keep everything hidden takes up any reflective capacity that is left. With all capacity used up, she is prevented from listening properly or learning effectively. The group of peers in her world may appear confusing to her a lot of the time as she struggles to work out how she is meant to act around them.

Step four – Become aware of the things that heighten anxiety such as homework or the threat of detention. Girls with ASD hate getting it wrong – they want to be seen as smart and popular. Connect with and validate the importance of this feeling by saying something like, "I feel it really matters to you to get it right. Let me help you feel a bit calmer before you do your homework; if you take a break and come back to it, then you'll find it easier to focus and do it to the best of your ability." Her focus on being smart may prevent her from seeing that, to some of her peers, this might be off-putting. Help her to become more aware of how she comes across in her group – by supporting her to mentalize herself.

Step five – Talk to your daughter about her interactions with her friends. It's likely that your teenage daughter has many of the same interests in make-up and appearance as her friends and is also interested in social media just like them ... except that often she does not understand the nuances of teenage girls' conversations. Sit down with your daughter and ask her to tell you some of the things her peer group talked about then help her to unpick the parts she didn't understand. Empathise with her that it must feel very confusing not to be able to follow it all the time.

Parenting boys with ASD and supporting their social skills

The prevalence of ASD in boys is approximately 3:1 by current estimates compared with adolescent girls and it is more frequently diagnosed in boys than in girls. The reasons for this are likely related to the more obvious signs of social difficulties and behavioural problems noticed in boys at a young age, and the greater understanding of male ASD among mental health and paediatric/general health professionals.

When we think of teenage boys with ASD, particularly prominent difficulties are most notably in their social relationships, especially in relation to their peer group. Teenage boys with ASD often speak of struggling to understand the banter of their peer group, including the sarcastic comments that are made about each other in everyday conversations. Sarcasm and banter are naturally harder for ASD teenagers to understand because they involve having relatively advanced "theory of mind" skills – the skills involved in holding one belief but expressing another. For example, I might understand that James wants to do well in his exams, but he doesn't want to appear a show off in front of his friends, so he might say after leaving the exam hall, "I didn't do well in that one, couldn't be bothered to revise." Someone with ASD is likely to be more literal, not thinking through how his comments could appear to the outsider, so might be more likely to say, "I revised for hours for that exam, so I'd better do okay." This type of comment could potentially lead to his peers thinking he's over-confident or arrogant and might put them off him.

As well as struggling with banter, teenage boys with ASD struggle with other areas of their social communication skills. For example, it's very difficult to take another person's perspective into account if you have ASD, so this often leads to teenagers talking about their own particular interests, and often with a level of intensity and preoccupation that's off-putting to other people. In these types of situations, it will help your teenager if you talk with them about how they can have a different kind of conversation with their peers, one that expresses an interest in other people's points of view. If you help your teenager to mentalize other people – showing curiosity, empathy and interest in other people's perspectives – they will learn the type of skills needed for making and maintaining friendships. Here are some steps to helping your teenage son get along with his peer group:

Step one – **Mentalize yourself – notice how you are feeling and thinking.** Make sure you are in a calm state of mind yourself before you begin to help your teenager with his emotions. It's sometimes difficult to manage your own emotional arousal around teenagers with ASD as their strong feelings will often unbalance your own state of mind.

Step two – **Help your teenager to notice how he feels.** Sometimes young people with ASD have a limited emotional vocabulary, so it can help them if you support them in expanding this. You can do this by suggesting different feelings that fit different situations, making sure you explain more nuanced feelings such as irritation, jealousy, frustration and confusion, as opposed to extreme feelings like fury and sadness. Teenagers with ASD often jump to extreme emotions, missing out on the feelings that build up to the extremes.

Step three – **Help your teenager to manage how he feels.** You can use the emotional thermometer discussed in the introduction to help your teenager notice when he is at either end of the thermometer and to explain the link between being in the too-hot or too-cold range, where it's much more difficult to mentalize – to notice what he and other people are thinking and feeling. Think with your teenager about strategies that will help him to manage his emotional temperature, for example, listening to music, walking while listening to a podcast (to reduce anxiety) or sitting in a quiet place without any sensory input. Get your teenager to see how different he feels when he is in a calm place and how, once calm, he can be more reflective about himself and other people.

Step four – **Help your teenager to understand other people.** Once your teenager has got himself into a calmer, more mentalizing, state of mind, help him start to be curious about other people. You might want to suggest some questions he could ask other people and help him plan social situations in advance. For example, say your teenager is going on a school trip with a group of friends and his tendency would normally be to talk about his own interests, suggest he has a series of questions in his back pocket to ask his friends on the journey, such as, "Did anyone watch the match last night? What did you think?"

Ultimately, it would be beneficial to your teenager with ASD if you could help them to understand themselves better. When a young person with ASD has this understanding, they can usually manage their feelings better, understand their reaction to social or confusing situations, and then use the strategies you've talked through together to recover their capacity to mentalize in these situations. When they have managed to do this, they might even feel comfortable or self-assured enough to tell others that they have ASD or ASD-type differences and that some situations feel a bit confusing for them. Young people are often surprisingly accepting of neurodivergence and having an understanding of their own identity is extremely important for your teenager's general well-being and mental health.

PAUSE AND REFLECT: YOUR TEENAGER'S SOCIAL WORLD

In a nutshell ...

Peers are essential to your teenager's survival so it's important to help your teenager learn how to understand and manage their friendships and relationships. Your relationship with their other parent or your partner will have a big influence on how they conduct their own relationships. Reflective Parenting reminds us how important it is to help your teenager to understand and manage how they feel.

Reflecting on yourself helps you ...

Understanding the importance of your teenager's peer relationships helps you to take a step back and allows you to support their relationships with peers as a vital part of their development.

Reflecting on your teenager helps them by ...

When you step back and allow your teenager to develop their social network, through friendships and relationships, you allow your teenager to develop more resilience compared with if you have too much proximity to them. Taking seriously their relationships outside of the one with you, taking a back seat at times, allows your teenager to develop a support system of friends, much needed for their development and eventual transition to independence.

Reflecting on your teenager – using a parent APP – helps your relationship by ...

In some circumstances, focusing on your teenager's feelings about their friendships, and helping them to feel understood – using the principles of attention and curiosity, perspective taking and empathy and validation – helps them to resolve difficult situations with friends. Understanding your teenager's difficulties in social situations and helping them to build mentalizing skills themselves, increases their understanding of complex social interactions. This is helpful for all teenagers, but particularly helps those with social communication differences and/or ASD.

Keep in mind …

- Use the "two-hands" approach to help your teenager manage their use of social media. This means, on the one hand, understanding their need for connection and acceptance in their peer group through social media use, and on the other hand, setting a boundary around how much time you allow them to look at social media.
- Helping your teenager monitor their use of social media and notice the impact it has on their mood (making them possibly more anxious or depressed) will help them learn to self-regulate.
- Mentalize yourself and note that it's difficult not to feel hurt at times when your teenager needs to connect with their friends in preference to you. However, your acceptance of this is crucial to maintaining your long-term connection with your teenager.
- Resist making assumptions about what you think you "know" is going on in your teenager's mind. Pause and reflect on what's in your own mind – using the parent MAP – and then try to mentalize what's going on in your teenagers, while keeping a position of uncertainty and curiosity.

6

YOUR RISKY TEENAGER

> *"This is risky for others but not risky for me, I'll probably be alright."*
>
> *"How did she get there in the first place? Why didn't she tell us?"*

Up to this point, we've looked at the type of problems you might face with your teenager that are the ordinary, expected parts of adolescent development, such as the need for autonomy and the difficulty in appreciating others' perspectives. In this and the following chapter, we will look at why teenagers take risks, how the context of the teenage years can increase the opportunity for risk-taking, and the impact that all of this has on you and your relationship with your teenager.

Understanding risk-taking in the teenage years

In adolescence, there is a strong urge to take more risks, particularly in peer groups, where experimentation is encouraged and the consequences of risks are unlikely to be thought through. Risk-taking in adolescence can take different forms, from risky behaviour such as drinking, drug taking and unprotected sex to practices such as self-harm, an increasingly common coping strategy for teenagers trying to deal with overwhelming or intolerable feelings (Figure 6.1).

Adolescents do need to take some risks in life as part of normal development. For example, going for a job interview involves taking a small risk. They might get rejected, might even feel humiliated if they completely dry up or feel inadequate if the questions are tough. It will undoubtedly involve some stress.

DOI: 10.4324/9780429459245-7

As a parent, you wouldn't advise your teenager never to take this type of risk. However, when it comes to other risky behaviours, such as drinking and taking drugs, you might have differing views about whether you would consider it a "normal" risk to take.

The risks your teenager is vulnerable to will be partly out of their and your control because their response to risk will have been shaped to some degree by your response to their feelings as a child, although there is much that you can do to change their response through increasing your connection via a reflective approach. For example, if when your child was six years old you encouraged them to talk about all of their feelings, not just the happy ones, and set an environment where it was OK to be miserable and lonely and to feel uncomfortable, and that you could sit *alongside* your child with these feelings, truly engaged with their experience, then this will continue into their adolescence and beyond.

In fact, today's teenagers take *fewer* risks than in previous generations. The current generation of teenagers at the point of writing, sometimes referred to as Generation Z – people born between 1996 and 2010 – are in this category. According to research statistics, this generation of 11–26 year-olds are the *least likely* in modern history to take risks: to smoke, drink alcohol, use drugs, have sex early or participate in criminal behaviour. In fact, since the mid-nineties, rates for all of these behaviours have dropped significantly, making this generation of young people possibly the most sensible (or careful, or anxious) teenagers in history. Therefore, we need to think about risk carefully and, first and foremost, the risk to mental health, which, while other risky behaviours are on the decline, has seen a steep rise in the past decade. There are many reasons why "traditional" risky behaviours have decreased and mental health problems have increased and these include:

- Parents are generally more involved in their teenager's lives and fathers especially spend more time with this generation of adolescents than in previous ones. Father involvement with their child has been found to correlate highly with reduced emotional and behavioural problems in adolescents. Parents are more vigilant of their teenagers and talk about risk in a more approachable way, so this has meant that teenagers have a more informed and sensible approach to risky activities such as drug-taking.
- Today's teenagers more frequently have what has been termed

"delayed independence." They learn to drive later, leave home later, have children later and often have sex later. This can mean they are less resilient, which impacts on their mental health.
- Teenagers are more anxious now than in previous generations. Anxious about the climate crisis, and financial independence and generally more anxious and pessimistic about their futures.

It is important to distinguish normal risk-taking behaviour in adolescence from serious and significant self-harm. However, although the latter clearly causes a greater level of distress for parents, any type of risk-taking can be seen as a form of communication, which is important for the teenager, and which mustn't be ignored by parents and significant adults around them. We will look specifically at high risk and self-harm in the following Chapter 7.

Let's consider the range of risks to your teenager, including some of the more "traditional adolescent" ones, together with newer risks, including those associated with social media and the online world, increased anxiety and social isolation and a decrease in in-person activities. Understanding the reasons why your teenager might take risks is an important first step for parents in responding to their teenager's risky behaviours.

- **Brain changes in adolescence** make teenagers more likely to take risks. Teenagers make good or bad decisions, or take big, small or no risks, based on the lack of maturity of the pre-frontal cortex, as discussed in Chapter 1. As adults, we often feel like doing something, but then the forward planning part of our brain – the prefrontal cortex – kicks in and we think, "Hmm, I'm not going to have that extra glass of wine because I've got an early morning meeting." Research shows that teenagers base their decisions about risk more on how they are feeling in the moment (because of the lack of development in the pre-frontal cortex), rather than on thinking ahead, so they are likely to act more on impulse. So their response might be more like, "Hmm, I fancy another drink, I'm having fun at this party." Even if there's an exam in the morning. In response to this, you might find yourself asking, "Why didn't you think about your exam when you went out last night?" or, "You knew that wouldn't be a good idea, but you decided to do it anyway, what a mistake!" In this situation, you're using your fully mature brain to apply logic to your teenager, who has a more impulsive brain. Your questions won't make sense to them and won't be welcome.

- **Adolescents take risks to feel pleasure.** Immediately following a risky event, we feel pleasure, and this can be heightened for adolescents. Take a rollercoaster ride at a funfair for example. The excitement that comes at the end of the ride is related to having survived the risk, and this is related to the release of the neurochemical dopamine, discussed in Chapter 1. This neurotransmitter sends signals to your brain that lead to dramatic feelings of pleasure and in turn thrill and excitement. Of course, we all want pleasure in life, but some people's brains seem more designed to seek it out than others. One interesting finding (1) showed that the reward system of the teenage brain may ignore a small reward but produce an exaggerated thrill reaction after a moderate experience of excitement. In other words, if your teenager is a thrill-seeker, they need to take a moderate or bigger risk to produce the desired sensation.
- **Teenagers may take risks because it affords them the popularity or respect** among their peer group they want. Even those who are not particularly big risk-takers may suddenly take a risk for this reason.
- **Adolescents may take risks because they "just felt like it."** This idea should not be underestimated, and it is important to recognise this is a legitimate response on the part of adolescents, who are acting on feelings.
- **Research** (2) **suggests that teenagers take longer than adults to work out what is dangerous** and what isn't. The pre-frontal cortex – which in adults inhibits risk-taking and stops us from acting on impulse – is not yet mature in teenagers, and so they are more likely to engage in risky behaviours without first thinking it through.

Other factors that lead to risk-taking

Some risk-taking behaviours are part of normal exploration and development, and your parental reaction to this and your ability to regulate your own emotions – using your parent MAP - becomes crucial. Using the emotional thermometer will be important to your ability to get into a space where you can mentalize yourself and then start to mentalize your teenager. You will then be able to think together reflectively about their experiences, without leaping to punitive or judgemental action, which will push your teenager further away. It's important to bear in mind that, where risk is concerned, if your interactions with your teenager cause them to be pushed further away, or retreat into their own world, it's likely that the risk to them will increase. So, how do you keep a connection with your teenager when they are engaging in risky behaviours that are raising your emotional temperature? Here is a quick step-by-step guide to follow before we look in more detail at the types of risks that concern you.

The risk "scale"

It helps to think of risk on a continuum and to accept that risk-taking is part of normal development during adolescence. At the very bottom of the scale, there are teenagers who don't take any risks at all. These teenagers are worrying as they don't learn about exploration and they are highly vulnerable to mental health problems later on when faced with life's challenges. In the middle of the scale there are the teenagers who take risks because they tend to think, "This is risky for others but not risky for me, I'll probably be alright." This accounts for the majority of risk-takers in adolescence who lack an awareness of risk, although they knowingly enter into it, enjoying potentially risky activities such as rock climbing, parachuting, drinking and using drugs at parties and with friends. Lastly, there is a third group at the top of the continuum who take risks, not caring if they live or die; they feel "it doesn't matter, so if I die, I die, who cares?" This group of teenagers are seriously risky and need support from professionals to help them with the underlying cause of their attitude to risk. Although it seems counterintuitive to us, there is sometimes a reason for doing something risky that serves as a reward for the teenager, for example, "doing this will give me status in my peer group or it might give me an experience I hadn't had before."

For us parents, it's important we reflect on the different meanings behind our teenager's risk-taking behaviour.

The risk to your teenager's mental health

Mental health problems such as depression are more likely to start in adolescence than at any other time of life, with up to 75% of mental health challenges emerging at this time. Given these statistics, mental health is most likely the biggest risk facing today's teenagers, and your main responsibility as their parents is to support their mental health and well-being. Teenagers need to talk about what's going on with them, and they need to feel equipped when their friends reach out to them – teenagers are more likely to talk to their friends about their problems. Your role as parents is to talk to your teenagers about the challenges they may deal with as they're growing up, particularly the ones that challenge their mental health.

Like physical health, we all have mental health, and the first step is to make this an everyday part of your conversations with your teenager. If you want to equip teenagers with the language for talking about their mental health, then they need to know it's normal and okay to sometimes feel sad, angry, alone and frustrated. These problems may become more persistent and might point to something else, and it will be crucial for you to be able to recognise the early warning signs so that your teenager can get help.

Mental health statistics

- One in six children aged five to 16 were identified as having a probable mental health problem in July 2021, a huge increase from one in nine in 2017. That's five children in every classroom (i).
- The number of A&E attendances by young people aged 18 or under with a recorded diagnosis of a psychiatric condition more than tripled between 2010 and 2018–19 (ii).
- 83% of young people with mental health needs agreed that the coronavirus pandemic had made their mental health worse (iii).
- In 2018–19, 24% of 17-year-olds reported having self-harmed in the previous year, and seven per cent reported having self-harmed with suicidal intent at some point in their lives. 16% reported high levels of psychological distress (iv).

- Nearly half of 17–19-year-olds with a diagnosable mental health disorder have self-harmed or attempted suicide at some point, rising to 52.7% for young women (vi).

The statistics are shocking, but the focus for parents is clear: we need to make our teenager's mental health our top priority and think about how we can help to support them to become mentally healthy young adults. Mental health problems, such as depression and anxiety, often underpin other risk-taking in adolescence. For example, trying alcohol for the first time at a party could be seen as a relatively normal, low-level risk, on the risk scale. Drinking excessively in an attempt to block out feelings of depression, anxiety, loneliness and social isolation, is much higher up the risk scale. As you go through this chapter, think about where your teenager is on the risk scale and how much of their behaviour is possibly related to their mental health.

Responding to your teenager's risk-taking

You probably know that, realistically, your teenager is going to try some things that you consider to be risky, but how you manage your own state of mind and help them to stay safe at the same time is quite a complicated process. Your focus should be on their well-being and ability to navigate their way through life. A balanced approach is advisable, as extreme punitive measures will be met with equally extreme reactions.

Some risk-taking behaviours are part of normal exploration and development, and your parental reaction to this and your ability to regulate your own emotions – using the principles of the parent MAP discussed in Chapter 2 – become crucial. Assessing your emotional state – using the emotional thermometer tool will be an important part of your ability to get into a space where you can mentalize yourself and then start to mentalize your teenager. You will then be able to think together reflectively about their experiences, without leaping to judgement or punitive action, which will push your teenager further away. It's important to bear in mind that where risk is concerned, if your interactions with your teenager cause them to be pushed further away, or retreat into their own world, it's likely that the risk to them will increase.

So, how do you keep a connection going with your teenager when they are engaging in risky behaviours that are raising your emotional temperature? Here is a quick step-by-step guide to follow, before we look in more detail at the specific types of risks that may concern you.

Teenage parties

Figure 6.1

The reasons why your teenager engages in risky behaviours are not entirely down to the maturity of their brain; they are also susceptible to several influences, from social media to peer relationships and the physical changes occurring in their bodies. Reflecting on the generally less risky generation of teenagers today, described at the start of this chapter, one of the risks to your teenager may be that they don't want to go to *enough* parties or to socialise much at all. One of the main reasons for the reduction in risk-taking behaviours in adolescents in recent times is the drop in in-person socialising among them. Teenagers are not going to parties as much as their parents' generation did. The picture is complicated, but the research suggests that parties have *not* been replaced by online activities. Also, the drop in attending parties has not led to a drop in drug use or alcohol consumption. Teenagers still engage in these things and in fact, those adolescents who are heavy gamers and social media users are *more* likely to smoke, drink and take drugs. It seems then that the context for engaging in risky behaviours has shifted from those risks that were previously taken outside of the family home, and those that are closer to home, but still kept separate or hidden from parents and family. Risks such as heavy gaming and social media usage are more prevalent than risks such as teenage pregnancy, drunken driving and unsafe sex. However, the intersection between these risks and social media is important to understand and consider how you approach these as a parent.

Risk is not restricted to our traditional parental worries of too many drugs, alcohol, sex, and driving cars, but has increasingly focused on the mental health of our teenagers. Let's first look at the scenario involving Connor and his mum, and some of the anxieties both parents and teenagers experience when social media and parties are involved.

Leah lives in a suburb near the countryside with her partner and two children, having moved from London when the children were small. Their teenage son, Connor, is 17 and their younger boy, Jamie, is 10.

The family went away for a weekend to a leisure park, where Jamie had lots of fun on the water slides, but Connor felt bored and out of place. He missed his friends. On the second evening, after weighing it up for a while, Leah and her partner decided to give their oldest son, Connor, some independence and let him travel back early to their home in Surrey to meet up with his friends, while they continued to enjoy the last night of their weekend at a leisure park. What they didn't know was that the meet-up with friends was actually a party at their house and that Connor was the host.

On their drive home, they received a phone call from Connor: "I'm really sorry," he said, "but Josh broke that standing vase in the kitchen scootering round the table." Leah and her partner were alarmed to find out that not only had Connor been hosting a party in their home without telling them, but also, even worse, what was meant to be a gathering of around 20 mates had spiralled out of control, enabled by social media, into a party of around 200 people.

The scene that greeted them at home included a bad smell from the ruined carpets, broken latches on the bathroom doors, a broken toilet seat and cigarette burns on Leah's favourite armchair. The cat was nowhere in sight and Connor said he hadn't seen her for 24 hours. He was visibly upset when they got home and seemed extremely anxious.

Leah and her partner dealt with this by immediately confiscating his phone and he was banned from going out for a while. They were both angry and distressed by what had happened behind their backs. Their main concern, aside from the deceit, was what *could* have gone wrong, without any adults on hand to pick up the pieces. The whole range of potential horrors ran through their minds from "What if someone had set the house on fire with their cigarettes and candles?" to, "What if someone had needed to go to A&E and there was no adult there to drive them the fair distance to the local hospital?"

Reflecting on Leah and her partner

What thoughts and feelings are in your mind when you read through this scenario? It might be a familiar scene or very far from your own experience. What would you have done in Leah's situation when you returned home? If you think about your own emotional response to this scenario, try reflecting on where it comes from – perhaps using part of your parent MAP, such as whether your own upbringing is influencing your response to this scenario, or perhaps something that's happening in your life at present. If you are reflecting on yourself – with reference to your parent MAP – you might think about what your parents would have allowed you to do, what their reaction would have been, and also some of the things currently going on in your life. If you are already feeling stressed and worried about your teenager and other things in your life, what kind of reaction would this scenario have likely provoked in you? Your own adolescence will also influence how you respond.

I felt shocked and sympathetic towards Leah, hearing this story. I then started to think about how she must have felt about not just her home, but also her teenage son, who had gone behind her back to host a party. It also made me wonder about my own family and whether there had been concealed parties I never knew about!

Reflecting on Connor

What did you think about Connor when you read the scenario? I wonder what it might be like for him to think about having to tell his parents and to have had a party that got out of control. Was his actual intent to have a party on this scale or simply to have some excitement, which then spiralled into a massive, out-of-control party? Despite all that happened, we might feel quite sorry for him when hearing about him phoning his parents. At the same time, we might think, "What *were* you thinking putting it on social media?" As we've seen in so many different scenarios, it's hard to regulate yourself when your emotional arousal level or anxiety starts to increase, and this makes it harder to think about what might have been in Connor's mind when he sent out the invitation.

Thinking together

What they found was that Connor was distraught. The party had got out of control, he spent the whole evening running around the house trying to prevent people from going into rooms they were meant to be banned from and had thoroughly hated the whole night; the mix of anxiety and anger around so many strangers had left him broken.

Although his parents banned him from using his phone, they knew that they couldn't do this forever and also that this punitive approach on its own wouldn't work. In fact, they suspected he would only dig his heels in further if they took to banning him from going out. Perhaps they might have considered getting their son to update his social media settings to private. As time went on though, and they listened to their son talking with friends about where the next party was, they knew that they couldn't keep him under lock and key forever. They realised that they needed to understand how this had happened in the first place, and how things could be different next time. They talked with Connor and listened to what he had to say. They came to understand that he had initially just wanted to have some independence, away from his parents. He had found the experience at the leisure park childish, and it made him crave his friends' company. He didn't want to feel like a kid on the water slides but wanted to feel the thrill and independence of having his own fun in a house without adults. His parents tried to understand his motivations in the first place (wanting to be popular and cool); his expectations of the party; his reasons for not asking his parents (he was sure they would say no, mistakenly), and his state of mind (frightened, anxious, guilty) when everything was turning to chaos during the party. It would have been easy for Leah to make Connor feel shame for his actions. By listening to Connor, Leah and her partner avoided Connor feeling shame, which could have made him feel as though there was something wrong with him; however, they did try to instil a sense of guilt over his actions, as they felt this would be helpful. For example, they might have said something like, "We just can't ever trust you to be responsible," which would have induced shame, as opposed to something like "We feel very upset, things have been broken" to induce guilt. It was important that Connor and his parents could restore trust in their relationship and also that Connor could feel happy with his friendship group and not ashamed of them around his parents.

Be realistic and be prepared. We left our house unattended one New Year's Eve, leaving just one (usually very trustworthy) teenager in the house. We told several neighbours we were going away and asked them to keep an eye and ears out for a possible party. We know this son hates social media, so the chances of anything being posted there was, nevertheless, a risk. But we insisted on keeping in contact and on him phoning us on New Year's Eve. Yes, he had a gathering of a few people, and our 9-year-old son found a (strangely full) bottle of Absinth behind the piano when we returned, but there had been many conversations before we went away about what we were and weren't okay with when it came to a party. One of the key things to emerge from this conversation was that it wasn't just us who felt uncomfortable with the idea of a big party in our family home but *he* felt the same way too. Just like Connor, the actual horror of a party that's out of your control, happening in your own home, is nobody's idea of fun. A few years later when this son was in his late teens, he reflected that the reason he had the party was not out of fear of us saying no, but more out of a desire for independence around socialising, noise, drinking, etc. I think this is a useful reflection from a teenager's perspective that where we might get hung up on authority and respect and keeping to rules, teenagers are striving for greater independence and autonomy and not necessarily looking to break our rules.

Let's think about another scenario involving risk for a teenage girl, where a party and substances are involved.

> Vicky and her eldest daughter, Jess, have always had a good relationship. At school, Jess is bright and popular and at home, she has always been the sort of child Vicky feels she can trust and relate to, seeing a lot of herself in her daughter. So, when Jess asks her if she can go to a friend's party on Saturday night, Vicky asks a few basic questions about who is hosting and readily agrees to her daughter attending the party as it's only three streets away from their home, with a friend she has known for years. Saturday night arrives and Vicky and her husband are sitting at home enjoying a relaxing evening with a glass of wine. As midnight approaches, Vicky starts to get a little worried she hasn't heard anything from Jess and sends her a text asking if everything is OK. She gets no reply. Half an hour later, Vicky is getting more agitated and wondering whether Jess needs her or her dad to walk her home; the party is just around the corner after all. The phone rings and a slurred voice asks, "Mum, can you come and get us?" Vicky says, "Where are you, love?" "Er, I'm near Slough I think." Vicky's mind starts spinning, "Slough?!" It's at least an hour away from their home, and, more importantly, neither parent had any idea that Jess had gone to a party so far away from home. Who's party is it? How does she know anyone in that area? Who is she with? How did she get there in the first place? Why didn't she tell us?
>
> Vicky is about to ask her husband to drive to pick Jess and her friend up when she realises he has had more than two glasses of wine so isn't in a fit state to drive, so she sets off herself into the night, a thousand worries racing through her mind. The journey home isn't easy. Jess is too drunk to speak properly, and Vicky spends the journey anxiously checking in the rear-view mirror to see if she can catch Jess' eye to gauge the state of her pupils. Were there drugs involved? Why did she deceive us like this? What on earth has gone on? As they pull up to the house, Jess staggers out of the back of the car and tramples over the flowers in the front garden, to the sound of Vicky exclaiming "No! Not my tulips!" Jess promptly vomits all over them.

I wonder what is going on in your mind as you read this scenario, and what sorts of thoughts and feelings it provokes in you. Let's mentalize Vicky first and then look at what might have been behind Jess' behaviour as we try to mentalize her.

Reflecting on Vicky

We know from the scenario that Vicky feels very close to her teenage daughter, Jess, and that she identifies strongly with her. It's likely then that being deceived in this way by Jess will come as a shock to her and challenge her perception of this closeness. We can imagine that she feels both shocked to learn of Jess' whereabouts, because she's been lied to, but also anxious and frightened about what she's been involved in at the party and if anything terrible has happened. She might also feel guilty that she didn't ask more questions about where her daughter was going, and that she and her partner didn't steer clear of any alcohol in case their daughter needed picking up. However, it's understandable that she trusted her daughter was close by, and we can imagine her feeling confused about exactly what happened that evening.

Reflecting on Jess

Jess has drunk more alcohol than she can cope with at the party and so is in no fit state to answer her mum's questions. She must feel both physically ill and worried about what her parents are going to do to punish her, knowing that she went to a party so far from home and lied to them about where it was. In Jess' mind, she was excited and flattered to be asked to a big party, away from her local area where everybody knows everybody. Being part of a different crowd gave her a feeling of freedom and independence, and by going along with a trusted friend, she felt she would be okay. Once there, she felt more anxious than she'd anticipated and, to deal with her social anxiety, she drank a lot and took a pill someone gave her, because everyone else was doing it. She suddenly felt her anxiety getting out of control and needed to get back home, where she feels safe, so she called her mum. She doesn't know how much to tell them; if she should disclose taking the pill or try to conceal that to minimise the damage.

Thinking together

We can see both perspectives when we read this scenario and I think that at the heart of this story is a close relationship between parent and teenager. It's evident how hard it will be for both Vicky and Jess to mentalize in this moment. Vicky is very worried and feeling slightly guilty and Jess is experiencing similar emotions, but also an additional feeling of shame that she has both betrayed her parents and failed to handle a party with some new people, whom she had hoped to impress. In some respects, Vicky has the more straightforward task of ensuring that her daughter is OK and getting to the bottom of what's happened. However, she also has to try to keep the channel of communication open between her and her teenage daughter, which is likely to close down if she becomes punitive and judgemental too quickly.

Jess has a more complex set of feelings as she is embarrassed about having to call her mum for a lift and then being so out of it to even speak. To top it all, she has been sick in the front garden, and wonders if anyone saw her stumbling home. When she wakes and sobers up, she will feel physically terrible and will start running over the events of the previous evening in her mind. She might not even remember everything that happened and could feel extremely frightened not knowing what she did at the party.

Taking substances

Parents will always be concerned about their teenagers taking substances that impact their physical and mental health, and most adolescents will be tempted to experiment with them, whether it's trying alcohol for the first time but then not developing a regular habit, or smoking weed at a party, the temptation to try something – especially when they are with their peers – is strong. Smoking has decreased dramatically, but unfortunately vaping has taken off since 2016, which suggests teens are still interested in novel ways to take risks, especially if there is an element of marketing which suggests to them that vaping is "cool." We still need to talk to them about the dangers of vaping (they seem to have understood the health risks of smoking).

Dealing with teenage drinking

There are very few teenage parties where alcohol isn't a feature. Along with drugs, it's such an area of vulnerability and is associated with so much risk-taking in teenagers. Often, the drink of choice today at teenage parties is spirits, in part because they are easier to disguise as water. However, teenagers are more likely to get drunk on spirits than on wine or beer – partly because it can be hard to know how much has been consumed when mixed with soft drinks – and subsequently, they are more likely to take risks. Unfortunately, the adolescent brain is more vulnerable to alcohol and other drugs than the adult brain and we don't fully understand why. We understand alcohol reduces inhibition and decreases our capacity to make good judgements, and these problems are multiplied further for teenagers. The risks that apply to everyone, such as inhaling vomit, driving a car, deciding to walk home alone at night, having sex with someone without thinking, and getting a lift from a stranger, are amplified with teenagers because alcohol has a greater impact on them, and they are developmentally more likely to make rash decisions.

The fact is that if your teenager has decided they are going to drink at a party then, short of policing them in front of all of their friends, you have relatively little control over whether they will drink or not. It's best to be realistic about this and acknowledge that alcohol is likely to be part of their social scene at some point, even though your teenager may choose not to drink, may not like drinking or may not even consider it for religious or cultural reasons.

There are several practical things you can do to help your teenager make some wise choices:

- Accept that at some point they may have some alcohol and encourage them to choose drinks such as beer that have a lower volume of alcohol (ABV).
- Buy alcohol for them. Sometimes standing with their friends in a supermarket leads to worse choices.
- Choose to drink only in moderation yourself. Children learn so much from our behaviour, so consider the effect if, for example, you regularly drink with friends in front of your children, or say, often took them for pub lunches when they were younger to socialise with other families and the adults drank a lot.

Whatever limits you set and advice you give, it's likely your teenager will find a way to push the limits and drink too much alcohol at some point during their adolescence, for all the reasons related to risk-taking in adolescence already discussed. When you talk to your teenager about the pitfalls of getting very drunk, do this in a non-patronising way that doesn't involve shame. For example, instead of saying, "You don't want to be throwing up on the carpet," say, "You'll have a better time if you keep within your limits." Talk to your teenager about ways to moderate drinking and discuss the dangers of excessive drinking, including the very serious implications this can have, such as stomach pumping and even early liver damage, taking into account that they are likely to switch off from extreme scare stories, thinking "that's not me."

Drug taking in adolescence

We know that teenagers seek stimulation and like immediate, rather than delayed, rewards. Alcohol and some drugs give teenagers an immediate reward by elevating their mood quickly, giving them a sense of confidence and belonging in their social group and even approval from their peer group. All these immediate rewards are far more salient to your teenager than the longer-term risks, which are harder for teenagers to relate to.

There is a stronger taboo around drug-taking than alcohol, although a major study in 2010 by the former government chief drugs adviser, Professor David Nutt, on the overall dangers of the entire spectrum of drugs both to the consumer and wider society ranked alcohol as the most damaging. Whatever your view, it is less likely your teenager will have been exposed while growing up to you or other people in their family taking drugs, than to seeing you drinking alcohol. However, drugs are more easily available and more dangerous in their toxicity to teenagers now than in previous generations. There is no single reason why adolescents misuse substances; they might be bored, feel low, want to fit in, want to seem older, etc. There could be any number of reasons, but the important issue is how you as their parent try to understand their desire or need to use substances – this is the mentalizing approach, to be curious and interested in your teenager's experiences, while at the same time using your two-hands approach to set a boundary in place and to advice on the harmful impact of using drugs. Many teenagers will take drugs or consume alcohol to fill an empty void in their emotional world. Mental health problems, particularly depression, are more likely to start in adolescence than at any other time (see the section on mental health below), and drugs and alcohol often serve as easy quick remedies for dealing with feeling low or depressed.

Your teenager's social scene may revolve around both drinking and using marijuana and perhaps other drugs. As with alcohol, sometimes friends urge one another to smoke marijuana, but it's just as common for teenagers to start trying a substance because it's readily available and they see some of their friends enjoying it. In their minds, substance use is a part of the normal teenage experience.

You might be starting to feel anxious even reading and thinking about this now, in which case it will hopefully be evident how important it is to mentalize yourself ahead of any conversations you have with your teenager about this tricky and contentious possibility.

- If you are thinking about having a conversation with your teenager about the dangers and risks involved in using drugs, try to do this as early as possible in their adolescence, so that they can think about your perspective and consider this alongside any pressure that might be starting to build up among their peers. It may not impact them enough to stop them from being tempted to experiment, but it's good to have started a conversation so that they are aware that you are open to talking with them about it. Any topic that becomes a taboo is likely to lead to more secrecy around that behaviour, and a disconnect from you.
- Provide accurate information. Your teenager might have friends who claim to be experts on various recreational substances, and they may tell your teenager that the risks are minimal. Your role can be to have an honest and open conversation with your teenager about the risks of taking drugs, and point them to the evidence, without shaming them. If your teenager has started taking drugs, be prepared to manage your emotional response to this if they are open to sharing this information with you. Speak in a measured and calm tone about the dangers, giving facts, for example, about the damaging impact of cocaine use on the heart.
- Be prepared for your teenager not to take an interest in your perspective. The tendency to act impulsively and to take risks among their peer group means that they are unlikely to care about any long-term consequences. If your teenager is going to parties where you know it is likely drugs are a part of the scene, give them advice about how to tell friends or call on you if they begin to feel unwell. Showing that you don't advise drug

taking, but will have your door open to helping them should something go wrong, will keep your teenager feeling connected where risk is concerned.

- Help your teenager understand that any substance they use will impair judgement and so they are more likely to find themselves in a potentially dangerous situation, such as driving drunk or having unwanted or risky sexual encounters.
- Speak to your teenager the way you'd like to be spoken to. If you build up to having 'the talk' then your teenager will be acutely sensitive to feeling patronised or condescended. Treat them instead like the adults you want them to become, so they can see you are listening to them and respect them.
- Always give your teenager a chance to speak and show that you are actively listening – you can use your parent APP to help you. Let them ask you questions too, modelling that you are open to sharing your knowledge and not scared of the topic of drugs and alcohol.
- Being aware of your own thoughts and feelings – mentalizing yourself – and through this process starting to understand where these thoughts and feelings come from so that you can manage to regulate them, will help you to have a calm and thoughtful conversation with your teenager about their experiences, without jumping to setting conditions and rules that they subsequently break.

Sex

There's no doubt that for many families, having conversations about sex feels awkward and embarrassing for parents and teenagers alike. However, research tells us that sexual contact can start between children as young as 10 or 11 years old, and this usually involves sexual activity in which girls are serving boys' needs, with little regard for the social or emotional needs of the girls. Girls find it hard to say no, particularly if they want a relationship with a boy. These are general trends, and it's not to say that there isn't pressure between same-sex relationships, but the more prevalent risk of coercion in relationships is largely boys to girls. Delaying substances, such as alcohol, for longer helps reduce the risk of sexual coercion and potentially risky sexual behaviour, as boys consuming alcohol tends to increase the likelihood of them putting pressure on girls to have sex, and girls consuming alcohol lowers their inhibitions and reduces their emotional regulation.

Having conversations about sex with your young teenager

Parents are often reluctant to convey their views and advice about sex because they fear resistance from their teenagers, but evidence shows that these discussions are best held sooner rather than later – before your child reaches their teens. It's important to hold on to your authoritative parenting role. Young teenagers don't need you to be their friend but rather need a parental perspective on their experience, otherwise, they get lost. At a young age, they can internalise something of your perspective and use it to help guide them, otherwise, they are at risk of feeling abandoned and overwhelmed. When you take a reflective parenting stance and use your mentalizing skills to reflect on your own and your teenager's perspective, you will find that when you give information calmly and respectfully, your teenager will want to talk and you will want to listen.

One aspect of your conversations about sex with your teenager should involve thinking with them about their sexual identity. Parents can often default to assuming their child is straight, particularly if they are heterosexual themselves. Make your conversations about sex *relational* so that there is always an aspect of the conversation where you are talking about the other person as well as your teenager's feelings. Give time and space for your teenager to reflect on their sexuality by saying things like, "If you decide you really like a boy or girl and you want to get to know them better" as opposed to saying, "If you like a boy" automatically to a girl. This will make it harder for her to open up if she feels more attracted to her own gender or feels bisexual or fluid in her sexual preferences.

Consent and abuse

Consent happens when all people involved in any kind of sexual activity agree to take part by choice. They also need to have the freedom and capacity to make that choice. Sexual activity doesn't have to involve penetrative sex but could be sexual touching or any contact or non-contact involving sexual intimacy. Any conversations you have with your teenager should involve a discussion about consent, and ideally, these conversations should take place as early as possible in their pre-teen years or in early adolescence when they are approaching puberty.

I remember when I was around seven years old, walking home from my friend's house, just around the corner. It was a lovely sunny day and my friend's mum had given me an ice lolly to cool me down during the five-minute walk home. As I walked along the road, a middle-aged man stopped me and said, "That lolly looks nice, can I have a lick?" I froze, unsure of the right thing to do, but handed him the lolly, thinking "This is being polite" and he sucked the lolly in a way that I now understand as suggestive of oral sex. I went home and felt uneasy and couldn't figure out what it was about. I decided not to tell my mum, as I didn't really understand why it was I felt unsure about this encounter. Then later that afternoon, my mum noticed I was quieter than usual and asked me if anything was wrong. I told her the story and she sat down with me and first just listened, then asked me what it was I had felt and why. She listened and validated how I felt, telling me that it had maybe felt "weird" because I didn't know him, and he had taken something that was mine and had been in my mouth and then put it in his. This made me feel validated in my feeling that this was something odd. It taught me that all of my feelings were important – not just the happy ones – and that my mum could empathise with me when I was feeling in my gut that something wasn't right. Later in life when I was flashed at by a stranger, I walked away quickly, knowing that he was potentially dangerous and that I was vulnerable. It stayed with me, however, and I felt violated and, albeit in a non-contact way, sexually assaulted by this stranger. Although I was in my twenties at the time, it was a horrible experience that impacted me for a long time afterwards.

The UK charity Rape Crisis reported that 9 out of 10 girls and young women in schools reported being subjected to "sexist name-calling" and receiving unwanted 'dick pics' or other images of a sexual nature. Despite parental attempts to control phone use, including putting parental controls on your teenager's phone, these statistics reflect the fact that girls in particular are at risk of sexual assault or abuse. We don't know the exact statistics for sexual abuse because many young people will be too afraid, too young, or too ashamed to tell anyone what is happening to them. Adults are also not always able to recognise the signs. The estimate is that approximately 1 in 20 children between ages 11–17 have experienced sexual abuse. It's important, therefore, for parents to listen to their teenage girls' concerns and experiences, but also crucial, to talk to their teenage boys about appropriate and respectful behaviour and crucially about consent. The onus should never be on the victim to behave differently, but to educate potential perpetrators of these abusive behaviours as to their consequences.

Coercive sex

Until recently, sex was deemed to be coercive only if physical restraint or force was used, but now we understand that it is much more nuanced than this. People can use pressure or influence to get your teenager to have sex and this may be done consciously through deliberate manipulative techniques, or more unconsciously, where it is assumed the other person is consenting. Sometimes drugs or alcohol can be used to remove the ability of the other person to object to or resist sex. Other times, more subtle methods can be used to force another person to have sex, such as using the status of the relationship or their gender; for example, "Sex is a way to prove you love me," and "If you don't have sex with me I'll get it from somewhere else," or "I'm a guy, I need it."

Rough sex and online sex

Sexual "choking" has become more prevalent in mixed-gender pornography and in young men's behaviour. Choking is actually a form of strangulation, although it's been increasingly brought into the mainstream and, worryingly, is seen by many teenagers and young adults as something that doesn't require consent. It involves pressing or squeezing the neck until the blood flow to the brain is cut off, causing light-headedness. It is usually done to girls by boys and, despite experts saying there is no safe way to engage in this act, many girls and young women report having been "choked" during sex because their sexual partner assumed it was something they were okay with. Consent was never asked. This might be one of the topics you choose to talk to your young teen about, in a very straightforward way. When you explain to them the importance of taking other people's feelings into consideration, as well as reflecting on their own, you are laying the groundwork for them to know what feels right for them and what doesn't. You are also teaching them how to reflect on other people, so if you're talking to your young teenage son about sex, keep the focus on treating other people with respect and try to help them keep in mind the other person's wishes and feelings.

Porn

It's important to acknowledge, too, that your teenager will have access to and be curious about porn, and that this curiosity is natural. However, it's equally important to have conversations with them about it and to make a distinction for them that most porn is not about real people or a healthy representation of real sexual relationships and that it usually distorts reality. It can be incredibly confusing for young teenagers to work out what's real and what's fantasy, and much of the porn industry thrives on feeding information to young people (and adults) that promotes a particular type of sex. For example, women are often objectified and their sexual pleasure is often not the focus. Also, dangerous practices such as rough sex are often promoted and consent is not a part of most porn. To many parents and carers, the risks involved in areas such as porn and internet sex feel like areas that are out of their control. This is where you need to be able to face up to your own awkwardness or lack of knowledge about these topics, do some of your own research and start conversations with your teenager as soon as possible about the potential risks. This needs to be done, as with all subjects, without shaming your teenager. So, for example, it would be good to start by saying something like, "I know everyone is curious about porn and that it can feel exciting at first. I wouldn't blame you if you had taken a look at it. I'd just like to tell you a bit more about it, and help you understand that it's seldom about healthy sexual relationships or real people." Before you say anymore, it would be useful to your teenager to show them that you want to listen to what they have to say, and to be prepared for their awkwardness and embarrassment, even acknowledging your own. The approach is no different for this conversation than it is for the one about alcohol or drugs – you are simply modelling an open and balanced mind (yours) that is interested in what your teenager thinks and feels.

It's important to be aware of these risks and that porn is an industry that is about selling products, so there are algorithms at work to get people to increase their use and to escalate the access and type of porn people watch. These algorithms work out how long particular images are holding your attention and then feed more similar images.

How you can talk to your teenager about sex

Having a mentalizing conversation with your teenager about sex is important, particularly in their early adolescence, when they are still forming their ideas about what sex means for them, what their personal gender and sexual preferences are and what is real and what's fantasy

Here are some suggestions for how to talk with your teenagers about sex and consent:

- Talk to your teenager about sex and relationships when they are younger, ideally before they reach puberty or around this time.
- Keep your focus on feelings and validate your teenager's. Speak to your teenager about not trying to please someone else when a sexual act doesn't feel right for them. If they risk being rejected or not liked, talk this through and emphasise the importance of listening to their own instincts.
- Equip young girls and women with the capabilities to decide if a particular sexual act is something they want to engage in. Talk to them about trusting their own instincts and about the importance of being consulted by a sexual partner about what they find pleasurable. The idea of pleasure in sex is rarely mentioned in sex education in schools.
- Explain to them the difference between sexual fantasy figures on programmes and on porn sites and real-life relationships. Emphasise the need to feel safe and respected.
- Listen to your teenager's worries and keep a close eye on their mental health. If they seem to be interested in sex because it will please someone else, focus on asking them what they think would make them happy/calm/content/safe and try to reflect on their state of mind.
- Create an environment where your teenager can talk about anything with you, no matter how embarrassing it feels to them (and you possibly!) at first. Model not being shocked, but being concerned for their safety, happiness and general well-being. Put these principles first and focus on managing feelings.

Another aspect of sex, and something that often gets missed in terms of risky behaviours, is internet sex. While for consenting adults, this can be part of their relationship, for teenagers, there are inherent risks. For teenagers, this can mean chatting to people through social media channels initially, which can then lead to direct messaging. From here, a teenager might be encouraged/coerced into practices such as sending nudes, and/or meeting up with a stranger, with all the risks this involves. If a teenager does send an explicit photo of themselves, they could potentially be put on a sex offender register, even if they were sending it to another person with their consent.

Let's look at the following scenario, where Cath is trying to work out how to help her young teenage daughter, Millie, manage her mixed feelings about sex. When reading this scenario, try to keep in mind what the risks are that Cath is trying to mitigate.

When Cath's 14-year-old daughter, Millie, started spending time with a boy and brought him back to her house, she started to worry that she hadn't spoken to her daughter about sex. One day after school, Millie went up to her bedroom with the boy when Cath was working in her office. When she called for Millie to come for dinner, she got a shock when they both came downstairs. She waited until after the boy had left before telling her daughter, "The rule in this house is 'no boys in the bedroom'." Millie asked, "Why?" and Cath said, "It's just a house rule, OK?" Millie muttered an "okay."

Straight afterwards, Cath started telling Millie the risks of teenage pregnancy, and talked about her lack of maturity and the importance of consent. Finally, she told her that if she absolutely insisted on having sex, then she must make sure that the boy had condoms. Millie looked horrified in response to her mum's lecture and said, "But I'm only 14, Mum." Cath realised that her mind had jumped way ahead of what her daughter was currently thinking about, and she had been way off the mark. At the same time, she felt a bit of relief that she had even had the conversation. Millie went up to her bedroom straight afterwards and stayed there for a while. Later that weekend, Cath decided to take a different approach and step back from giving more rules and instead just be curious about what Millie was feeling about the boy she was seeing, rather than lecture her. Millie said that she was just "getting to know" the boy and liked him, but he wasn't a boyfriend yet. Millie told Cath that she didn't want to have sex yet, but just liked hanging out with both boys and girls as friends.

Reflecting on Cath

We can see in this scenario that Cath was so shocked by her daughter going up to her bedroom with a boy she hadn't met, her mind immediately jumped to the worst-case scenario for Millie. In her mind, her daughter wanted to have sex – or the boy might make her – and was heading for a ruined life. Her emotional temperature rose so fast that she reacted by giving her a set of rules for behaviour, without first finding out what Millie was thinking and feeling. When they had a bit of time and space from each other, and Cath had managed to regulate herself better, she was able to start to be curious about what was in Millie's mind. From her reaction, we can imagine that she perhaps hasn't had many, or any, conversations with Millie about sex and relationships. When she is suddenly confronted with her daughter and a boy she panics.

Reflecting on Millie

To Cath's surprise, Millie was feeling "scared" about what had happened to her friend. She wasn't identifying with her friend at all but was clearly very worried for her. At first, she wasn't able to tell her mum about this feeling because she felt she was being told off – as if she had been the one to have had sex at 12. She was annoyed with her mum for assuming that whatever her friend had done, Millie would surely do the same. She may have felt insulted that her mum made this assumption about her.

Thinking together

In this scenario, it's easy to see how the emotional temperature of the parent got in the way of her being able to show any interest or curiosity in what was going on in her teenager's mind, which many parents will be able to relate to. As we saw in the scenario with Josh and the party earlier in the chapter, the teenager's upset is far from the parent's mind because the parent is so emotionally dysregulated, albeit understandably. You can see from both scenarios that when a parent has been able to manage their own emotions, it leaves a space for them to mentalize their teenager and to use the parent APP – expressing curiosity and interest in their perspective. This allows the teenager to say what they are feeling, which might often be far from the parent's perception of what was in their mind.

Social media and the risks for adolescents

In Chapter 5, we looked at how social media and the online world are relevant to your teenager's social world. Here we think about some of the risks this exposes them to. Social media use increased during the Covid-19 pandemic, and research observed the negative impact of social media use on the mental health of adolescents and students (3). The most noticeably observed were anxiety, depression and stress. The study, which looked at over a thousand records found that more **active** and **prolonged** social media usage was associated with a negative impact on MH of adolescents and students. Two studies recorded some potentially positive effects, such as support in coping and providing a sense of connection for those who were isolated due to social distancing measures. The review focused on the early period of the pandemic, and more research is needed to see the effects after the two-year period of lockdowns and social distancing. Given social media and online activity are universal features for nearly all of us, the important focus of your parenting is to help your teenager, and yourself, to *self-regulate* use.

An inherent problem in talking about social media from the perspective of someone my age, or even younger, is that developments in social media technology and its usage mean it is changing at a faster pace than our understanding. The key then to understanding the impact of its use and potential risks including the pros and cons, is to speak with teenagers and young adults and to understand how the different social media platforms affect them.

How does your teenager use social media? I wonder if you can answer this question. When asked, most teenagers will say they are just "wasting time" by scrolling or using their phones the same way that older generations used television – to watch movies, favourite shows, or sports highlights.

The fact is, we cannot control the messages, images and videos our teenagers send and receive, the number of likes they get to their posts, or any of the inappropriate pop-ups they receive when they

Figure 6.2

are idly watching YouTube or scrolling through TikTok. We *can* maintain a conversation with them about their online life, and their feelings about their friends, or would-be partners and we can help them understand that it's best not to post something online that they wouldn't dream of doing or saying in real life because they can't take it back once it's posted.

Social media clearly heightens the insecurities of those competing online for superficial attention. We are all susceptible to counting the number of "likes" we get to a post, and teenagers even more so, and there is a dopamine boost involved too. The pressure to be popular and interesting in adolescence is enormous and all-consuming for many, and it takes a great strength of character to rise above this. Young people can feel a lot of pressure to keep up with what is going on and so are exposed to arguments and issues getting blown out of proportion, as well as feeling under pressure to post things about their "amazing" lives. A lot of adolescents feel more ambivalent about social media than the mainstream discourse would suggest. Some teenagers find that regular breaks from social media improve their mental health and ease anxiety, while others have very minimal or no involvement with social media to support their mental health and general well-being.

Thinking about the risks related to phones, let's look at this scenario with Yameena who gets exposed to great unkindness by her friends, and subsequently, this impacts her mental health and she develops poor self-esteem (Figure 6.2).

> Yameena was in a friendship group in year 12 at school that used a WhatsApp group to communicate about their social plans. There were daily messages on this group, mostly concerning plans for meeting up at parties or small gatherings. During one half-term break, Yameena saw a photo appear on the group chat of all her friends at a party in a place she didn't recognise. The words underneath said, "What goes on in Ibiza stays … .." It took a moment to realise her friends had all gone on holiday together without asking her. She burst into tears but didn't want to tell her mum and dad, who didn't particularly like the friendship group, but were also often preoccupied with their own worries as their older daughter had severe learning difficulties and was very challenging at home. Day after day, Yameena looked at the group photos and messages, none of which mentioned her absence. She felt trapped. Leave the group and she would be cut off from them socially. Stay in the group and be subjected to daily torture of the antics of her friends. She said it felt like "torture" and her predominant thought

was, "What's wrong with me?" She was convinced they must not like her because of a fault in her. She spent the whole half term in her room, pretending to her parents to be studying, but feeling extremely low and ever more anxious as she looked at her phone. Her stomach would lurch every time the phone pinged. She lost sleep and started to dread going back to school after half term. She started restricting her eating, believing she was partly left out because she looked overweight in her bikini.

When I hear a story like this in my consulting room, I must mentalize and regulate myself. My immediate feeling is upset, and I feel protective and angry, probably as a parent would if this happened to their daughter. In this scenario, we can see that Yameena's friends have been extremely unkind by not inviting her to their planned holiday, but then exposing her to pictures of the trip and party. It would take an extremely strong and self-assured character to not be deeply hurt by this behaviour, and Yameena's situation is compounded by the fact that her parents' attention seems to be focused elsewhere. I wasn't surprised to hear that she turned this on herself but, in this type of situation, it's critical to help a young person to recover their capacity to mentalize – to think reflectively about themselves and other people – and in this case to help Yameena understand that their behaviour reflects on them, and not on her character. Her parents need to empathise with her and validate her hurt feelings, acknowledging that this is a horrible thing for anyone to do and that being hurt and feeling left out is appropriate. Following that, it's important to help Yameena not to turn this on herself, seeing it as something she is lacking, but rather to support her in making different friendship choices. None of this is easy and it will probably take a bit of time before Yameena is able to regulate herself well enough to feel able to mentalize and take a balanced view of the situation.

Social media and mental health risks

When social media use isn't controlled or a teenager is unable to regulate their responses then this could have a detrimental effect on mental health for some, while for others, there may be problems with addiction. Young adolescents, already struggling to understand themselves and others, are vulnerable to being hurt by comments and microaggressions online. The UK NHS survey of the mental health of children and young people (2022) found that 1 in 8 11–16-year-old social media users reported that they had been bullied online. This figure rose to more than 1 in 4 among those who had a mental health problem.

Parenting that validates *all* types of feelings, not just the positive, happy ones, is crucial to helping our teenagers manage risk so that they can protect themselves and know instinctively when something doesn't feel right to them. Help your teenagers from as early an age as you possibly can to feel validated by you in how they feel. If they feel like a "loser" because they haven't gotten a text back from a group when they reached out to try to arrange a social gathering, validate this feeling with empathy and understanding. If your teenager says, "I only got a couple of likes for the post of my prom dress," don't say "At least you've got someone out there who likes how you look." Listen to them and validate their feelings. Once you have empathised with them, try to bring in another perspective; for example, you could say, "I guess there might be other friends who really like how you look but aren't always checking other posts to send likes, they might prefer to say it to your face." Comparison with others is also a risk to mental health (first discussed in Chapter 5).

Risks of gaming

As we saw in Chapter 5, gaming is a big part of teenagers' lives, particularly young adolescent boys. The risks involved include online gambling, becoming addicted to a game, and having highs and sudden lows after a loss on a favourite game. If teenagers get involved in excessive gaming, their system becomes flooded with dopamine as there are frequent opportunities for "winning." These are the moments when you hear your teenager whooping with excitement during a game. Unfortunately, although dopamine release is a pleasurable experience, if it happens very regularly, then the brain begins to down-regulate its sensitivity to dopamine. This means that the everyday experiences your teenager might have previously enjoyed, such as playing football, dancing to music, or playing a game with you, will suddenly feel inadequate. The brain has been trained to respond to the pleasure of online gaming and everything else pales in comparison.

This means that, unless you offer your teenager some alternative experiences, or talk to them about their feelings about gaming and their online activities, it will get harder over time to engage them in any alternatives.

Managing risks of social media

There are times when staying connected to your teenager can be helpful and can help them to manage certain risks.

Many parents have tracking devices on their children's phones, follow them on social media and have some great text conversations that they never have in real life. One parent of an adolescent with ASD said that her daughter can communicate far more emotionally and reflectively by a text message, when she's had the time to think about what she wants to say and when she wants to say it, in a way that she finds much harder to do face to face when she feels "on the spot." Some parents will say they feel their teenager is far safer when they can Facetime them to show them that they are on their way back home.

Parenting styles and managing risk

A 17-year-old got involved in smoking weed. He would walk over the local common with his friends, saying he was going for "a walk" and then come back stinking of cannabis. His dad would go out of his mind when he was out, not knowing if he was going to get attacked by local gangs, be mugged, or get so high he lost consciousness or any sense of where he was or of what danger he might put himself in. The dad made the decision to give his loft over to his son and his friends, even installing a pool table up there. His thinking was that he could give his son a space in which he could be safe and take controlled risks while not wholly advocating for what he was doing.

If you ban your teenager from smoking cannabis, does this mean they will never be tempted when they're out with their friends to smoke? If you keep them at home, telling them they aren't allowed to go to parties or see "risky" friends, will they do exactly what you ask? Well, some teenagers will. There is a percentage of young people who will respect the values of their family and cultural norms, who might never be tempted to smoke or drink because these are firmly held beliefs and values that they have embraced themselves. However, some young people might take a different position if their parents take authoritarian measures and this can result in them being pushed to take greater risks to evade authority. Then there is the risk of not taking risks, which we've already discussed, but that needs to be considered whenever you're thinking about your teenager's behaviour. Try to think about the risk scale, and where you and your teenager are on this scale.

A permissive parent might let their adolescent set the rules for their risk-taking, and a neglectful parent will be absent when their teenager is potentially at risk. A more authoritarian parent is likely to take a highly punitive approach to their teenager after they've done something risky. All these parenting styles are highly likely to put your teenager at further risk. Trying to be their friend, in a permissive parenting way, will leave your teenager unclear about the boundaries and expectations of their own and other people's behaviour. For example, if you don't set any guidelines about appropriate behaviour, your teenager will feel unable to distinguish between low-, medium- and high-risk behaviours. Some parents do this, believing that modelling a relaxed approach to risk helps their teenagers, but it actually makes them feel more unsafe and unsure of how to tackle risky situations. The most helpful parenting approach to risk is to take an authoritative – reflective parenting – approach. By doing this, you will be setting clear expectations while still listening to your teenager's perspective, and they will be open to listening to your perspective and will internalise it so that it helps inform their decisions about risk in the future. By taking this approach, you keep your teenager closely connected to you in a warm, loving and safe relationship.

The following principles can help guide you when you are parenting a teenager where you are concerned with helping them understand and manage risk

- **Focus on earning trust**

One of the common themes that runs through each of these vignettes is the need to establish trust in the relationship between yourself and your teenager, so that a whole range of thoughts and feelings can be thought about together (when your teenager is in the right state of mind to share them). Crucially, this needs to be done without entering into a conversation that leads to feelings of shame in your teenager, as discussed below.

- **Help your teenager to problem-solve**

Problem-solving is a helpful skill to help your teenager learn. When your emotional temperature has gone down and you can face having a calm and rational conversation with your teenager, it's helpful to start by trying to get them to figure out how they might have done things differently. If they can see you listening to this and taking seriously their attempts to work out for themselves what went wrong and why, then you've got a chance of keeping a connection going with them, and of keeping their respect.

- **Don't be afraid to set boundaries**

Knowing what the limits of behaviour should be is containing and helpful for your teenager. When thinking about setting limits, balance is key. Simply laying down the law – usually done at high volume and with lots of conditions and arbitrary laws – will simply shame your teenager into feeling bad about themselves. Instead, use the two-hands approach to set sensible limits and boundaries – balancing curiosity about the meaning of their behaviour with a limit-setting. Do this alongside a thoughtful conversation in which you help your teenager to see what risks they took, and how they might do things differently next time. Stay in an authoritative, parental role and don't try to be their best friend.

- **Support your teenager to self-regulate**

Being a reflective parent and taking a mentalizing approach increases your teenager's ability to regulate their emotions. They can begin to reflect on their own thoughts and feelings more when you mentalize them, showing them that you understand them. This helps your teenager become more self-aware and helps them to manage a risky situation differently, or to regulate their use of social media and gaming more consciously.

- **Always avoid shaming your teenager**

When your teenager takes a risk, as they almost inevitably will, it's your responsibility not to shame them. This is important because the consequence of shaming on the brain is to shift it to a negative bias where your teenager feels that everything is their fault. When the brain feels shame your teenager feels pain. When we feel shame, two specific areas of the brain are activated. First, the default mode network is activated. This area of the brain – in the posterior cingulate cortex and the ventral medial prefrontal cortex – is involved in rumination and having an awareness of self. When this is activated, an individual tends to default to thinking about what's wrong with them, what other people think about them, and what's wrong with other people. Secondly, shame activates the part of the brain that is involved in our perception of pain in the anterior cingulate and anterior insula areas. This means that some people can physically feel pain in their body when they are experiencing feelings of shame. This in turn leads to shut down and dissociation – becoming disconnected from feelings – which leads to negative thinking and an inability to problem-solve so that the teenager becomes even more vulnerable to risk.

Some parents shame their teenagers perhaps without realising it. Parents sometimes have a conviction that they *know* why their teenager did something. For example, they may accuse their teenager of throwing a party behind their back because they are a deceitful person who doesn't show respect. This causes the teenager to feel shame and risks damaging the connection between the parent and teenager.

PAUSE AND REFLECT: YOUR RISKY TEENAGER

In a nutshell ...

Teenagers are more likely to take risks than young children and adults, based on changes in their brains. A lack of maturity in their pre-frontal cortex means that they will act more impulsively, respond more to reward than punishment in the short term, and take more risks when they are with their peer group. Some risk-taking is important for your adolescent's growing independence and autonomy.

Reflecting on yourself helps you by ...

By understanding that there is a risk scale and that taking risks is part of everyday life for your teenager, and important for their development and survival, you can shift your perspective and manage your own strong feelings. Becoming aware that everyday adolescent risky behaviours are normal helps you to not over-react and to resist becoming over-protective. Mentalizing your-self and using your knowledge will enable you to get your perspective across when you want to talk to them about more serious risks.

Reflecting on your teenager helps them by ...

When you mentalize your teenager, you can start to see where their risky behaviour comes from. Reflecting on the inside story of their behaviour helps you to understand that there are brain changes that both increase their likelihood of taking risks and inhibit their understanding of any medium or long-term consequences of their behaviour. It helps when you mentalize them to understand that their perspective is equally valid, but very different, to yours.

Reflecting on your teenager helps your relationship by ...

Understanding your teenager's experiences and perspective sends them a message that you *want* to understand them, even when they are taking risks. This prevents you from judging or shaming your teenager and keeps a connection going between you. This in turn builds trust between you and makes it more likely your teenager will talk to you about their worries, whether that's in their friendships or about how they see themselves.

Keep in mind ...

- Think of yourself as the safe harbour to which your teenager can always return. When they are struggling in life, remind them that you are always there to help them.
- Mentalize yourself first and think about the things that influenced you as a teenager, whether you took many risks or not. How have these experiences influenced your view of your own teenager?
- Consider the "hidden" risks to your teenager in their online world. Help your teenager to self-regulate and to notice how they feel when they have social media breaks.
- Check that you are armed with facts to guide your teenager about the safe levels of substances and be realistic about their exposure to them.
- When you have managed to get yourself into a calmer state of mind, show curiosity and empathy for your teenager. Perhaps they took a risk that was too much for them and they are struggling to admit they feel bad for a mistake. If you work hard to develop trust in your relationship, they will

know that they can tell you how they feel and that you won't make them feel shame.

- Educate your teenager about the risks of drink and drugs and model a healthy, fun lifestyle yourself.
- Attachment is the opposite of addiction. Keep up your close and secure attachment with your teenager to avoid them needing to use substances to deal with complicated or confusing feelings.

7

UNDERSTANDING SELF-HARM

"How could I have missed this? Where were the signs?"

In earlier chapters, we looked at the various factors that can affect our ability to mentalize; how, for example, our values and beliefs, backgrounds, influences and how stressed we feel in the moment – our emotional thermometer – can all affect our capacity to reflect on the thoughts and feelings of ourselves and others. Self-harm is a manifestation of a significant loss of this capacity, where a young person turns to self-harming measures to deal with overwhelming and intolerable states of mind that they feel unable to manage or express in any other way (1). In a therapeutic context, the aim is to help these young people move out of this non-mentalizing, self-harming, state, into a more mentalizing one – where intolerable thoughts and feelings can be understood, digested, empathised with by the therapist, and ultimately tolerated without the need to harm the self. In this chapter, we will look at how you can take this approach with your own teenager if you are worried about self-harm. Even if your teenager doesn't engage in this type of behaviour, it is important to be aware of the reasons young people use self-harm to cope with difficult emotions and to learn ways to reduce the risk of them starting to do so.

Some clinicians refer to "superficial self-harm" when the harm has been carried out as a way of gaining support and attention for feelings that can't otherwise be processed. Self-harm is often a repeated behaviour, but it can also be a one-off response to a situation. It can mark the difficult interpersonal transitions from adolescent to adult relationships with peers, parents and within the home and school environment. In some cases, self-harm can represent an attack on the body as a deliberate act of

 DOI: 10.4324/9780429459245-8

aggression against a parent – representing a "safe" alternative to attacking others. In more severe forms of self-harm, it often manifests in adolescents with what's known as "emergent personality disorder," where many of the women have experienced childhood sexual abuse. Self-harm is then a way of managing feelings such as anger and unhappiness, which have not been managed by a parent who can contain these experiences in their early childhood (which affects our secure attachment, as discussed in Chapter 1). Distinguishing between types of /reasons for self-harm is helpful for parents as, while self-harm is understandably terrifying for parents, they can understand that it is not necessarily a reflection of any deep, underlying traumatic experience or mental health struggle.

Any episode of self-harm indicates a need to be heard and validated. When I was a 19-year-old teenager, after an unexpected breakup with my boyfriend at the time, I impulsively stabbed myself in the arm with a breadknife at his house in a state of extreme upset. I didn't think he could see or hear how I felt, and this seemed to be an obvious way to get him to notice. It was a one-off in my case and there will be many adolescents who do something similar in a temporary state of heightened emotion, when it feels impossible to reflect on alternative coping strategies – when mentalizing is too hard – and luckily for many people, these states are not frequent or persistent.

The narrative around self-harm has altered over the past couple of decades. Traditionally, self-harm was thought of as a response to early trauma within the family, with factors such as sexual abuse, neglect, maltreatment and poor emotional regulation from primary caregivers all contributing factors. More recently, there are more young people self-harming who come from loving families with secure attachments. They are experiencing the same challenges in adolescence that their predecessors experienced 15–10 years before them in this stage of life, but their mechanism for dealing with this has become much more normalised.

What do we mean by self-harm?

Self-harm refers to intentional and deliberate acts of harming oneself without the intention of committing suicide. It can range from superficial self-harm to more serious and repeated acts of self-harm. It is important to distinguish both from attempted suicide – discussed later in this chapter – and to note that, although self-harm can accompany suicidal thoughts or attempts, it will very often not lead to it. The intention of self-harm is often to replace an unbearable feeling with one that is more easily tolerated (the injury), or it can be an attempt to get care and attention (someone else cleaning and caring for their wounds is an important part of what an adolescent often wants), and it can be an attack on parents and other important people around an adolescent. It can take many forms, including cutting, burning, scratching, hitting, or biting oneself. Adolescent girls are at an increased risk of engaging in self-harming behaviours. According to researchers from the University of Warwick, UK, girls aged 14 are the new risk group. This is linked to several factors including childhood poverty, neglect and abuse, exam pressures, and bullying using social media – all of which have driven up the rates of self-harm among girls. Another report in the same year (2020) in Lancet Psychiatry said girls were more prone to self-harm than boys because "poor mental health among women and girls is often closely linked to violence and abuse, such as experience of physical abuse from a partner, sexual abuse as a child or sexual abuse as an adult." In the Warwick study, of the 11,000 students interviewed by researchers, 15% were found to be indulging in self-harm. Of them, 73% were girls, and 27% were boys. More teenage girls, than boys, reported experiencing negative moods. Among a quarter of the teenagers who reported feeling unhappy, more girls said they felt unhappy than boys. Teenagers also reported having feelings of poor self-image with girls experiencing this three times more than boys.

Researchers also found, that for both girls and boys close to their parents, the chances of self-harm and building a negative self-outlook were less.

Importantly, research also reveals that the more frequently a young person self-harms, the more severe their self-hatred and the higher the chance of them experiencing suicidal thoughts. (2). It is crucial therefore to take self-harming extremely seriously and find ways to help your teenager if they are hurting themselves, especially if this is on a frequent basis.

Data about young people's mental health in England:

- The number of A&E attendances by young people aged 18 or under with a recorded diagnosis of a psychiatric condition more than tripled between 2010 and 2018–19 (3)

- 83% of young people with mental health needs agreed that the coronavirus pandemic had made their mental health worse (4)
- In 2018–19, 24% of 17-year-olds reported having self-harmed in the previous year, and 7% reported having self-harmed with suicidal intent at some point in their lives. 16% reported high levels of psychological distress (5)
- Suicide was the leading cause of death for males and females aged between five and 34 years old in 2019 (6).

Nearly half of 17–19-year-olds with a diagnosable mental health disorder have self-harmed or attempted suicide at some point, rising to 52.7% for young women (7)

The last statistic is from NHS data for 2017 and what we know about how trends have changed since the pandemic is that this statistic has since risen, with current modelling by the Centre for Mental Health suggesting that 1.5 million children and young people in England will need either new or additional mental health support because of the pandemic. Services have reported a rise in young people attending A&E for this reason.

In the following scenario, we consider the actions of a young teenager who has superficially self-harmed and her dad's reaction to her. Following on from this, we look at how a mentalizing approach can help both Ellie and her dad understand the meaning of her self-harm.

Ellie is 14 and is usually top of her class in most subjects. She lives with her two parents, Beck and Nelson, who are loving and warm while holding high expectations of her academic achievements. They have always considered Ellie to be their "perfect little girl" and value her attractiveness and high status at school. She is popular among her peers and revered somewhat for having "perfect" thick, long hair. After the end-of-term tests are over, Ellie is massively disappointed to get her maths mark which is lower than usual and places her lower down the class compared with her peers. She tells her parents about her mark, which is still a high 89%. Her dad comments, "What happened to the other 11%?" which leaves Ellie distraught.

The next evening over dinner, Ellie sits at the table wearing her school uniform. Her short-sleeved shirt reveals a number of scars on her left arm and Nelson immediately notices them – they are easily visible.

Nelson is horrified at the sight of his "little girl's" arm covered in marks and says, "God! What have you done to yourself? You'll ruin yourself doing things like that!" Beck leans towards Ellie and tries to touch her hand gently, but Ellie pulls her hand away. Beck tells Nelson to "shush, you'll make her feel worse."

Ellie feels a rage build up inside herself and, struggling to think, pushes her chair back from the table and shouts at her dad, "Just shut up! Shut up! OK? I hate how I look!" She pushes her plate away towards her dad and runs upstairs, slamming the door behind her.

Reflecting on Nelson and Beck

In the heat of the moment, when Nelson sees his "perfect little girl" with self-inflicted marks up her arm, he can't mentalize at all and his anger and upset take over. He feels a sudden pressure to fix things and wants his daughter to immediately stop what he sees as this self-destructive behaviour. In his mind, his daughter is beautiful and perfect and he can't understand why she has attacked herself in this way, "ruining" her looks. Beck, on the other hand, can see that Ellie is in distress, she doesn't know how to respond to it and is also struggling to understand, but reaches out to Ellie in an attempt to soothe whatever distress she's feeling that's caused her to act this way. Beck is upset with her partner about his reaction to Ellie and can see he isn't helping the situation.

Reflecting on Ellie

We can imagine how Ellie felt when she got her test result, which didn't live up to everyone's expectations of her. On receiving the test result, we can imagine she might have experienced a mixture of emotions; disappointment in herself for not achieving her usual high mark, anger at her parents for putting constant pressure on her to be perfect and perhaps a desire to destroy the image of physical perfection pushed onto her by her parents and peers. This all builds up in her mind as a huge pressure to get everything right and, unable to tolerate these feelings, and not wishing to physically harm her parents, she turns the attack on herself instead, knowing this will upset her dad especially. In addition, this is a time of her development when Ellie most needs the approval of her peers and is the most susceptible to feeling rejected by them (8), so, unable to mentalize, Ellie sees her test result as a devastating blow to her popularity at school.

Thinking together

When Ellie gets her test result she can't mentalize herself or anyone else. She assumes her parents will reject her because the comment from her dad "What happened to the other 11%?" left her feeling she wasn't good enough. It also made her furious with her parents and, unable to talk about her feelings because her emotional temperature was so high, she cut her arms superficially to make sure her parents could see how she felt. When she was reprimanded rather than comforted by her dad, she became so angry she was unable to tolerate being in the same room. Something that is too painful for Ellie to think about – that she needs to always be perfect for her parents and she has let them and herself down with her mark – gets enacted instead through the act of cutting herself. Ellie's parents will probably feel under pressure to fix the situation for Ellie, but the more they try to fix this the more Ellie is likely to push them away, as the pressure of achieving has become too much for her. Instead, Nelson and Beck should focus on learning to tolerate uncertainty and allow their teenage daughter to be herself and simply do the best she can, rather than pressuring her to meet Nelson's expectations.

The link between eating disorders and self-harm

When we think about self-harm among teenagers, we include eating disorders. This is because eating disorders such as anorexia nervosa, binge-eating disorders, bulimia nervosa or orthorexia (an unsafe obsession with healthy food) seldom occur independently of other mental health difficulties and behaviours, and it is common for people with eating disorders to also cut themselves or engage in another form of self-harm. Adolescent girls are more likely than boys to develop eating disorders and the root causes of this are often similar to other forms of self-harm. Anna Motz (9) writes that "the gender difference in self-harming rates may reflect social conditioning, which requires women not to express anger, and to value their appearance and social acceptability above all else." We can see anorexia nervosa – involving controlled and restricted eating – as a means of exerting control. Motz goes on to suggest that women use their bodies as a means to communicate underlying damage and to exert some control. Adolescent girls typically use their bodies as a way of identifying themselves and social media emphasis on body types clearly exacerbates this. Restricting eating and damaging the body is therefore a way of self-harm that symbolises how they are feeling inside. There has been a significant rise in the past decade in the number of young people with eating disorders, which are typically related to an adolescent's need for control. Unsurprisingly, along with some other mental health difficulties, eating disorders increased further during the pandemic as young people experienced an increased sense of loss of control.

Why do teenagers self-harm?

- Self-harm can provide a sense of control. Adolescents may feel as though they lack control over other aspects of their lives, such as their relationships, academic performance, or family dynamics; for some, self-harm seems to provide a way for them to exert control over their own bodies and emotions.
- Self-harm is more prevalent in girls than boys. As stated above (in the eating disorders box), social conditioning requires women not to express anger and attacking the self may be one of the few ways they can legitimately express this. It is also an explicit attack on the idealised way that others, including parents, may have positioned them.
- Adolescence in particular, with its many changes and pressures, increases the likelihood of self-harm. If we put ourselves

into the mind of an adolescent, then one of the most important things in our world is the way our friends see us and respond to us. If we feel they are rejecting us, or simply uninterested, we are more likely to turn this negative feeling on ourselves than to blame others. This makes us highly susceptible to feeling critical of ourselves and hypersensitive to what our peers think of us.

- Research shows that the most common reason for self-harm among young people is to get relief from painful thoughts and feelings.
- Self-harm is a sign that there is a problem with your teenager's mental health and not a signal that they simply want attention.
- Forensic psychotherapist and clinical psychologist, Anna Motz, sets out an understanding of self-harm without suicidal thoughts as a choice to preserve life and not destroy it. Motz argues that the main purpose of self-harm is to escape unbearable pain, and this fits with the mentalizing approach we are using throughout this book. It is in one part an aggressive attack on the self, and in part an attempt to create some meaning and order in an otherwise confusing and disturbing chaotic world.

If you try to hold this adolescent's view of the world in your mind, it will help you to mentalize your own teenager better. Self-harm may also serve to alleviate emotional pain, that can be caused by several factors, including social rejection, or a sense of academic failure, even if only temporarily. If a teenager feels that they are unable to express their emotions or communicate their distress to others, self-harm can serve to signal to others that they are struggling.

If you are the parent of a teenager who regularly harms themselves to cope with overwhelming feelings they have no way of expressing, this is an unbearably distressing and terrifying situation to be in.

Initial reactions

Parents or carers of young people who self-harm can feel desperate to change their teenager's feelings (Figure 7.1). Many of these parents try to make their children happy, understandably thinking that if they could get them out of this state of mind with distraction – happy thoughts and events to look forward to – this

Figure 7.1

would somehow lift them out of this dominating and depressing state of mind. It makes complete sense that if you have a teenager who experiences very low moods and feels that they are worthless, you will do anything to make them feel happy. Unfortunately, the strength of feeling they are experiencing means that attempts to distract and cheer up a young person who is feeling this low don't work on their own. Here are some other things that **don't** work when you have a teenager who is injuring themselves:

- Making every day a special day so that life feels more worth living.
- Offering comparisons of other people's lives who are "worse off."
- Distracting from the negativity all the time.
- Not talking about the self-harming and ignoring the darkness and seriousness of the situation.
- Telling yourself self-harming is "part of being a teenager" and they will "grow out of it."
- Getting angry at them for feeling so low and "spoiling everything" for the rest of the family.

- Assuming you know how they feel and what their world looks like. You can't read your teenager's mind and you don't know everything about them (even though you might think you should).
- Comparing with your own experience as a teenager. They are not equivalent, and their experience is different from yours.
- Telling them that their being sad is making you sad and that you can't cope.

Why mentalizing is relevant to self-harm

Evidence shows that mentalization-based therapy can reduce self-harm and depression in adolescents, one of the few approaches that have been shown to be effective. (10) For parents of teenagers who are self-harming and experiencing very low moods, understanding how taking a mentalizing approach with their teenager can be helpful, and is therefore extremely valuable. The changes to the adolescent brain described in the introduction mean that young people are especially prone to losing their mentalizing capability. We know that adolescents are hypersensitive to triggers in their social world; for example, they can often misinterpret/misread the facial expressions of other people (especially other young people). This means that if they are already struggling with their mental health, they will become even more vulnerable to misinterpreting the facial expressions of other people in their social world. This can lead to adolescents interpreting certain faces (or actions) as rejecting, as shown in the scenario with Chloe later in this chapter. Rejection is one of the most difficult and stressful feelings an adolescent can encounter, and it can lead to a feeling that their emotions are beyond their control. For some adolescents, sometimes the only way they feel they can exert some control over these horrible feelings is to self-harm. Mentalization-based therapy helps adolescents to regulate their emotions and manage impulsivity, which go hand-in-hand. It seems that the positive changes that result from increased mentalizing can lead to better-functioning relationships, in turn, playing an important part in reducing self-harm and depression in adolescents (11). The reflective parenting approach described throughout this book can therefore be an invaluable tool for how you conduct your relationship with your teenager if they are struggling to manage overwhelming and intolerable feelings and, as a consequence, impulsively harming themselves.

Here is an example of a young person with a pattern of significant self-harm. As you read through, notice the sensitivities she shows and where you can spot her difficulty in mentalizing others.

> Chloe is 17 years old and has requested to be put in care after a long history of difficulties in her relationship with her mother, who has struggled to understand how Chloe feels and what's going on with her. Her mother has had a series of boyfriends who Chloe has come into conflict with. Currently, she is living with a foster carer.
>
> She has made several suicide attempts during her young life and regularly self-harms. She has been admitted to the hospital on a number of occasions, and each time discharged without follow-up treatment. Chloe joined a mentalization programme for young people who self-harm.
>
> One evening after dinner, Chloe confides in her foster carer about something that happened at college that day. She tells a story about her peers at college who all get up to leave the refectory one lunchtime without her, leaving her feeling "abandoned." Her carer listened intently to this story, thinking she was empathising and showing a level of understanding when suddenly, Chloe explodes, "You f****ng bitch, don't you dare." She storms out of the room after throwing over the chair. After 6 weeks of trying to speak to Chloe, sending text messages and asking her what happened and asking her to come out of her room and "please talk to me or to your therapist." Chloe finally tells her foster carer, "I left because you raised your eyebrow at me."

Reflecting on the carer

It took six weeks of Chloe's foster carer trying to talk to her about why she had stormed off. She encouraged her to talk about it in her therapy, but said she wanted to apologise and she couldn't figure out why Chloe had been so angry but, "Please tell me, I want to understand." before she agreed to come back and see me. When Chloe eventually told her about the raised eyebrow, we might wonder what this really meant and whether her carer could understand. Her carer is possibly thinking that she has no idea what she did or said to make Chloe so angry, as she had thought she was listening and they generally had quite a good relationship. We can imagine that her carer was listening to Chloe's story about the feeling she had in the refectory, and possibly feeling very empathic towards her, and perhaps also curious about why Chloe had felt so rejected by then. We could perhaps speculate that the raised eyebrow was her way of showing curiosity and interest in what Chloe had to say.

Reflecting on Chloe

When Chloe sees her carer raise her eyebrow after she's confided in her that she had a horrible experience with her friends, she is possibly feeling extremely self-conscious and full of insecurities about whether she is really likeable to her friends. At this moment, we can imagine that she is feeling sensitive to any reaction that doesn't feel empathic and understanding of her feelings. As her emotional temperature rises and Chloe struggles to mentalize, she could easily get into a mode where she is unable to accurately read her carer's expression, and she might start to attribute a negative intention behind her raised eyebrow. In this moment, we can imagine that Chloe feels her carer doesn't believe or, perhaps thinks she is being silly or exaggerating her feelings and what happened.

Thinking together

When Chloe saw that her carer was making repeated attempts to speak to her, and this went on for six weeks, she started to feel that her foster carer wanted to repair the damage between them and wasn't dismissive of her reaction. Her carer showed persistent interest in what Chloe had to say and showed she was listening. Eventually, Chloe replied, "I told you my friends abandoned me, and you doubted me." Her carer was then able to wonder what Chloe thought was in her mind when she perceived her carer to have raised her eyebrow. "That you didn't believe me … more that you thought I was being stupid or exaggerating and I felt f****g angry that you didn't get it, how bad it felt when they all walked out on me. It was like you thought I was making it all up in my head."

It seems that Chloe's foster carer made a big effort to show Chloe that she was sorry she thought this was what she was thinking, and she could understand how she would be very angry if she thought she didn't believe her or take her and her feelings seriously. It was helpful to Chloe for her carer to show a different perspective to the one she had. By stressing that this was *not* what she had been thinking or intended and also saying she wasn't even aware that her eyebrow had been raised at the time. Finally, and tentatively, her carer asked her if she thought there might be any other reason why she had raised her eyebrow – inviting Chloe to consider a different perspective, using the ideas from the parent APP. Chloe was angry and said she couldn't think of any other reason why she would do this, and didn't she understand that "when someone looks at you this way it makes you feel s**t." Her carer needed to respond with empathy – using her parent APP again –saying she could definitely imagine that it would make her feel this way if she thought the person she was confiding in about something that made her feel abandoned and rejected seemed not to believe her or take me seriously.

The parent APP helps your teenager to mentalize – start to reflect more on their own thoughts and feelings, and on other people's – so with this approach, Chloe became calmer as her foster carer spent time empathising and validating her. This led to Chloe commenting to her carer, "Maybe you were just not understanding me properly?" and then she offered, "Or maybe you just wanted to know a bit more?" As Chloe's emotional temperature came down, she was able to mentalize her foster carer better and see that there were other possible explanations for how her carer had acted.

What you can do as a parent

As explored throughout the book, mentalizing – reflecting on states of mind in yourself and your teenager – is very helpful i.e. to help your teenager to see themselves and relationships in a more balanced, reflective way. To look at themselves as someone who might have difficulties but who is lovable, respected and valued by others. For Chloe – so sensitive to feeling rejected and abandoned – she interpreted her foster carer's behaviour as further rejecting and shaming her and this led to her outburst. If you don't take your teenager's feelings seriously (even if you don't agree with them, or feel they are out of proportion), you will leave them feeling shamed; this could lead to an outburst, either against you or against themselves (leading to further self-harming).

Work out your state of mind

When thinking about how to support your teenager if they're self-harming, the first priority is to establish that everyone is safe right now. Then think how far apart you are in terms of your mind and your teenager's mind. Ask yourself, "Am I over-worrying or worrying too little?" It is important not to under- or overreact to your teenager's state of mind, and instead to work on keeping your own emotions regulated – thinking back to Chapter 2 and the parent MAP can help if this feels difficult. Notice what's going on in your mind, and where it comes from, and then try to manage your emotional temperature by doing something that will help you to feel calm enough to consider what's going on in your teenager's mind.

Identify your support network

Of course, this is not easy when your teenager is harming themselves and you are feeling extremely frightened. Sometimes taking this reflective stance will feel nearly impossible to do on your own; Chapter 8 looks at how you can draw on your available network of people if you are struggling to manage your emotional response in the face of a teenager who is at risk. It can be very hard to think about who is on your "team" when you're in full panic mode, but it's also hard because it involves showing your vulnerabilities as a parent. Although parents can often be highly competitive with each other, letting this go and acknowledging that showing your vulnerabilities will bring you closer to other people, particularly those who understand your experiences can be hugely beneficial, as discussed in Chapter 8.

Be a figure of trust/be available

Your aim should be for your teenager to experience you as a parent who is an available attachment figure, that is, someone who is actively trying to reach them in a way that makes them feel listened to, respected, connected and loved. When your teenager is struggling with their mental health, it is important that they feel they can trust you because it's at these low points – when their emotions feel unbearable – that they will be least likely to be able to mentalize the people around them. In other words, people in their world will feel untrustworthy, or even persecuting.

It's important to ensure that your teenager receives the message that they can trust you, and that you may even have valuable advice or experience you can pass on to keep them safe and reduce their risk of feeling low or perhaps self-harming. This is a delicate balance because, as discussed in previous chapters, there is a need for us to be simultaneously available to them while also letting them go. There needs to be a shift in how you think about your relationship with your teenager, and this will allow them to think about the relationship differently as a result. As child and adolescent psychiatrist, Dickon Bevington, put it, in adolescence, "parents need to be the safe harbour rather than the lifeboat." If you can frame yourself in this way, you stop being the lifeboat for your child – the one who rescues and makes it all better – and move to being the harbour that is always there to return to. This might feel extremely challenging – risky even – if you have a teenager who feels that life isn't worth living. You will want to be as close to them as you can, possibly feeling you've got to keep watch over them, and it could feel too risky to step back. This isn't about being detached, though; rather, mentalizing your relationship with them means being very aware of your own emotions, how you manage them and offering this safe harbour consistently to your teenager.

Keep the conversation going

At times you will be lost for words; barely able to regulate your emotions, particularly if your teenager has told you something you feel extremely upset by. At these times you might simply say, "I don't know what to say right now, but I'm just really glad you told me that." Maintaining a connection with your teenager is the most important task. Being overwhelmed with the feeling that life isn't worth living and that they feel utterly helpless and hopeless usually occurs when your teenager feels a sense of anomie – that is a feeling of disconnection or alienation from society or the world around us that gives a sense of there being no attachment. This feeling can lead to other feelings of hopelessness and despair. It's important for people experiencing this sense of anomie to seek help from friends or family or, if needed, from mental health professionals. If you feel your support isn't enough, therapy and counselling can help reduce your teenager's feelings of hopelessness and despair and develop a sense of purpose and meaning in their lives.

Check-in regularly

The importance of attachment in your relationship with your teenager cannot be understated. Despite everything they may say to you about wanting to be left alone, it's vital you don't leave your teenager alone for long periods of time. Popping your head around the door says, "I'm still here, even if you don't want me right now. I'm not going anywhere and I'm here for you." Keep your door open, even if their door is closed. Maintaining connection and a sense of attachment are all important if your teenager is experiencing unbearable and intolerable feelings they can't control.

The theory of psychic equivalence

If your teenager feels extremely low and has an urge to self-harm, it's important that you don't get into a state referred to in mentalizing theory as "psychic equivalence," which means that you think that what you feel is the reality. For example, a young child who fears there are monsters under the bed will think this is the reality, and it's only when they get older that they can understand the distinction between their fears and reality. Psychic equivalence is one of the *pre-mentalizing modes* we looked at in the introduction, and adolescents can get into this mode when their emotional temperature is either too high or too low, i.e. when they are unable to mentalize. When we are unable to mentalize, say because we are extremely anxious about our teenager's well-being, as parents we can get into thinking that our anxiety is the reality. For example, a parent might think, "I know my teenager doesn't like me" is a *feeling* but when we can't mentalize as parents, we believe this to be the reality. If we mentalize, we might be able to start to see that this is our fear and underlying this fear (of our teenager not liking us) is an underlying longing to be close to our teenager. Similarly, your teenager, feeling helpless and hopeless believes that they *are* hopeless. They are not able to mentalize themselves sufficiently to see that this is a feeling that will pass, and that feeling low or bad about oneself doesn't have to mean that they *are* bad, but more that some things in their life have made them feel this way.

> It is important to your teenager's well-being that you are able to get yourself into a mentalizing zone where you can think reflectively, without overwhelming anxiety, about their experiences and feelings and how you can support them.

Supporting your self-harming teenager.

Keeping in mind the mentalizing tools that are part of the reflective parenting model can help you provide crucial support for your teenager at this time.

- Understand and regulate your own emotions first. You are in no position to help your teenager if you are unable to control your own thoughts and feelings.
- Be more curious. Ask what feelings led them to self-harm, and what it feels like afterwards, and if they don't know, don't push.
- Help your teenager to learn that they can trust you and that you are reliable and steady. Then make sure you communicate that you will always try to understand and validate their feelings.
- Get closer to the problem than you would feel comfortable with to show your teenager that you can listen to any difficult thoughts and feelings they are experiencing.
- Validate how your teenager feels, even when you don't agree. For example, if they say, "Life is just shit," don't tell them it isn't. Instead say something like, "It can feel like that sometimes. It's so hard."
- Sit alongside your teenager and acknowledge that how they feel is a terrible, terrible feeling that they can't control.
- Offer empathy.
- Tell your teenager there is no time limit on your listening to them.
- Say that you can handle what they are telling you and will help devise a plan to help them through it.
- Model honesty, problem-solving and being flexible. When you do this, it is likely that your teenager will pick up and use these skills, too.

When suicide is a risk

While there is a strong link between suicide and mental health problems, particularly depression and excessive alcohol, many suicides happen impulsively in moments of crisis with a breakdown in the ability to deal with life stresses, such as relationship break-ups or the loss of a loved one. They also happen at moments where there is a complete breakdown in mentalizing and a young person tragically cannot see any other solution to their problems.

Suicide rates are also high amongst vulnerable groups who experience discrimination, such as refugees and migrants; lesbian, gay, bisexual, transgender, and intersex (LGBTI) young people. By far the strongest risk factor for suicide is a previous suicide attempt. It goes without saying then that if your teenager has expressed suicidal thoughts or ever tried to end their life, you should take this as a very serious signal that they need additional support, and you may want to turn to Chapter 8 where we discuss the importance of getting support from a network of people.

There is good evidence that if a young person is planning on attempting suicide they will have given some warning signs; for example, by saying they feel "hopeless" all of the time, alone, or they will have spoken of suicide, even jokingly. However, one of the most terrifying aspects of suicide risk for parents is no obvious sign that a young person is going to kill themselves. Sometimes a young person may have been behaving completely normally up until the point where they took their own life. This is clearly terrifying for friends and family who struggle to make sense of their teenager's actions and ask, "How could I have missed this? Where were the signs?" Parents of course want to think that their teenager would never do anything so terrible, or that at the very least they would talk to parents beforehand. Sadly, there is no strategy that will guarantee that if parents take it up, their teenager won't have suicidal thoughts or, worse, attempt suicide. However, we do understand that when a young person attempts to take their own life, they are at a point of feeling so utterly alone and hopeless, that there seems to them to be no other alternative at that point in their life. In Chapter 8, we look at how a network of people can help to support a teenager, but here the focus is on what parents can do.

There are so many potential reasons why teenagers and young people experience suicidal thoughts and feelings, and for most people, these feelings will be fleeting and pass quickly. If your teenager has frequently thought about it, you may or may not know as it's so hard for them to talk about such thoughts without experiencing feelings of shame or failure. If your teenager has suffered from depression, anxiety or bipolar disorder, these problems make it difficult to manage emotions and cope with stress. When your teenager feels they can't cope, this often leads to feelings of inadequacy and despair, which, for some, is when suicidal thoughts may follow. Another reason why teenagers and young people experience suicidal thoughts is when they've experienced a traumatic event, such as abuse, neglect or loss of a loved one. Trauma can lead to feelings of helplessness, guilt and shame. As we've discussed, relationships with peers are crucial to teenagers and if these relationships prove difficult or confusing, this can lead to your teenager feeling rejected or isolated; both feelings of which can increase risk. While some teenagers deal with these feelings by self-harming alone, for some, repeatedly feeling this way can lead to suicidal thoughts. Finally, abusing alcohol or drugs can have a significant impact on mental health and increase the risk of suicidal behaviour as they increase impulsivity and blur clear thinking and problem-solving.

All of this can feel so overwhelming for parents and it can be incredibly difficult to know where to start helping your teenager. However, there are some things to do if you have a teenager who is either self-harming and/or having thoughts of suicide:

- Minimise the risk of them feeling shame by letting your teenager know that you understand how they feel and that you can listen to how they feel, no matter how big and scary those feelings are.
- Ask your teenager more than once if they are okay. The lauded UK "Ask Twice" campaign, launched in 2018 by the charity/organisation, Mental Health Today, encourages you and your teenager's friends to ask more than once if they are okay. Don't worry about being intrusive or prying when it comes to serious risk – it's good to ask more than once.
- Your teenager is self-harming to avoid an intolerable feeling and to escape the pain they can't bear. You can help your teenager by using the security your relationship offers, by being consistent and clear in your intentions to listen and be curious about your teenager's thoughts and feelings. The security your relationship offers can be an alternative to cutting or self-harming.

- It may feel so shaming to your teenager to talk about it, so offer an alternative such as communicating their thoughts and feelings with you via phone messaging for example.
- Try to focus on what's causing them to self-harm or feel suicidal instead of on the self-harming behaviour itself.
- Encourage your teenager to tell you when they've self-harmed if possible and try to keep calm when they do. Clean any wounds and if the injury is serious, they should get treatment with your support at the hospital.
- Talk to your teenager about other things that may help them when they have the urge to self-harm; for example, they could paint or draw in red ink; hold an ice cube in their hand until it melts; listen to music; scream into a pillow or punch it; talk to friends, family, mentors; exercise, and other similar distraction techniques.
- Help your teenager build their confidence back up by reminding them of all the things they do well and try to focus on their personality rather than factors such as academic achievements.

Particularly vulnerable teenagers

While this chapter describes some of the common risks most teenagers take, there are groups of teenagers who are particularly vulnerable to greater risks to their mental health. As previously mentioned, LGBTI adolescents, who are on the receiving end of discrimination and prejudice, have higher rates of mental health problems and higher rates of suicide than their peers. Equally, adolescents who have experienced trauma in their early lives will be at greater risk.

Risk of suicide for ASD teenagers

Teenagers with ASD represent a particularly high-risk group when it comes to mental health. Research suggests that autistic people are at an increased risk of suicidal thoughts and attempts, compared to non-autistic people. The exact numbers, however, are unknown, but estimates put the increased likelihood as up to twenty-eight times more than non-autistic young adults. Of course, we can never know the full extent of the reasons someone resorts to this act, but we do know a lot about the mental health needs of adolescents who access mental health or general health services who have ASD. We know that aspects of daily life can be generally more challenging for people with ASD and, for teenagers who are already more confused about their relationships with their peer group, it becomes an even greater pressure when they have differences in understanding social situations and relationships. Also, not being understood or accepted by non-autistic people can increase anxiety and stress. This can lead to social isolation, rejection and low self-esteem.

Autistic people may face other experiences that can cause them to feel suicidal, including:

- Repetitive thinking which may lead to an intense focus on suicide.
- Unmet support needs/poor access to healthcare.
- Difficulties recognising, managing and regulating emotions (alexithymia).

According to the National Autistic Society, some autistic people suggest that an earlier autism diagnosis may have prevented thoughts or attempts of suicide. They feel it would have given them better self-understanding and access to support, which would have improved their mental well-being. This is a common experience for therapists working with young people with possible ASD and, whilst diagnostic assessment is an individual choice, my experience is that when an adolescent has this understanding of their identity, it brings a sense of relief and self-understanding for the majority of young people. If you are parenting a teenager with possible or likely ASD, it is extremely helpful to them for you to use a mentalizing, reflective parenting, approach to help your teenager start to notice and name how they are feeling and to understand that in certain situations their emotional temperature will increase because of a degree of social anxiety. Some other interventions that help teenagers with ASD include:

- Social stories.
- Social communication skills training for teenagers who want to understand others more easily.
- Support in learning to recognise and name emotions in themselves.
- Validation and empathic support for an ASD young person's identity, including educating neurotypical people on the sensitivities and differences they need to be aware of.

Self-harm and suicidal thoughts can impact other people in your teenager's life. In this scenario, we see a friend's perspective.

Paul is 20 and spoke about how he felt about an experience he had when he was in year 13, aged 18. His school friend, Will, started withdrawing from their friendship group and messaging to say he felt too low to come out with them. The lockdown during the pandemic had impacted the group already and they were only meeting up to hang out in the local park with a few tins of lager at the weekend, but it had felt good to Paul to have this regular meet-up. When Will stopped coming on Friday evenings, Paul messaged him to ask if he was OK. He didn't hear from him for a few days and when he contacted him again, neither Will nor his family responded.

Paul went round to Will's house a few times and knocked for him, but when no one answered the door, he went on to Will's playlist to see what songs Will was listening to and was shocked when he saw they were all about ending it all and suicide; this raised a red flag in his head. Paul contacted a couple of their other friends and asked if they'd come to Will's house again with him. This time, after banging on the door and throwing pebbles up at his bedroom window, he answered the door after an hour. Paul offered to go for a walk with him to listen to him and initially, Will agreed. They set off, but halfway down the street, Will said, "I can't do it," and went home. At this point, Paul had no idea what was wrong, but it was clear to him that his friend was really struggling, so Paul and his friends gave him the message that they were there for him and wouldn't be judgemental or think of him any differently because of what was going on with him. Paul said he didn't understand what was going on with Will and felt confused. He sent a text message, telling Will, "If you want to talk any time I'm here but only when you're ready. I'm here, call me and we can go for a walk." One week later, Will messaged back and asked to go for a walk. On the walk, he broke down and started saying how bad he'd been feeling. He told Paul he's been feeling suicidal, but when Paul asked if he had "tried something" (attempted suicide) he started crying and broke down and said how bad he felt. Someone he was close to, his girlfriend, had died very suddenly following an illness, and he didn't know what to do with his feelings. He hadn't shared this with his friendship group, feeling unable to find the words. Will explained that he felt he couldn't talk to his family because they were strict and he didn't talk about emotions with them. Will said his dad definitely couldn't talk like this and so didn't have any outlet. After this conversation, Paul said he just "let him do his thing" and waited for him to approach him, but in retrospect, he thinks he should have initiated more. Paul reflected that he didn't approach his friend too much because he felt worried he might be interfering. Over time, Will started to become more involved in social meetups and got a bit better, but Paul kept messaging him to make sure he was OK.

Thinking back two years later, Paul said he hadn't been worrying since about Will because he wasn't his closest friend, and he thought if it had been a much closer friend at home or at university, he would have been more affected by it. He wasn't sure if this would have made it harder or easier for him to help. He thought he had probably tried to block it out, partly from fear of being too involved and partly because he moved away and went to university. Looking back, he recalled that his first thought when he was first worried about Will was fear of the outcome, of what would happen if his friend committed suicide. This had made him feel anxious and preoccupied with worry as he ruminated on what the best thing to do might be.

Reflecting on the parent

In this scenario, we have limited information about Will's parents. What we do know is that they are "strict," particularly his dad. We also learn that they don't usually talk about emotions in the family, so we can imagine that they might be largely unaware of what their son is currently feeling. This puts him at greater risk. Where there isn't a culture of expressing emotions in a family, young people learn to keep their feelings to themselves, sometimes even feeling ashamed of these feelings and lacking any language for emotional expression. In Will's case, this has partly contributed to his thoughts of wanting to end his life, as he is unable to get any help with his emotional processing from his family. However, we don't know anything about his parents' stresses or lives, and we might imagine that they are struggling to understand their son and perhaps see his withdrawal and unwillingness to communicate with them as a signal that they should leave him to be on his own. They are possibly struggling to understand how they can help Will, so they might want to turn to Will's support network or turn to other people in their extended family or Will's school, for extra support.

Reflecting on the friend – Paul

In this scenario, we can understand Paul's confusion and anxiety about his friend. At first, Paul didn't see Will's fear, just his disappearance from the friendship group and his refusal to answer the door or his messages. Paul was able to think about what Will was like before this incident and could easily notice how his friend had changed. It's important to be vigilant of any changes in your teenagers; for example, have they stopped doing something they used to do, lost motivation for activities, or spent less time with friends and more time on their own? In this scenario, Will has suffered a traumatic bereavement and his friend is the only person who seems to be keeping an eye on him. For a while, Paul is able to keep Will in mind and keep the relationship going, providing communication, trust and care. Eventually, though, it becomes too much responsibility for him.

As Paul becomes increasingly worried about Will's state of mind, we can see the impact Will's suicidal thinking and behaviour have on Paul as he attempts to regulate himself around Will, but also his fear of how much he can do to support him. He is aware that Will's family, particularly his dad, doesn't have conversations about emotions. This makes Paul feel more helpless, perhaps because he feels the weight of responsibility for helping his friend and having the type of conversations with him he can't have at home. Through Paul's curiosity and willingness to listen, Will *does* open up sufficiently to tell him what has made him feel so low and also why it's hard at home. It's quite overwhelming for Paul and eventually, he justifies his withdrawal by saying he wasn't a very close friend. We might understand this as Paul wanting to hand over the responsibility for Will's well-being to someone else. Despite this, Paul keeps up contact with Will and messages him consistently.

Reflecting on Will

When a young person is in a depressed and suicidal state of mind, feelings become overwhelming and it's impossible for them to imagine how they can manage them. How Will feels is how he thinks he *is* – he is in "psychic equivalence" mode, discussed earlier in the chapter – where his feeling that life isn't worth living equates to him thinking he doesn't deserve a life. He doesn't have an outlet at home and his family doesn't appear to be available or able to listen to him and offer any empathy or alternative perspective. This leaves him at a complete loss as to how he can process his feelings. When Paul first goes for a walk with him, his initial feeling is he can't cope with the closeness of the interaction and feels unable to articulate his feelings, so he withdraws and goes home. On their second walk, Will opens up to Paul. He might subsequently feel a sense of shame that he has told his friend he feels suicidal, but also some relief and connection to Paul that he has shared details about the death of his girlfriend. Even managing to put the basic details into words so that Paul can understand how he's feeling seems overwhelmingly positive.

Some of Will's difficulties are due to his family's inability to communicate meaningfully, but they are also related to the trauma of his girlfriend's death. The sudden nature of her death changes the way he sees things – it colours his view of everything in the world, including his friends and even himself.

What could Will's parents do?

I wonder how you felt, reading this scenario? It's quite likely you felt upset that Will was going through such a terrible experience without the support of his parents. You may then have wondered *why* they didn't talk about emotions in the home and what he meant by them being "strict." We might assume that this is a household where they are authoritarian rather than authoritative parents. Perhaps *their* parents brought them up not to express emotions, but rather to exert authority and control. In authoritarian parenting, there are lots of rules and very little warmth, which usually results in a disconnect between parent and teenager. In contrast, with authoritative parenting, the teenager knows the rules and boundaries in the family, but they are implemented with warmth, and the focus is on keeping a close connection through a secure and loving attachment relationship. The "two-hands" approach, discussed in Chapter 1, reflects an authoritative parenting stance, as parents make efforts to understand the meaning of the behaviour while simultaneously creating a sense of safety for the young person. In this scenario, it would have been more helpful for Will if, following the death of his girlfriend, he had been able to tell his parents that he felt suicidal – safe in the certainty of their warm response – and they could have validated and empathised with his feelings of loss and despair and make him feel loved and less alone.

In conclusion, getting alongside – seeing things from their perspective – your teenager when they are at their most vulnerable, lowest point will show them that you are able to listen to them and understand their experience. It will help them to know they are not alone and that, despite any despair they may feel, for example, that they are hopeless or because they feel rejected or not accepted by others, your support for them is unwavering. This is hard work for any parent, but if you put in the work to help your teenager feel listened to, understood and validated in their feelings, then you can help them to become less impulsive, so that they pause and think about possible alternatives to their current situation. By doing this, you will be helping them to mentalize – to see that there are other possible perspectives to their own situation, and that these ones contain hope for their future and their general wellbeing and happiness.

PAUSE AND REFLECT: UNDERSTANDING SELF-HARM

In a nutshell ...

Self-harm can take many forms but is usually a way for teenagers to deal with feelings that become intolerable and too overwhelming to manage. The act of self-harm can offer temporary relief from these intolerable states, but can also be a way for your teenager to try to get rid of parts of their personalities they don't like, or an attack on people around them who they feel can't understand or accept them. Understanding the reasons adolescents self-harm is important to how you manage your own response to it and support your teenager.

Reflective parenting helps you by ...

By mentalizing yourself first, you can start to become more aware of your thoughts and feelings about your teenager's self-harming behaviour. You will understandably feel highly anxious or terrified about your teenager's safety, but if you allow these feelings to overwhelm you, it will be extremely hard to help your teenager manage their own feelings. If, on the other hand, you can regulate yourself, you will be able to think of ways you can help your teenager, either by using other people for support or offering it yourself.

Mentalizing your teenager helps them by …

By modelling a reflective mind – one that is open to thinking about different perspectives and listening with empathy – you will teach your teenager something important about how they can manage their own emotions. This will help them to regain their capacity to mentalize after stressful times and encourage them to talk about their intolerable feelings, instead of resorting to self-harm. By validating that sometimes life does feel terrible for them, and showing empathy, you will keep their trust in your relationship and they will be able to use your support to problem-solve.

Reflective parenting helps your relationship by …

When you have a risky teenager, it can be easy to become quickly alienated from one another, because emotional temperatures are running high in both of you. Reflecting on your own mind so that you can become calmer and more regulated in your emotions, and then reflecting on what's happening with your teenager, embeds a sense of trust and security in your relationship. This offers a safe harbour for your teenager to come back to when they feel alone or overwhelmed by a sense of hopelessness and perhaps having suicidal thoughts, and also when they have taken a moderate risk that has left them feeling frightened.

Keep in mind …

- Helping your teenager to manage their feelings is the most important task you can achieve when you want them to find alternative coping methods and reduce self-harm.
- Mentalizing can help reduce feelings of depression and the urge to self-harm but it is hard to do when the emotional temperature is too high. Talk to your teenager about having an emotional thermometer and encourage them to note down when they feel they are getting too hot or too cold.
- Don't make too many statements or guesses about what you imagine is going on in your teenager's mind. This helps with

much younger children but with teenagers, it feels intrusive and can distress them further. Instead, show empathy and listen to what they have to say.

- Work on controlling your own emotional response to your teenager when they are at risk. You may need to speak to a partner or friend or consult a professional if you find that you are struggling to help your teenager. This is perfectly valid and shows your teenager you are trying to work out how best to help them.
- If your teenager becomes extremely distressed, use validation to help them manage their emotional arousal level. This means using a less emotional voice and expression than when you are empathising, and it works well to bring down the temperature. When you validate, you agree with your teenager about how hard/confusing/unfair/scary everything is from their point of view, but your tone of voice is one of competence and seems clear-sighted.
- It's normal to need additional help and you should seek professional help for your teenager if they are high risk. Model help-seeking to your teenager so that they understand this is acceptable and appropriate.

8

USING A NETWORK OF SUPPORT

"I have no idea what I need, so I don't know how to ask anyone to help me."

When you encounter times where you find it extremely hard to understand and help your teenager, your relationship can be tested to the limit. For example, if you are worried that your teenager is taking risks or you're very concerned about their mental health, you may feel overwhelmed and struggle to think clearly and reflectively. This is completely normal. At these times, you may feel you can't manage on your own, or even with a partner's support, but that you need a wider network of people around you – to help you manage your own feelings and to get support both for yourself and your teenager. In this chapter, clinical psychologist and colleague, Laura Talbot, who works with professionals providing mental health support for young people, adds her voice to help to shine a light on the importance of supportive networks for parents and families. Together, we will look at how you can reflect on your supportive networks and who best to ask for help; how to overcome barriers to seeking support; and, ultimately, highlight the importance of having more than one mind to help you problem-solve in more difficult times.

Support for families has decreased considerably from the days when it was genuinely "a village" that helped raise a child, where communities actively looked out for each other. Today, it is often the sole responsibility of parents, or one parent alone, to manage the pressure of this job. We did not evolve to be the sole carers of our children and teenagers; we are genetically predisposed to have a network of caregivers – there should be grandparents, uncles and aunts, cousins – an extended family network. Today's increased

 DOI: 10.4324/9780429459245-9

mobility means that parents are often living far away from their extended family network and can be extremely isolated in their role of raising children and teenagers. Fortunately though, by nature, all young people exist within a system, or network, of friends, school, clubs, and family, and not in isolation with one or two parents or carers. Networks can be a source of help for parents, particularly when times are difficult and the sense of isolation you can feel as a parent becomes an unbearable pressure.

By drawing on help from your network, and truly acknowledging your need for this support, you can regain your own capacity to think, and this will make you a more available and useful presence in your teenager's life, so they don't feel they are overwhelming you with their difficulties. More importantly, they will have another experience of you, as a reflective and resourceful parent, who can think about their needs and who can best support them, and this will leave them feeling more closely connected and trusting of you and their relationship with you.

Turning to others for support

By thinking beyond the relationship between you and your teenager to the role of some of the other relationships around you, you can build on the ideas and influences that make up your parent MAP, discussed in Chapter 2. The parent MAP makes you think about what influences our parenting and state of mind, but beyond this, our relationships can influence how manageable or not parenting feels. For example, if you're currently parenting under a great deal of external stress (from your job, money pressure, other carer responsibilities) these current influences can make it more likely you will need to reach out to others for support, and getting this support will help you to mentalize better. In addition, the relationships within and around your family can be extremely influential in determining how manageable the task of parenting a teenager feels for you as a parent or carer. For example, maybe you disagree with some of the other adults in your teenager's life, which can mean you find yourself in conflict with others on the best approach to parenting and supporting your teenager. Perhaps you feel that you lack others to turn to for support to help with some of the challenges you face as a parent, which leaves you feeling quite isolated in your parenting role. In this chapter, we will look at how thinking about who the key people are around you and your teenager can help you to identify a supportive network and in turn draw on them when in need, to help you be a reflective parent. We will also explore how taking a mentalizing stance can help you to address any difficulties that may arise in the wider relationships around you and your teenager.

Why might parents need help from other people sometimes?

Parents can find themselves in all sorts of different circumstances with their teenagers, some more or less challenging than others. While we know that reflective parenting can be such a valuable approach, the constantly changing emotional context of parenting and family life means that we will all experience fluctuations in our ability to hold a reflective parenting stance in relation to our children. When challenges become more significant, for example, *"Should I be worried that he spends all his time alone in his room?"*; *"Why is she coming home so late?"*; *"Why is he constantly so disrespectful towards me?"* These kinds of struggles, similar to those discussed in Chapters 6 and 7, can impact family life in a number of ways and there's no doubt that parenting a teenager in these kinds of contexts, no matter how strong the relationships are around us, can be highly stressful.

When your emotional temperature is too hot

If this is something that you're currently going through, it is likely that this is impacting your emotional temperature and state of mind. You may have the feeling of generally "running a high temperature" (e.g. being generally in a state of increased emotional arousal) as well as experiencing moments of "temperature spikes" when particularly challenging situations or interactions come up within the generally difficult period that you're experiencing. At these moments, when we feel we might need extra help, we are likely to be experiencing a spike in our emotional temperature, making it impossible to reflect on what we think and feel. This is entirely normal, and we will all have spikes in our daily lives when things become particularly difficult emotionally, and we struggle to think in a reflective way. As outlined in the introduction, we are probably all only mentalizing around 30% of the time. It's worth remembering this statistic when you are struggling to think clearly. If you are also trying to manage pressures or stresses in other areas of your life outside of parenting, then this will impact the way that you are feeling and thinking further.

When parents have ongoing worries about a teenager and are dealing with emotionally charged situations, it seems unrealistic to imagine that they can parent at their best. In contrast to situations that raise our emotional temperature just moderately, where we can usually manage to bring ourselves back to a more emotionally regulated place, particularly challenging situations can mean we need the help of others. This is because when our emotions feel overwhelming, it is much more difficult to shift our emotional state and mindset on our own. For example, we might feel a bit anxious about our teenagers starting at a new school, but we probably wouldn't need to ask for support from others, and we would more likely be able to manage this feeling and know that it will pass. When our emotions feel more overwhelming, it is much more difficult to shift our emotional state and mindset on our own. For example, if you have a teenager who is being repeatedly bullied at school and they are becoming more depressed and withdrawn, you may feel that the situation is too overwhelming for you to deal with on your own because your own anxiety is hard to overcome.

How others can help

Our mentalizing capacity can be powerfully restored through positive relationships. What this might look like will vary according to your situation. Essentially, though, being able to connect with others can give us the support and time that we need to work out what is going on in our minds. A supportive network can show us empathy and provide validation for what we are experiencing and also help us to begin to explore different perspectives and responses to our situation. For instance, in the example of worrying about your teenager being bullied, you might feel you need to speak to another parent who has experienced a similar situation, or a teacher who understands the dynamics in the school and who you feel understands your teenager. So, in effect, you may need others to extend to you the principles of the parent APP – attention and curiosity, perspective-taking and providing empathy and validation – before you can regain your capacity to mentalize yourself and your teen, making effective use of both your parent MAP and the parent APP.

As you are reading this, you might already be thinking about examples of when people in your life have supported you in this kind of way. Support can come from a range of people in our lives. In certain situations, you may seek professional help, but support can also come from a partner or co-parent, family members, friends, colleagues, neighbours and people within our wider communities, for example, in faith groups, or those we encounter during leisure activities or when volunteering. You might be able to think about exchanges that have happened with others that have been supportive or useful to you in some way; perhaps someone has offered you a listening ear, given you space to get something off your chest, shared with you their own highs and lows of parenting or given you advice about something. Some of these supportive exchanges might have happened spontaneously within the natural flow of conversation, without you explicitly seeking advice or having been particularly aware of needing support at that moment. We can probably all think of times when we've shared difficulty in our relationship with our child or teenager with another parent. As a result, you may not have framed these exchanges as "getting help." When we become aware of how helpful and supportive some of our existing relationships can be, this offers us opportunities to draw on this support more consciously when times are challenging.

How do you feel about asking for help?

Asking for help, whether or not we have access to a network of people who we think can help us, is something that many of us find harder than we might care to admit. In the context of parenting, while we might "know" that experiencing some struggles is a very normal part of adolescent parenting, how do we really feel about letting people in to see a little (or a lot) of what our version of these struggles looks like?

For many of us, even the mention of the word "help" and the suggestion we might need support can feel uncomfortable. "*Well it would be nice if I had people in my life who would help me like that*" or "*There's absolutely no way I would confide in anyone else about what's going on in our family.*" Both of these experiences are important to acknowledge as it is sadly so common for parents to feel isolated and alone, even when they do have networks of people around them. It's also very easy to fall into thinking that we are the only parent who somehow hasn't managed to get a handle on our teenager. Because parenting can feel competitive at times, it can feel hard to admit our vulnerability or acknowledge any sense of failure. When this happens, our feelings of shame, vulnerability and failure can be so powerful that they shut down our help-seeking instincts, often leaving us feeling even more alone with our struggles and without the help we might need to be able to work out a way forward, or if you're happy to seek help but are unsure who to approach. The points on our parent MAP, including our attachment styles, will influence how readily and comfortably we ask for help.

Studies into how we seek help offer us some understanding of what can promote help-seeking behaviour and what can get in the way of us turning to others for support. Research published in 2005 by psychology professor Debra Rickwood and her colleagues outlined four key stages that were important in young people seeking help in relation to their mental health. This model can also be useful in making sense of help-seeking behaviour in a range of contexts, including parenting. The stages are as follows:

- **Awareness** (*of need*). The help-seeking process starts with us having an awareness that we need something.
- **Expression** (*of need*). We then need to find a way to express this need that feels comfortable for us.
- **Availability** (*of helping source*). Next, we need to perceive that there is someone available to us who could help.
- **Willingness** (*to use source*). Lastly, we need to feel willing to approach this person or people for help.

The following scenario brings this to life.

Claudette, a single parent, has a 13-year-old son called Jaden. Jaden has never liked school, but in the last few months, Claudette has really struggled to get him up and out in the mornings and he's now missing a couple of days of school every week. Claudette herself did not have a very positive experience with education, and she wasn't expecting her son's teenage years to be a smooth ride but has always wanted Jaden to fare better in education than she did. She's getting increasingly angry with Jaden for what she sees as him wasting a chance to get a good education; as a result, most mornings are filled with shouting and arguments. Claudette's manager at work is losing patience with her for frequently coming in late and she's dreading a meeting she and Jaden have been asked to attend at school next week. She is worried she won't even be able to get Jaden to the meeting and feels she will be blamed and judged for what is happening. She has had quite a lot of criticism from her mum and sisters over the years about being too soft on Jaden and so is worried about how they would react if they knew how bad the situation had become; however, she feels things are getting to the point where she can't manage it on her own and will need to seek help.

Reflecting on Claudette

What comes to mind when you think about how Claudette might be feeling about asking for help in this situation? It seems very understandable that Claudette has reached a place where she feels that she needs some support navigating the situation around Jaden's school attendance. We could imagine that she might be feeling under a lot of pressure to get him to school partly arising from her own (very reasonable) hopes for Jaden's education, but also from her workplace and school. It's also easy to see how her family experiences might lead her to anticipate that she's going to get a similarly critical rather than supportive response from school and have caused her to have some reservations about approaching her family for help. Connecting to the above help-seeking model, Claudette has some *awareness* of her need for help, but may not be fully sure about how she might *express* this to some of the people who do not yet know the full picture, namely her family. In terms of people being potentially *available* to help, she has school, her mum and her sisters on hand, but her *willingness* to draw on those people for support is being strongly influenced by both her past experiences in those relationships and some of the things she imagines might come up if she were to ask for help.

This example illustrates some of the complexities that can arise when we consider asking for help and why we might find this hard to do. Looking in more detail at each of these stages can help you begin to think about how they might apply to you and your thoughts and feelings about help-seeking as a parent or carer.

Awareness

In the hustle and bustle of family life, it might be hard to find a moment to pause to check in with ourselves about what we are experiencing, thinking and feeling in relation to how things are with our teenager. Some of us might be juggling parenting with other commitments outside of the home, such as work or wider caring responsibilities. We might have the feeling of being constantly in "doing" mode or of having a head brimming full of all the things that need to be done. This can mean that there's not much time or headspace to stop and take a step back to consider how we are coping: what is going on for us, what is going on for our teenager and do we need to give some more thought to what is happening in their life and with them. Perhaps we are just focused on surviving on the treadmill of parenting.

Another experience might be that we are conscious of some needs or difficulties, but rather than allow these to come into our full awareness so that we can begin to think about them, we try to push them away, perhaps more or less consciously. We might feel that we don't have time to deal properly with the issue right now or, we might want to avoid some of the difficult thoughts and feelings that we fear might come up if we did address the issue. Sometimes it feels much easier to pretend something difficult isn't happening and hope for the best, rather than to confront it head-on. At times this can be a useful coping strategy if this is applied only temporarily. However, for more persistent difficulties, remaining in a state of unawareness risks a situation deteriorating further and also prevents us from discovering what might happen if we were to try to engage with the issue. For example, perhaps it is more possible to sit with and work through than we had feared or perhaps we find other ways of looking at it, or allow it into our awareness sufficiently that we then seek help from others, who may be able to see a way forward.

You might find particular points stand out to you here in relation to how easy or difficult you find this awareness stage of help-seeking. This in turn might link to how easy or hard you find it to mentalize yourself when you're using your parent MAP. For example, are you someone who finds it difficult to tune into what is happening in your mind, either in specific situations or generally, on an ongoing basis? Later in this chapter, we will think about some of the ways that people can help us to be more aware of what's happening around us.

Expression

If we have managed to become aware of a particular need, we might find it straightforward to put this into words or we may struggle to **express** it. It's likely that many of us can relate to being in a situation where we think *"I don't even know how to begin to explain what's going on for me"* or, *"I have no idea what I need, so I don't know how to ask anyone to help me."* We might also struggle to express our need – is it something that feels more easily done face-to-face or would we prefer to write it in a message? The context within which we express the need might be important to us, too; for example, is it something that we would be happy to express only if someone directly asked how we are doing, or would it feel okay to bring it up with someone unprompted? Our minds might even fast forward to imagining what it might be like to talk to someone about it. We might get caught up thinking, *"Will I be able to say what I want to say? Will I make sense? Am I going to be overcome with emotion?"*

Did you connect with any of these points? Are there particular aspects of putting your needs into words that feel more or less difficult for you? Of course, how you feel about expressing your needs to someone might be hugely dependent on the situation's specifics and who you might be considering doing this with. For example, would you feel very comfortable telling your closest friend, or your sibling if you are close to them, but too vulnerable to tell someone at your teenager's school or college? If you can relate to this being tricky, an understanding of some of the specific blocks that might come up for you in relation to this stage of help-seeking could be useful in enabling you to begin to problem-solve them. Perhaps in the example of Claudette, she might feel able to turn to a friend to get some help with working out how she is going to approach her mum or sisters for help with getting Jaden to the school meeting. Either way, although sometimes challenging, it will be helpful for Claudette to mentalize herself and think about what it is that's worrying her or putting her off approaching others for help. By doing this, she will be better able to manage, or regulate, her emotions.

Availability

Whether or not there are people who we perceive as or who are **available** to help us is another key aspect that influences our help-seeking behaviour. It might be that we don't have a ready-made network around us that we can tap into, maybe through being a solo parent, having difficult relationships with key family members, living in another country from some of our family, losing touch with friends or moving to a new area and struggling to form new friendships. Or it may be connected to our current mental health. Even if we do have people around us, we might see reasons as to why those people are not really in a position to help us. It can be common to think, *"I know that they've already got so much on their plate – I don't want to add to their load"* or, *"I don't think they will want to help; I haven't been in touch with them properly for so long"* or, *"I've tried talking to them in the past and they just don't get it."* You might also be in a situation where people around you know of some of the difficulties that you are having with your teenager and therefore be thinking, *"I'm sure if someone was wanting to help, they would have already offered."* This could lead to you feeling resentful towards others for not helping, or having overwhelming feelings of hopelessness or inadequacy about yourself for not feeling resourceful enough. As legitimate as some of these concerns might be, if you find yourself looking around your social circle and finding reasons to rule out approaching nearly everyone, it might also be a signal to pause and explore whether there is some underlying reason why you feel this way, perhaps connected to your parent MAP. For example, have you experienced people being unavailable to you in some way in previous relationships? Has it been hard to rely on other people for help? Have you been dismissed, invalidated or shut down? Many parents who haven't experienced their own parents and close family as supportive and available to help don't expect others to want to help, and often don't think of themselves as worthy of that help. Perhaps some of the people who you've had these experiences with are still in your life and are therefore understandably people who you have mixed feelings towards; as a result, you may struggle to see how asking them for help is going to have a different outcome. Being aware of some of the expectations that we might have of others and being compassionate to ourselves in relation to where these expectations come from, can sometimes allow us a bit of space to consider whether other relationships around us might offer us the opportunity to have a new experience of how we are received and responded to when we try to seek help. This might mean changing life-long patterns of how you relate to other people, which can of course be challenging. However, taking some small steps towards this, by perhaps sharing our low expectations can help. For example, you might share a concern with someone you trust who might be able to offer support themselves or think with you about who else you could turn to for support. Sometimes seeing a problem through someone else's eyes can be extremely helpful in introducing another perspective. This can help us to become a bit more curious, and to let go of set ideas we might have about other people's minds and likely responses.

Willingness

If we do identify people who we think we could approach for help and support, our willingness to use those sources influences whether or not we actually go ahead and seek help. As with our readiness to think about who is available, our willingness to accept help can be influenced by factors such as our direct experience of seeking help from those people before, our experiences of seeking help from others, and some of the beliefs that we have around whether seeking help is something that we should or shouldn't do.

Your parent MAP might be revealing some of the specific challenges that could come up for you when thinking about your willingness to turn to a source of help. For example, what aspects of your early family experiences and relationships influence your willingness to seek help from others? What messages have you been given, either directly or indirectly, from those around you about what it means to seek help? These messages might be strongly rooted in our culture or other aspects of our social identity, such as our age, ethnicity, religion, gender or class. Perhaps you are a female parent who has grown up in a family where female caregivers ran the household and took on the majority of the responsibility for parenting, seemingly without the need for support, and this is part of what you feel is expected of you. Perhaps aspects of your cultural identity mean that there is shame or stigma attached to acknowledging and seeking help for a family matter, which makes it difficult for you to share your experiences with those around you, even though they might be available to help you with other purely practical aspects of your life.

Some of the current influences on your parent MAP may also get in the way of your willingness to ask others for help. Maybe you're surrounded by people who tell only rosy stories of family life, leaving you feeling that you have to keep up the pretence that "all is well." Perhaps you fear being seen as a "bad parent" or someone who is "not coping." Or you're aware that some of the people close to you hold very strong views that clash with your own and would therefore offer little of value to you. You might always be the person who others turn to for help and it feels somehow shameful to acknowledge your own needs. Some parents might also be trying desperately to keep things to themselves because they do not want to alarm, disappoint or distress people who they care about.

When these worries fill our minds, it can be all too easy to find ourselves writing off our own needs and getting stuck at the final stage of the help-seeking process. We find ourselves feeling in two minds about what to do for the best, aware of our needs, but also aware of both the pros and cons of enlisting other people to support us. A useful way to support our ability to self-mentalize around a decision we feel unsure about is to use a pros and cons table. This is a therapeutic tool used in an approach called "motivational interviewing," which supports people who feel ambivalent about change. The type of table below, used in this approach, helps parents to mentalize themselves and explore the thoughts and feelings that they have in relation to things they feel ambivalent about, including decisions around seeking help. The example below explores how Claudette might sum up her pros and cons if she were thinking about asking her family for help in relation to Jaden.

Pros of seeking help	Cons of seeking help
• It might mean Jaden gets to school. • I wouldn't feel on my own with this. • I might start getting on better again with Jaden. • It might get my boss off my back.	• I don't know what reaction I'll get. • I'm worried I'm going to be judged. • Is anyone actually going to do anything helpful or will it be more stressful?
Pros of not seeking help	**Cons of not seeking help**
• I won't be risking a fallout with my family. • Jaden isn't going to be mad at me for involving other people. • There's less shame for me this way.	• I'm worried this is going to get worse and I won't be able to get him back to school. • I can't carry on having mornings like this. • It's giving me sleepless nights and my health is suffering.

Reflecting on the pros and cons of seeking help

While the cons of not seeking help may seem most serious, if we were helping Claudette to think through this situation, we might also be particularly interested in understanding some of the pros of not seeking help that she has listed. It seems as though finding a way forward might involve her thinking about how to frame her request for help from her family, perhaps including being clear with them about her worries that they might fall out, which she is keen to avoid. She might also want a bit of help – either from a member of her family, if she manages to approach them, or someone else could also help her to think about a way to speak to Jaden about her decision to involve other people – both to acknowledge that he might have a particular perspective on this, but also to share her reasons for needing to have a bit of support. She could talk to Jaden about wanting to find a way forward where involving others helps to improve the situation for them both, to hopefully make life feel less, rather than more, stressful.

Pulling this together: what will strengthen your ability to seek help?

The box below contains an exercise to help you reflect on the themes we have been exploring in relation to help-seeking. Hopefully, a few questions might stand out as being particularly useful for you to think about. You could consider how some of your responses could form part of your parent MAP. Observe and make a note of any thoughts you have about what might make the process of seeking help feel a bit easier to navigate.

Reflective exercise:

- How comfortable do you feel with the idea that at times you might need help and support as a parent?
- What would help you to feel more comfortable about asking for help? Is there anything that you could say to remind yourself of why getting help is important?
- How easy do you find it to be aware of your needs?
- What will help you to bring more awareness to your needs in your daily life?

- How do you tend to find the process of expressing your needs? Is it uncomfortable or can you do this easily?
- What do you need (from yourself and others) that helps you to do this?
- Do you feel able to identify people in your existing network who you feel would be available to help you if you needed it?
- Are there objections that come up in your mind when you think about other people's availability to help you?
- What influences your willingness to seek help? What are some of the pros and cons of this?
- What do you think would help increase your sense of willingness to seek help?

Who's in your network?

Now that you have explored your thoughts and feelings on seeking help – mentalizing yourself - you can think about how some of these reflections might apply within the network of relationships that surround you as a parent. One way to do this is literally to draw a diagram (Figure 8.1) to capture who some of your key people are and what your connection with them is like. There are no strict rules to this exercise as to who should be on there; the aim

Figure 8.1

is to start thinking about the people who feature regularly in your life in some way.

In doing this exercise you might feel a little clearer about some of the ways in which those around you are already supporting you; you might also have some additional ideas about other ways in which these people can help you. Exploring your relationships in this way may or may not be something you've given much conscious thought to before, and we know that tuning into what is happening in our relationships with others is not always a comfortable or natural experience. It might highlight that we are not as closely connected to other people as we might wish, or remind us of some of the conflictual, distant or strained relationships that are in our lives. Of course, it's completely normal for relationships to have both supportive and stressful elements, or for us to have periods of time where things are working more or less well between us and some of the people in our lives. If you do decide to sketch out a diagram, the one you create is just a current snapshot of how things are feeling from your perspective. It may well fail to fully capture all the richness and complexity of these relationships and will no doubt continue to shift over time.

The following guide can help you draw up your network.

Exploring your network

1. **On separate pieces of paper, write down the names of the important people in your life who support you in some way as a parent.** It's up to you who you include – every parent's network is different and is affected by so many factors. You may wish to consider including family, friends, other parents you know, neighbours, people in your local community, colleagues – whoever applies most to you. Write your own name down on a piece of paper.
2. **Place yourself at the centre, then arrange the other names around you in a way that reflects how these relationships currently feel from your perspective.** The people who you feel most connected to as a parent should be placed closest to you, then work outwards from there. Move people around as needed as you add others in.
3. **Read through the questions below** to think about the role that different relationships play in your life. Your

responses to the questions may help you to add some details to your network list about how different people play a role in your life at present. Some of these questions may feel more relevant to you than others, so focus on the ones that feel most useful. **Jot notes down by each name**, according to anything relevant that you feel characterises that relationship.

- Who do you have the most contact with?
- Who makes you feel good as a parent?
- Who shares your values and approach to parenting?
- Who do you feel you can be open and honest with?
- Who encourages and challenges you in your parenting?
- Who knows you best?
- Who helps you to be at your best?
- Who would you go to if you had a problem related to your teenager?
- If you were struggling, who would notice first?
- Who do you feel you can be yourself with?
- Who would you go to for a listening ear?
- Who gives you emotional support?
- Who would you turn to if you needed help?
- Who gives you honest feedback?
- Who would you trust with a worry or concern?

So, how did you find that? What are some of the thoughts and feelings that came to mind as you were working out who is in your support network and as you look at it now? Was it useful to think about some of your relationships in this way? To illustrate how this exercise might help, can you think about a time in the past when you've been helped in some way by a person/people on your support network list with an aspect of parenting in relation to your teenager? You might have been in a different place then. What happened that enabled that helping to take place? What did it look like and how did it feel? Sometimes reflecting on past experiences can be useful in generating ideas about seeking help for something we are currently struggling with, by reminding us of how this became possible before.

Reflecting on your network of support

You could try this now by thinking about whether there is something currently bothering or troubling you in relation to your teenager. Take a look at the list of people on your network and think about whether anyone on there is already helping you in some way with this issue and if so how. Is there anyone else on there who might also be able to support you in your current situation? It can help to consider the different kinds of support you think you might need and whether different people can offer different types of support, rather than help coming from one person only. For example, you might feel that one person will be better at offering emotional support, while another person's problem-solving skills could mean you choose to go to them when you're ready to take some action, as they are good problem-solvers. There might be some people who you feel have been through something similar, who would simply "get" what you're going through and possibly also have ideas about what would help. Others might be good at helping you think about different perspectives. These people can act more "impartial" compared to someone who feels so protective towards you that they would be naturally most focused on your needs. There might be certain things that it's easier to talk through with someone who also knows your teenager well, or conversely, perhaps you would find it easier to confide in someone who didn't know them very well. Setting out your network in this way can provide a resource that you can return to whenever you want to think about how you might turn to help with a particular dilemma or problem.

Making changes to your network list

If, in considering your network, you become conscious of a lack of support, this can be difficult as inevitably it makes you feel vulnerable and possibly alone. Working out who is in your network now could bring up painful losses, for example, important people you have lost through death or separation. This realisation can feel overwhelming and may highlight a need to express this feeling of loss to others, who may then offer new avenues of support. It's perhaps surprising to you to think that making yourself vulnerable to others can in itself allow them to help you when you most need it. If you have found this activity difficult because it has highlighted ways in which your current network doesn't offer the kind of support you wish you had, you can think about ways in which you can change or adapt your network model. Maybe relationships around you at the moment are not as you would wish, either in quantity or quality. Maybe this was already on your mind or perhaps doing this exercise has brought it into your awareness more. While setting out your network in this way might help you to make sense of why things feel so tough, it might also feel hard to sit with.

Parenting with a lack of support can be challenging, as can the potential for conflict within your support network. Where one or both of these are present, this can feel very isolating and stressful and can make the task of parenting feel incredibly overwhelming. There are unlikely to be quick fixes to these situations, particularly since they can also require others to be open to making changes, for example, by resisting being critical or confrontational. However, there are ways you can think about adapting or expanding your network.

Moving people on your network

If there are elements of your network diagram that aren't working, moving people around on your map can help you think about how relationships might work more effectively. Don't worry about how exactly these changes would come about, just focus on how things would look on your map. Who would you like to move closer to you? Are there key people close to you who are in conflict with each other in a way that is affecting you? For example; perhaps your partner and one of your parents don't see eye to eye and each has opposing views on how to approach a current difficulty with your teenager. If you were to move these people a bit closer together, to reflect them getting on better, or perhaps one person taking a step back to be slightly less involved, how would that be? Sometimes, viewing people in different positions can be useful and help us to think about some of the things that might be involved in getting this to happen. This could just involve thinking about a first step towards this change rather than having a plan to create the change in full.

Expanding your network

If drawing up your network felt challenging because there are not as many people on it as you feel would be helpful, think about the kinds of gaps that you'd like to see filled. What kind of supporters are you lacking? Do you have any ideas about where you might begin to build up more of a network? As well as increasing real-life connections, some people find solace in online communities, where being anonymous is an option and where there is the potential to reach a far wider range of people and views. In online environments, you can also read about others' experiences and dilemmas without needing to share your own and you can choose to be in a supportive role to others, both of which can give us insights into our own situation. Thinking about these changes isn't necessarily easy, so if you're struggling to envisage how you could adapt your network/optimise your network, you might even want to enlist the help of a particular trusted person to help you do this.

Planning your conversation

Once you have reflected on the network of people and your views on seeking help, you are likely to feel more assured about approaching someone to ask for help. It can be worth investing some time in thinking about this, as there are some things that might help to increase the likelihood of us getting a response that feels helpful when we approach others for support. Once you have identified who you wish to ask for help, whether that's one person or a range of people, you can start to think about how to get the most from this supportive network.

Once you have identified who you wish to ask for help, whether that's one person or a range of people, you can start to think about how to get the most from this supportive network. You might already have your own way of doing this that works for you, but in case you're struggling to find a way to have these conversations, the four-step model below can help you plan your conversation and keep it on track. Thinking about asking for help in such a structured way may feel unfamiliar but can be a useful starting point for working through problems and deciding what action you need to take. If you're able to bring down your own emotional temperature to a point of feeling reasonably regulated ahead of any conversation, even if the content of the dilemma is quite emotive, you can hopefully hold this structure in mind to guide the conversation:

1 *Mark the task (working out your goals)*

Work out what you want the focus of the conversation to be and what you want from it. You might find this tricky initially because stressful events and the thoughts and feelings about your dilemma are filling your mind. However, clearly establishing your goal will increase the likelihood of having a productive conversation. Taking a step back to consider what you might need help with can feel challenging but is an important first step in being able to return to a mentalizing state of mind, enabling you to use your reflective parenting stance and think through situations more clearly.

The type of tasks you might want help with could be:

- Working out your own thoughts and feelings. Dealing with your teenager's challenging behaviour may mean it's difficult to think clearly about your own feelings/to mentalize yourself.
- Understanding something that's going on for your teenager and how to talk to them about it. For example, you may want them to help you figure out why your teenager isn't talking to you and seems so unhappy, or why, for instance, they are finding it hard to go to school. Or you may need advice about how to approach a conversation with your teenager about a specific worry, which could range from concerns about why they seem so angry with you to worries about their disordered eating.

2 *State the case (sharing key details)*

Once you have identified the task, share the key information that the person you're approaching for help needs to understand to be able to support you. Try to stick to the key points to summarise recent events. Being disciplined about this will prevent you from getting bogged down in reliving the story, which in turn makes it hard to step back and think about it clearly. Dealing with a "manageable" amount of information will also ensure that the person you're seeking help from understands what's happened but isn't overwhelmed by detail.

The following conversation illustrates how you might summarise a situation:

- **Give a brief description of the problem:** *"My son has been staying out really late, sometimes not coming home until 2 or 3 in the morning."*
- **Say how long it's been going on for:** *"He's been coming in later and later over the last few months. Now he ignores any agreed time we've set and just does what he wants. This seems to have started since he started hanging around with this group that I'm honestly not that keen on."*
- **Give a recent illustration:** *"For example, last weekend, he suddenly announced he was going out with his mates after we'd finished dinner. I didn't have time to think about it. I said okay, but where are you going and what time will you be back? He just ignored me and left. I lay awake waiting for him to come back and he didn't get home until gone 2.30 am."*
- **Explain the impact this is having:** *"We've been arguing a lot about this. He says my rules are unreasonable and all his mates can do what they like. It's having an impact on his schoolwork and on family time at weekends – he's just lying in for hours after one of these nights out and we're all hanging around wondering if he's ever going to get up."*
- **Say what you've already tried:** *"I've tried being strict, saying he can't keep asking me for money if he's not going to do the basics and respect my curfews. It made no difference and he stayed out even later. I've also tried being casual about it all, mainly to try to get more information out of him about what he's getting up to, but I think that annoys him. My brother has offered to talk to him about it, as he thinks he's being out of line, but I don't know how my teenager would react."*

Avoid going into more detail, for example, recounting specific conversations or listing different occasions when something happened. In this way, you can be sure you are focused on what you want, rather than get lost in detail, and confident that the person you're approaching has grasped the problem. It might be helpful to check that they have understood the situation.

3 *Reflect on how you and your teenager feel*

Once you've set out the situation, ask for help to focus on the thoughts and feelings of you and your teenager – to mentalize you both. To achieve this, both parties in the conversation need to stay focused on this task. Together, you can think about the emotions you're aware of and why you might feel them. The person you are talking to might offer some thoughts on how they think you might be feeling and may even help you look below the surface as to why you might feel this way. For example, underlying a lot of anger or frustration can be feelings of worry or hurt that we may not be aware of. Mentalizing together in this way can help you feel understood and you might begin to feel a shift in your emotional state, perhaps experiencing a lightbulb moment. For example, "*Yes, that's exactly how it is*"; "*I think I've actually been feeling like this is somehow all my fault so no wonder this is weighing me down so much*"; "*You're so right, I hadn't realised, but when you said I must be feeling worried, I think I have been, I just haven't been letting myself go there.*"

Next, think about your teenager's thoughts and feelings and consider who they would accept help from, whether that's a family member who is closer in age or who your teenager looks up to as a role model; or a teacher, sports coach or some other trusted adult; or perhaps a mental health professional if your teenager is open to this suggestion. When you start to explore who could support your teenager, put the principles of the parent APP into action.

A – use **attention** and curiosity. Ask your teenager about who they get on with best – who they trust and who makes them feel good about themselves and understood. Your teenager will appreciate your interest in finding this out, especially if you hold back from making any assumptions or from assuming that you know best or can read their mind.

P – show that you understand that your teenager holds a different **perspective** from you. Display a willingness to accept that they might want more separation from you than you would like or feel comfortable with, and validate this (see below). Show curiosity in how things look from their perspective. If they tell you that a peer or other family member is better at understanding them than you are, try to manage your feelings about this and support them in getting help from this other person.

P – provide empathy and validate how your teenager feels about getting support. If they seem as vulnerable as you feel to asking for outside help, connect with this and show that you understand how difficult this can be. Try not to judge or push for them to get support from someone who *you* think will be helpful and instead, if they agree to seek support, validate their choice and their need perhaps to take their time before they speak to someone else.

What your teenager benefits from most is the experience of feeling truly understood and validated in their own experience of the world.

4 *Return to the purpose of the conversation*

Focus on returning to the task that you made the focus, or marked, at the beginning of the conversation and think about what this means for your next steps. Rather than immediately jump into problem-solving together, taking some time to reconnect with your original dilemma can help you notice an immediate difference in how you're feeling; you may have a steady flow of ideas about what you might do next or are struck by how you were actually focusing on the wrong thing initially. For example, by thinking about your co-parent's perspective, you may think that the next step is to have an in-depth conversation with them, rather than approach your teenager directly. At this point in the conversation, agree together what will feel most helpful to you and whether the person you are talking to can help you figure out a way to follow a particular course of action. Or is there someone else that could help you with that? If you need to, take a few days to mull over your next steps.

When perspectives differ

Sometimes the help that you need as a parent relates to feeling stuck in a situation where you feel in conflict with others in relation to your teenager. For example, you might disagree with a partner or co-parent about the best way to approach a situation with your teenager; you might be clashing with other members of your close or extended family about your approach to parenting; or perhaps you find yourself at loggerheads with your teenager's school because of how they are responding to their needs or behaviour. These differences might make it very difficult to move forward with tackling a problem your teenager is experiencing. When people pull in different directions and respond to your teenager in different ways, this itself can compound some of the challenges. For example, if your teenager is struggling to attend school you might be concerned for their mental health, while your teenager's school might be more focused on increasing their attendance and believe they are truanting without good reason. Or you might have a particular approach you're trying to take with your teenager, but you feel that your efforts to follow this are being undermined by the input of others. Trying to manage these differences of opinion could begin to feel as hard to manage as the actual issue with your teenager.

Inevitably, when we experience such stressful dynamics in our relationships, both our emotional temperature and our capacity for reflective parenting are likely to be challenged. Even if some of these conflicts are familiar – perhaps because they are aspects of our relationship and life history that are captured in some way on our parent MAP – it is very difficult to parent at our best when we are struggling to agree or collaborate with others who are involved in our own or our teenager's life.

So, how do we make sense of these situations and begin to move forward in a helpful way? In addition, the more people there are in your network of support, the more different perspectives you have to consider. This involves the same work of reflecting on your own thoughts and feelings first, and when you are in a calm place, reflect on the different points of view held by people in the network.

Let's take an example that most parents of adolescents can probably relate to – that of working out how to respond to a teenager when they say hurtful things to a parent during an angry outburst. As their parent, your approach might be to give your teenager some space, recognising that this is not likely to be the best time to talk to them in the heat of the moment, but perhaps something you say might follow up with them at a quieter moment at the weekend. However, if your partner, co-parent or your teenager's step-parent is outraged by how your teenager speaks to you in these moments they may think an immediate response is needed. In addition, your teenager's older sibling may tell you that you let their younger sibling get away with things in a way that you did not with them. They say that your lack of strictness has created a pattern where their sibling doesn't show respect and so you only have yourself to blame. When you seek a supportive ear from your mum, she reminds you of how busy you've been at work lately and says this is probably your teenager's way of trying to get more of your attention; she suggests that you're spreading yourself too thinly, especially with the arrival of your partner on the scene a few years ago and that you could spend more time with your teenager to make up for this.

How do you think you might think and feel if you were the parent in the centre of this network of relationships, hearing all these differing perspectives trying to make sense of your teenager's behaviour and offering advice on how you should be responding to it? You might feel criticised, and as a result your confidence in your own sense of how you see things and what might be helpful could be easily undermined. You could also feel hurt by other people's take on the situation and have a sense that whatever you do, you will be met with disapproval from somebody else. You might also feel under pressure to go along with some of the suggestions others are proposing, to prevent further disagreements or conflicts within those relationships, particularly if these relationships are supportive or helpful in other ways that you don't want to risk losing, for example, if your parent often helps out when you're busy with work. The impact on your teenager of being surrounded by these different voices and views might also be on your mind. You might worry about the message they are receiving about themselves from hearing the way others make assumptions about their intentions or from the conflicting ways in which they are being responded to. You might feel that you and your teenager are getting a bit lost within this sea of opinions, and that what's going on inside each of your minds is getting harder to make sense of.

Where is your partner coming from?

If you have a co-parent, you might want to reflect on what you know about some of the past and current factors that might be influencing their parenting.

- What do you know about their relationships with their early caregivers and how this has influenced them as an individual and a parent?
- What are some of the aspects of their identity that influence their parenting in some way?
- Are there things happening in their life currently that might be affecting how they are thinking, feeling and relating to others?

Perhaps there are similarities and differences in your approaches to parenting that you have considered together before or perhaps particular situations are bringing these into focus for the first time. If you are able, try sitting together and exploring your respective parent MAPs. This sounds incredibly formal but it could be a casual conversation where you ask your partner about the things that they think influence them in their parenting; the ones they are fond of and the things they think are not so helpful. There might be information you overlooked that you hadn't connected to your current disagreement, or you might unearth new information about each other that could be relevant and help to make sense of how you're reacting to your teenager. Stepping back from the immediate conflict that you are entangled in might give you a chance to consider together which aspects of your approach to parenting feel the most shared and which aspects you are finding it most difficult to agree on. You may find it takes several conversations to work out how to build a more shared approach to your teenager, allowing you both to step away if emotional temperatures are raised and return to the discussion another time. Where communication with a partner has broken down, support from others, whether a trusted family member or friend or a health professional, may be needed to work through differences and parent in a more united way.

How different perspectives look

Certain situations, for example, where a teenager is self-harming, missing school, or hanging out with a risk-taking group of people and/or getting into serious trouble, can mean that a range of people are brought together and there is, therefore, a high potential for conflict as the different groups try to find a way forward.

Farida is having a challenging time with her 14-year-old daughter Amani. She is feeling very stressed and overwhelmed by Amani's behaviour. She feels her own mother blames her for Amani's behaviour and she is struggling to get on the same page as Amani's school and youth worker in relation to what a helpful course of action would be to improve things. Here's what the thoughts and feelings of each person involved in Armani's life might look like:

	Teenager (Amani)	*Parent/carer (Farida)*	*Grandmother*	*School*	*Youth worker*
What is the problem?	My mum and I don't get on.	Amani is out of control. She does what she likes.	Farida and Amani don't get on. Farida is stressed and not coping.	Amani's school attendance is low; she gets lots of behaviour points for bad behaviour.	Amani is unhappy at home and school. Her confidence and mood are low.
Why is the problem happening?	She gives me a hard time; there are too many arguments and too much stress.	I have no help with Amani. I can't get her to listen. She needs help with her anger.	Farida is too soft on Amani because she doesn't want to upset her.	Amani finds it hard to get on with teachers and students. Perhaps she is stressed by problems at home?	Amani may be stressed at home and at school. This means she can't always manage her emotions. She goes out to get away from it all, with a new group of friends.
What should be done?	Let me go out when I want. Being at home is just going to lead to problems.	She needs a mental health worker. The school needs to put something in place.	Farida should be firmer and stand up for herself.	Support is needed for Farida and Amani.	Support for Farida and Amani is needed to improve their relationship. A plan with the school can help Amani manage better there.
Who should do what?	My mum should back off.	Amani needs to go and have therapy.	Farida needs to take charge of the situation.	Amani needs to talk to her youth worker about this.	Farida, Amani and the school need to work together, maybe with my help.

What stands out to you as you read the above? Do these grids make it easier to step back and begin to "see" more clearly what is going on within the minds of people in a network? If we look at all the different perspectives, we can start to work out where the shared views are and where there are big conflicts. While mentalizing all the people involved in your teenager's life might feel too much, if it does feel helpful, you could have a go at drawing up a similar grid to the one above. Where you can see that views are shared, this might help you identify where people could work together to help your teenager. Similarly, by flagging up areas of conflict, you might be prompted to think of ways to resolve disagreements and move forward. If this task feels too overwhelming or too complex, then simply noting down the people you think could be most helpful to you and whose perspective you would value, is a good place to start.

Although a grid does not solve the problem of Amani and Farida arguing and Amani staying out late, it may help those involved to have a shared understanding of what might be going on and some ideas about what could help. Finding someone you trust who is not directly involved in the situation could help you think about how a similar grid might look to you. This person might also be able to help you consider how to approach others in your teenager's network to draw out their perspectives and discuss ideas and plans. This trusted person can help you to keep going, keep thinking and keep trying things out to improve the situation for you and your teenager.

At times, parenting a teenager is extremely hard, and it can feel incredibly lonely if your teenager is struggling and you feel helpless to support them. Ask others for help whenever you feel stuck and you will notice how helpful it is, to both you and your teenager to have more than one mind reflecting on your teenager.

PAUSE AND REFLECT: USING SUPPORT NETWORKS

In a nutshell ...

There are times when parenting your teenager will feel too overwhelming or even unsafe for you to do without additional support. The "thinking together" model helps you to identify what you want to focus on getting help with (what your main struggle is) and noting down those people who you find most helpful, and the key people in your teenager's life will help you gain a new perspective on a difficult situation.

Reflective parenting helps you by ...

By mentalizing yourself first, you can start to become more aware of your thoughts and feelings about asking for help. If you use your parent MAP, you will become aware of your feelings about asking other people to support you – perhaps there are things getting in the way of asking for other people's support. Becoming aware of any barriers to help, but also reflecting on those people who you could approach, is an important aspect of mentalizing yourself.

Reflective parenting helps your teenager by ...

When you start to reflect with your teenager on who might be most helpful to them, using your parent APP – modelling attention and curiosity, perspective taking and providing empathy to your teenager – you show them that you want to understand from *their perspective* what and who might be most helpful to them. By validating their feelings and showing them that it's helpful to have other people's support, you help your teenager regain some control by providing a different perspective from your own.

Reflective parenting helps your relationship by ...

Bringing a mentalizing approach to trying to problem-solve with your teenager helps them to see that you are open to new perspectives when it comes to understanding their difficulties. When your teenager feels your empathy and realises you are on their side, they will feel able to trust your opinion. If your teenager is overwhelmed by hard-to-manage feelings or is in conflict with someone, they might feel unable to ask for your help or unable to see how you *could* help them. Working out your network of helpful people teaches your teenager that you are open to other perspectives and this flexibility in your thinking will help your teenager to feel close to you and understood by you. Equally, they might feel worried that their problems are too much for you and appreciate being able to speak to other people outside of the intensity of your relationship.

Keep in mind ...

- When your emotional arousal is too high for you to think, you will struggle to be as helpful to your teenager as they need you to be. Reaching out to other supportive people will help you manage this arousal level.

- Having more than one perspective on a difficult situation enables you to get out of a "stuck" feeling when it comes to helping your teenager.
- Reflecting on why you struggle to ask for help (mentalizing yourself) can help you unblock these barriers and open you up to taking a different approach if you aren't used to asking for help.
- Have a conversation with your partner or closest family member and remind yourselves that you have different perspectives. Show curiosity and empathy for your partner's perspective and ask them to listen to yours.
- Have a series of conversations with your teenager about who they trust most in their network of friends and family. Ask their permission to contact this person and show them that you respect their judgement.

9

FOSTER CARERS AND ADOPTIVE PARENTS

Parenting your teenager who has a history of trauma

"Everyone I've ever got close to leaves me in the end, so I'm just waiting for the time when they give up on me and I move on."

Parenting a teenager is challenging enough when you know their history and have shared in their early experiences, but caring for a child who has a history of trauma brings unique challenges. As a foster carer or adoptive parent, it's likely you won't know the full extent of their history and experiences, so trying to understand the meaning and intentions behind their behaviour – mentalizing them – will be harder. Parenting for foster parents and adoptive parents presents unique challenges, however, many of the principles of reflective parenting still apply. You need to be more equipped than birth parents as you may have to deal with the effects of your teenager's trauma.

Jackie has been fostering for more than 10 years and now has three foster children living with her, two of whom are teenagers. Summing up her experiences as she trained to be a co-facilitator of a mentalizing group for foster carers she said, "I didn't think anything could shock me anymore, I'd seen it all. But I find myself being shocked again and again." This reflection sums up the experience of being a foster carer where it's possible to feel you are never fully equipped for the challenges a young person will bring with them when they come into your care.

Recent research (1) showed that children in care were 12 times more likely to have post-traumatic stress disorder (PTSD) than the general population. Is it helpful to think about a label like PTSD when you have a fostered or adopted child? Perhaps it makes you worried that you are looking after a young person who is too damaged to care for. However, one of the benefits of

DOI: 10.4324/9780429459245-10

thinking about your teenager in this way is that you can offer them an understanding of what they're feeling. Generally, young people with PTSD will suffer from more than one mental health problem, but if their PTSD is severe, understanding what they are experiencing and why is likely to be helpful. When a young person has had early trauma in their relationships with their main caregivers – often referred to as developmental trauma - this leads to the type of symptoms we see in PTSD that might be experienced by someone who has an acute traumatic event. For example, the PTSD experienced by soldiers returning from a war has been compared to the type of symptoms that children and young people experience when they have been abused and neglected by their families.

Developmental trauma can be a helpful way to understand a young person's needs, but it is a catch-all that doesn't capture the complexity and individual experience of each person. What we do know is that young people with a history of trauma, who have been let down by a lot of people, often struggle to trust adult carers and the professionals they encounter. This chronic mistrust of other people often leads to breakdowns in foster placements and, more generally, difficulties in relationships. A lot of these adolescents refuse to access mental health services because they've been so badly let down in the past; the chronic mistrust your teenager naturally feels will be brought into their relationship with you, their carer.

Trauma and the developing brain

The relationships we have with other people in our early life play a key role in shaping how our brain grows and develops. In early relationships where there is abuse and neglect, these experiences can affect brain development and have a long-term negative impact on children. Whether or not you have details on your teenager's early life, it can be helpful to understand how early experiences of abuse and neglect can shape a teenager's brain and worldview.

- Our brains adapt to the environment we've been raised in; this can mean that a brain that has adapted to survive in a threatening or unpredictable world may struggle to adapt to a non-threatening environment. Research carried out by neuroscientists Eamon McCrory and Essi Viding (2) on this group of children found that experiences of early traumatic experiences in the family can create what is called "latent vulnerability" – where early abusive or neglectful experiences with carers put children at greater risk of experiencing mental health problems. This incredibly useful research has helped professionals working with young people in care and their carers to understand how common experiences, such as moving to a new school and finding it hard to understand the intentions of school friends, can cause disproportionate fear and stress in these young people.

Neuroscientific research helps us understand that experiences of domestic violence or physical abuse can lead to hypervigilance, where the brain reacts more to threats or perceived threats. This might help a child stay safe in an early adverse environment, but it can cause problems in more ordinary environments (Figure 9.1). If you are a foster carer or parent to a teenager who has a history of trauma, you should anticipate that they might be more hypervigilant. It is helpful if, instead of seeing this as their fault or as a sign of damage that can't be fixed, you can understand that they had to be hypervigilant in their early childhood because it helped them to adapt to their threatening and abusive environment.

Figure 9.1

- If your teenager grew up in a world where their basic needs for care and attention were not met, this can shape the brain's reward system – the part of the brain that helps us learn about positive aspects of our environment and motivates our behaviour over time. As a result, the brain's reward system can learn to respond differently to positive social cues for example.
- For teenagers who grew up in an environment where there was abuse, neglect or maltreatment, negative memories appear to become more salient, which means they become more prominent than positive ones, and everyday memories can also become less detailed. This causes a problem for your teenager in a social environment, as we all need to draw on past experiences to help us deal with new social situations. If these past experiences are negative or confusing, it will make all relationships much harder to understand. If you approach your relationship with your teenager armed with this knowledge, it can help you to understand that they are using the only way they know to adapt to a new environment or relationship, and that they need time and your support to build trust and understand there are other ways of interpreting relationships and other people's intentions and behaviours.

What happens if we don't learn how to reflect?

Let's go back and imagine being a baby again, as you did at the start of this book in the introduction. This time, think about what the baby's experience is like when their parents can't meet their normal developmental needs. The baby needs to be kept safe, cherished and respected as an independent being, to have a sense of belonging. Sometimes, parents, for many different reasons, such as their current mental health, past history, and current circumstances, cannot meet these needs. What is the young baby's experience in this dynamic? The baby wants to develop and experience life. When we mentalize, we can step back and think about why they need these things and what we can do to meet them. Thinking about a baby's needs, imagine that their mum has just had a row with her partner. The baby cries and it doesn't make her feel concerned, it makes her say, "Shut up, I'm not in the mood for this right now." Mum is saying, "I've got my own needs." In this dynamic, her facial expression isn't concerned and warm, it's an angry one that says, "I don't want you here right now," which will make the baby feel unsettled. Imagine a baby whose cry isn't effective, but leads instead to them being blanked, or an angry or to a hostile, resentful response from other people. As the baby doesn't have the words yet for "sad," "hurt" or "lost," they feel these emotions in their body. So they feel hot, or cold, or their tummy clenches up. These memories are held in the body and create the experience of trauma that is carried on into the future.

Later, as a child, this baby goes to school filled with fear and trepidation, thinking, "People might not like me or help me." These feelings might have names by now, because the child has language, but trauma will still be held in the body so the child might have a tight feeling in their tummy, or feel too hot or cold, or sick. Furthermore, if the child hasn't had an experience of an adult face responding to their feelings in a genuine way, or has experienced adults responding in frightening ways, they are likely to become hypervigilant, looking for the threat before it is there. At school, they will be hypervigilant to the faces around them and might read them incorrectly. The other children will greet them with all sorts of feelings, e.g. surprise, curiosity, "Maybe I don't want her to get in the way of my friendships." In return, they look at the expressions of the other children through one lens, which says "This person is not going to be friendly to me, this is not going to help me."

Later on, in adolescence, we can often see the effects of not being responded to as an infant in a teenager's expression and body language. For example, if we see a teenager with their eyebrows furrowed and their fists clenched, at a surface level we read this as, "This person isn't nice." You might look at your fostered teenager and think, "It's hard to like him, he looks ready for trouble." This possibly arouses a negative, punitive response in you as the teenager's foster carer or adoptive parent.

Stepping back from your foster teenager

However, if you step back and think about what the expression on the face and the body is hiding, the hidden feelings of being rubbish and worthless, then it's easier to empathise with your teenager, take a step back, and understand the experience of the child. When you take a reflective parenting, empathic, approach towards your teenager, it's more helpful to understand that the surface signals are not sending the message about the hidden feelings underneath, and perhaps there's a dejected baby underneath. It's helpful to remember that the body language of a traumatised adolescent tells the underlying story.

Overreacting and avoidance

Hyper-reactivity to threats can lead to overreaction and sometimes violence. Ruby, who frequently witnessed domestic abuse as a child, overreacted to a playful, encouraging nudge in the changing room, and the consequences had the potential to negatively impact her sense of self-worth, as well as her chances of building a network of friends. In some cases, where a teenager has had a chronic experience of abuse in their childhood, a pattern of avoiding friendships. This avoidance pattern is associated with unusually low brain activation in the threat system – the system that processes the response to a possible threat called the amygdala – which may lead to a child withdrawing or feeling anxious, even in safe environments. Try to remember that your teenager might have very few, if any, experiences of positive, helpful, and trusted relationships in their past. Withdrawing from friends and other people could reduce their opportunities to learn and increase their reactivity to stress and rejection. Past trauma can increase the intensity of emotions and result in poor emotional processing, leading to an increase in mental health problems such as anxiety and depression. By showing your teenager you want to understand their thoughts and feelings, using your parent APP from Chapter 3 to mentalize them – showing attention and curiosity, perspective-taking and empathy – you will be giving them a different experience of a mind that wants to understand theirs.

Your fostered or adopted teenager, who may have a history of several caregivers, will be especially susceptible to inferring negative intentions from you. For example, you might ask your teenager whether they've done their homework, in what to you feels like a friendly or neutral manner, with a curious expression on your face. They could easily perceive your tone and question as persecutory or aggressive and your curious face might be mistaken for a judgemental and hostile one. It's easy to see how this can lead to multiple misunderstandings between you and conflict escalating quickly as a result. Teenagers coming into care also often struggle to be aware of their own emotions and to feel empathy towards others. Early deprivation and environmental stress have a massive impact on the ability of these young people to form secure, reliable and trustworthy relationships.

We know a young person's brain has the capacity to continue to adapt and that this continues well into their twenties. For this to happen, they need our help to build and maintain trusted relationships, manage everyday stresses and reduce the risk of new ones from happening. As their carers and parents, we can encourage them to try again when they are knocked back and believe outcomes can be different. This is far from an easy task and takes time. Using a reflective parenting approach with teenagers who have experienced traumatic relationships in their past can help them build trusting relationships and create opportunities for their brains to adapt in new, more resilient ways.

Let's look at the example of Ruby.

> Ruby has been in three different foster placements in the past four years. Her birth parents neglected her needs, and shouting and violence in her home meant that she was often confronted by threatening voices and faces. When she was upset, her mum used to tell her not to make so much noise as it was making her ill. She frequently witnessed her dad hitting her mum and she often went to bed hungry if her mum and dad were too preoccupied arguing with each other.
>
> She is only 11 years old and has just started year 7 at secondary school. The change from her small primary school to a large secondary school came only three weeks after moving in with her current foster carers. She enjoys playing netball, is good at most sports and is chosen for the school netball team in the first term.
>
> Before her first match, as she walks from the changing room to the netball court, a teammate gives her a friendly nudge and says, "Play your best out there, Ruby." Ruby feels angry and hurt and gives her a hard shove back, resulting in the PE teacher calling her to one side. The teacher tells her that she can't tolerate this type of behaviour and tells her to wait in the changing room as a substitute. She says, "I'll think about putting you on the team next time, after you've thought about your behaviour." Ruby feels confused and angry that she's been left out of the team when it was someone else who pushed her first.

Reflecting on Ruby

For Ruby, with her history of trauma and multiple caregivers, the experience of moving to her new school feels daunting and stressful; new faces appear threatening, and she misses the positive social cues from her classmates and teacher. She is finding it hard to trust new people. We might imagine that she would enjoy joining a new sports team because she's good at netball, but even these kinds of experiences can be challenging. Her past traumatic experiences of relationships cause her to place too much focus on potential threats and to miss out on positive social cues, such as a playful nudge from her teammate, who thought she was encouraging Ruby to play well. These past experiences can also cause an overreaction, which leads to an increased risk of conflict. She sees her teammate's nudge as an attack and gets stressed and defensive in the face of what she sees as aggression.

This type of common experience can make it even harder for a child such as Ruby, who feels unconfident and anxious inside, to deal with everyday challenges. This, in turn, makes it harder for her to build and maintain relationships over time. As young people like Ruby become teenagers, they can lose friends and the support of adults and so miss out on opportunities to grow and develop. This phenomenon is called "social thinning" and can increase the risk of mental health problems in the future. In Ruby's case, feeling criticised and misunderstood by her teacher rather than valued leads her to feel angry at them. Her response to both her teacher and her teammate means she is excluded, which leads to further difficulties in developing and maintaining friendships.

Reflecting on the teacher

Ruby's PE teacher has interpreted her behaviour as an act of aggression. She probably thinks she is teaching Ruby a lesson about sporting/team behaviour by banning her from the game. We can probably assume she is unaware of Ruby's background and just knows that Ruby is keen on sports. This might mean that she interprets her behaviour, incorrectly, as Ruby being competitive with a teammate.

Even if you are the most reflective, mentalizing caregiver in the world, your capacity to mentalize – reflect on your own thoughts and feelings and on the mind of your teenager – when you are in a caregiving relationship with a teenager with a history of trauma and possibly abuse and neglect will be significantly compromised, because of the challenge of caring for a teenager who struggles to understand emotions (3). At times you may seriously doubt your own mind. It becomes more of a challenge, but even more important, to mentalize yourself when you have a looked after or adopted teenager; being a reflective adoptive parent or foster carer can help you and your teenager to stay connected through what can be extremely challenging times.

Simone and Eddie have been fostering for 15 years. They have offered emergency placements to babies, young children and many teenagers, but have never felt quite so challenged as they do when looking after 17-year-old Shanice. Shanice first came into care when she was 12 years old, when her mother decided she was beyond her control. At her mother's request, she was placed in foster care by the local authority. Since Shanice was around 11 or 12 years old, there have been numerous referrals to social services, predominantly regarding the relationship between Shanice and her mother, which is reported as being "cold and aggressive" and lacking in emotional warmth.

Between 2016 and 2018, Shanice went into three different fostering provisions: two foster families and one residential home, before she came to Simone and Eddie, who said that they felt experienced enough to offer Shanice the parenting she needed. They went into the fostering arrangement with their eyes wide open, armed with the knowledge that Shanice had a history of putting herself at risk. The long list of safeguarding concerns social services passed on to Simone and Eddie included exchanging sexually explicit pictures and messages by mobile phone with an older male, struggles with maintaining friendships and being told what to do, "explosive moods followed by withdrawal and sullenness, and using dysfunctional methods to manage stress, such as consuming alcohol and smoking cannabis (weed)." She had formerly engaged in self-harm, cutting herself to regulate her emotional distress. She had also engaged in risky sexualised behaviours, showed acute sensitivity to loss and perceived or real rejection from others and seemed to struggle with maintaining healthy relationships.

One evening, after Shanice had been living with the family for six months, Simone, Eddie and Shanice sat down for dinner. Shanice asked politely if she could go out and see some friends and Simone and Eddie asked who they were and where they lived. Shanice was somewhat vague about the details but said she would take her mobile and keep in touch, and that it was just a "small gathering" and "no big deal"; she promised she would be back by midnight. Midnight passed and Simone and Eddie made several attempts to contact Shanice but each time it went straight to voicemail on her mobile. Simone and Eddie started to discuss whether they should call the police or Shanice's social worker; the focus of their conversation became her sexual history and the fact that she was not currently taking any contraception and refused to. Simone and Eddie knew that in the past Shanice had requested a pregnancy test while in school, which was negative. They worried that part of Shanice wanted to get pregnant and to have a baby to care for at 17; the same age her mother was pregnant with her.

After contacting the duty social worker, who informed the police, Simone agreed she would be the one to stay up while Eddie went to bed, as he had work early in the morning, although he knew he wouldn't be able to sleep. At just after 2 a.m., the door opened and Shanice came into the sitting room, shocked to see that Simone had stayed up for her. Simone managed to keep calm and asked where Shanice had been and told her how worried she was. Shanice looked extremely sad and told Simone she had never expected anyone to be thinking about where she was. She then shared that there was a picture of her on the internet with hardly any clothes on, and "friends" were circulating it.

Reflecting on the scenario – what is your emotional reaction to this? What questions and thoughts are running through your mind? Can you relate to any of the feelings Simone and Eddie are having, and does it make you reflect on where your response to your own teenagers comes from? Try to notice your emotional temperature when reading this scenario and thinking about your own teenagers.

Reflecting on Simon and Eddie

Meantlizing Simone and Eddie, what must it be like for them? You might have imagined all the possible scenarios that were running through their minds about what was happening to Shanice and how responsible they must have felt for her safety, and at the same time perhaps felt helpless. You might also think that they could be angry that she had betrayed their trust, after seeming to have promised to be home at a certain time. Perhaps you imagined they were extremely frightened, or they were thinking this behaviour was "typical" and that Shanice was always going to be "out of control."

Reflecting on Shanice

What do you think was going on in Shanice's mind? Did you wonder if she had any thoughts about how Eddie and Simone would feel about her being out so late? She seemed to be quick to confide in Simone and surprised that someone had waited for her. We could feel a bit hopeful for her relationship with her foster carers and the fact that she has already developed an idea that they can help her when she's in trouble. We might start to wonder about the influence of her past relationship with her mother on her behaviour and emotions and how this led her to stay out so late without word to her foster carers.

From Shanice's perspective

If we try to step into Shanice's shoes and see the world and her relationships in it through her eyes, let's imagine what she might be thinking and feeling. "I don't expect people to bother about me really, so I was surprised to see Simone waiting for me when I got home. Why does she care? Everyone I've ever got close to leaves me in the end, so I'm just waiting for the time when they give up on me and I move on. It's not worth the effort of getting close to them and, anyway, even if I wanted to, I wouldn't really know how to. I just didn't think about them at all when I was out. There was a guy there, Ashley, who said he wanted to have some fun with me. I know he's probably not that great, but, you know, I feel good when I'm with him. He's a bit troubled, I mean, he's been in prison, but he says I'm really nice. When we slept together, he told me he didn't believe in using protection because it didn't feel as good. I wouldn't really mind you know, if I got pregnant. I'm young still, but my mum had me at my age. It would be nice to have someone to love who was just mine. I'm upset and angry that my so-called friends put a picture of me in my bra and shorts on social media. Everyone abandons me in the end, so it's not worth bothering. I'm just disgusting and not worth bothering with anyway."

Thinking together

Let's think a bit about developmental trauma and what it means, keeping Shanice in mind. Psychiatrist and trauma expert Bessel van der Kolk (4) described a person who has experienced developmental trauma in the following way:

> Expectations of a return of the trauma permeate their relationships. This is expressed as negative self-attributions, loss of trust in caretakers, and loss of belief that somebody will look after them and make them feel safe.

If we think about Shanice in this scenario when she left her home with Simone and Eddie to go out with friends, we can start to imagine that she was expecting the cold and aggressive responses and feelings of abandonment she experienced with her birth mother to be a feature of her relationship not just with Simone and Eddie, but with other people she gets involved with as well, such as Ashley. The loss of trust comes when she stays out later than she agreed. Her shock when she returns home is an expression of her loss of belief that there could be anybody who would look after her and make her feel safe. With these beliefs running so deeply in Shanice's mind, it is not surprising then that she doesn't have a concept of Simone and Eddie as trustworthy, safe attachment figures who have her best interests in mind. She doesn't have any previous experience or "model" of this so there is nothing she can access when she's away from home and in a vulnerable situation. Moreover, at the time she goes out, she doesn't recognise herself as being vulnerable to the abuse or exploitation of others; rather, she re-enacts an experience of rejection and maltreatment by sleeping with someone who refuses to use contraception, and she behaves in a self-sacrificing manner, where she has no self-value and places other people's needs ahead of her own. The hopeful part of this scenario is that seeing Simone has waited up for her and looks concerned, Shanice trusts her enough to tell her about something she's worrying about, which allows Simone to find out more about her evening.

This scenario shows how caring for someone who has no previous experience with people as being helpful, trustworthy, available and protective is extremely challenging. Simone and Eddie have managed to create a relationship in which Shanice can show them some vulnerability. We might imagine they have communicated that they are there to support her and are concerned for her well-being. They are trying to show Shanice that she can trust them and that they want to trust her. Foster children and teenagers can often feel that there are preconceptions about them as untrustworthy or bad. I vividly remember working with a teenager from Afghanistan who, when he came into foster care in England, was not given a key by his foster family because they had had a bad experience with a previous foster child, who had stolen from them, so they automatically assumed he was also untrustworthy. He had to knock on his own front door every day to get in.

Difficulties in mentalizing for carers and adoptive parents

There is good evidence to suggest that if your ability to reflect on the thoughts and feelings of yourself and your foster child (to mentalize yourself and them) is low, this can lead to increased behavioural problems in fostered or adopted children and teenagers (5).

Having understood how stressful it is caring for a young person with a history of trauma, and how important mentalizing – reflecting on thoughts and feelings – is to their behaviour, it seems essential to help you try to manage this stress through increased reflective capacity. The less able you are to manage stress and increase your reflectiveness, the more this will interfere with the skills you need to help your teenager manage their emotions. Research by Tina Adkins supports the view that foster carers, as those providing the most consistent relationships in the lives of children in care, should be offered help to build the skills of reflective parenting. A large body of evidence has demonstrated that achieving this leads to increased security and stability, and promotes a child's ability to regulate and manage their own emotions (Figure 9.2).

When, as a foster carer or adoptive parent, you are faced with extreme challenges, your emotional arousal – or emotional temperature – goes up. In this scenario, we can imagine that Simone and Eddie's temperature went through the roof as they sat up into the early hours, not knowing Shanice's whereabouts. We can imagine they might have felt a mixture of feelings including fear, anger and helplessness, and that all of these feelings interfered with their capacity to mentalize. A reflective parenting approach that

Figure 9.2

has been adapted for foster parents and evaluated in a clinical trial called the "Reflective fostering programme" would start with helping Simone and Eddie to reflect on their own thoughts and feelings – using the parent/carer MAP in Chapter 2 as a guide. The temptation, particularly for foster carers, can be to feel that you must strive to understand your foster child's behaviour. This feeling can be exacerbated when you have the added pressure of feeling under the watchful scrutiny of social services. Doing this, though, can be incredibly unhelpful to both you and your teenagers. Being a reflective foster carer starts with tuning in to your own emotional response and thoughts about your fostered or adopted teenager so that you can understand your own reactions better, and ultimately regulate these very difficult feelings in the face of regular challenges.

In the "reflective fostering programme"(6), the aim is the same as reflective parenting – to encourage carers to mentalize so that they can help both the teenagers and themselves to regulate emotions, ultimately resulting in better behaviour. Returning to Shanice, she hasn't had the experience of a relationship that helped her to understand her thoughts and feelings, so she has very little prior knowledge or experience of understanding others or herself and is a poor judge of relationships. In a reflective fostering or adoptive parenting relationship, you help your teenager to understand their own thoughts and feelings by looking at the meaning *behind* their behaviour which, as we know, is the main tenet of a mentalizing, reflective parenting, stance.

Since the 1970s to the present day, with the renowned work carried out by child psychologist Alan Sroufe and his colleagues, researchers have found that caregivers are not only responsible for helping their children and teenagers to keep their emotional arousal within manageable bounds but also, they help them to develop their own ability to regulate their arousal in the first place. In other words, for a normally developing child in a safe and secure environment, the parent is both the teacher of how they manage their own emotions and also influences the emotions the infant feels in the first place. For a fostered or adopted child who didn't have you as a regulator of their emotions, they will be regularly pushed into a state of hyperarousal and are likely to react in an impulsive way to social cues and misjudge situations regularly. Sroufe's study (7) showed how, where a caregiver hadn't helped a child to develop their own ability to regulate their emotional arousal, by the time these children had reached adolescence, over half of them had diagnosable mental health problems. Some of the features of these young people might be familiar to you; for example, they clamoured for attention and were easily frustrated when faced with even a small challenge. Because these children were in a state of almost constant arousal, this made them extremely anxious. Their ever-present need for reassurance and attention inhibited them from playing in a normal, carefree way and the result was they grew up chronically nervous. In school, these are often the teenagers who are so aroused throughout the day they can't settle and, coupled with the lack of parental comfort they have experienced, are often disruptive, oppositional, and aggressive. Their disruptive and aggressive behaviour makes them unpopular and provokes more rejection and punishment from both teachers and peers.

As a foster carer or adoptive parent, by being aware of how early trauma can affect behaviour and being "trauma-informed" you can start to notice the differences between what would be expected behaviour and what you see in your teenager. For example, when non-abused girls report a distressing event they've experienced, they show a normal level of distress. A study from 2011 (8) showed that, over time, girls who had experienced sexual abuse became less distressed when they talked about a, usually, distressing event. They shut down and became numb, almost seeming to have no emotional reaction at all. If you recall, Shanice showed no emotions, particularly when she spoke of having unprotected sex with a boy with a history of offences so serious he had been in jail. Equally, when she learned that the revealing pictures of her that friends had posted on social media had been widely shared, this elicited very little response from her other than some embarrassment. The normal range of distress signals that would be sent to a protective caregiver to say, "I'm in trouble, I need help," had been shut down and instead, she reported feeling "nothing."

When a young person shuts down and withdraws in this way, the real danger is that professionals, including teachers and carers, can miss the fact that there is something very serious going on. The other dangerous feature of this shutdown is that it means that none of the usual protective strategies are deployed as the young person fails to see themselves as being vulnerable and at risk. A further risk can be that once sensitive and reflective caregivers become withdrawn and rejecting in response to a looked-after teenager who seems not to need them. The following scenario shows how carers can use mentalizing to develop an understanding that there is still an underlying need for this type of teenager to connect, but they don't know how to send out this signal.

Eamon and Christopher are adoptive dads to siblings, Aron (aged 15) and Scarlett (13). They adopted the teenagers six years ago when Aron was nine years old and Scarlett seven, following a brief period the children had spent in foster care. The siblings' birth family was characterised by excessive alcohol use by their mother and grandmother and domestic violence in the relationship between their mum and her boyfriend. Aron and Scarlett were taken into foster care after a neighbour alerted the local authority when she heard the children screaming late one night and called around to find no adults in the house and signs of drink, drug paraphernalia and a pan of burning food, about to catch fire, on the kitchen hob.

Aron was extremely challenging from the moment he arrived at Eamon and Christopher's home. He made demands on them and seemed to get a lot of satisfaction from having new things; toys when he was younger, and now games and add-ons for his games console or phone. If he didn't get what he wanted, he would shout at his dads and tell them they were the "worst parents in the world" and that he used to get all the toys he wanted in his other (birth family) home, where he could also watch any programme he wanted to on TV. Eamon and Christopher find Aron very difficult but can understand why he always wants new things. They talk to him about this and help him manage his emotions by reassuring him that they love him and won't abandon him. This seems to calm Aron for a while and now after an outburst, he usually apologises to his parents, telling them he just couldn't control his anger.

They find Scarlett a lot easier as she makes very few demands on them and seems withdrawn and not in need of a lot of attention from them (in their view). They describe her as "self-contained" and "a bit shy and quiet"; as a result they let her spend a lot of time in her room, where she mostly reads and listens to music on her phone. Over time, they notice that Scarlett never seems to want to go to friends' houses or parties and prefers to come home after school and go up to her room, where she stays for most of the night while they deal with Aron. In an attempt to get her out, Eamon organises a trip to the local shopping centre to get Scarlett some new clothes, thinking this will make her happy. Scarlett walks quietly around the shops, following Eamon into one shop after another, before he persuades her, somewhat against her wishes, to "try something on" in a clothes shop. Scarlett stands in the changing room feeling uncomfortable, bursts into tears and asks her dad to please take her home.

Reflecting on the parents

Eamon and Christopher appear to think they understand both of their children's needs – that Aron needs more attention and Scarlett is apparently content to be on her own in her room.

In their parenting of Aron, although they find him hard work – demanding a lot of attention from them and getting satisfaction from material things – they seem to understand this as his need to feel wanted by them. In relation to Scarlett, they don't seem as capable of mentalizing her; because she places very little demands on them, they seem to respond to this by thinking that her quietness means she is happier spending time on her own. However, when they notice that she isn't being invited to friends' houses in the way other kids in her class are, they decide to take action and get her out of the house on what they think will be a fun trip to buy some clothes. We can imagine that perhaps Eamon feels quite shocked and confused when she bursts into tears in the changing room, and he is possibly lost as to what he can do to respond as he's so used to leaving Scarlett to her own devices. He may not have experienced an outward expression of emotion like this from Scarlett before and might even feel that this is too much on top of all the behaviour they have to deal with when it comes to Aron. He may feel quite helpless in the face of a usually withdrawn teenager and perhaps thinks that this is "out of character" for Scarlett.

Reflecting on the teenagers

Aron and Scarlett experienced trauma in their birth family for most of their childhoods. They are relatively old for adoption at nine and seven years of age, and so their way of dealing with their emotions and experience of relationships are well established by the time they are adopted by Eamon and Christopher. Aron has developed a strategy to get his needs met by demanding things from his parents. Given how overt Aron's behaviour is, they have been able to understand the meaning behind this behaviour, talk to Aron about it, and help him regulate his emotions and bring his emotional arousal down (perhaps by being aware of the concept of our emotional thermometer). We might imagine that Aron feels understood from time to time by his parents, but also he might feel quite powerful because he has a strategy for getting both attention from his parents and some material things that could make him popular among his peer group (and connect him to them via his gaming).

Scarlett is quiet and withdrawn, possibly as a response to her louder and more demanding brother. She has learned to keep her needs to herself and to not demand anything from her parents or take any normal risks, such as going to friends' houses or inviting people to stay at hers, risking the rejection of them saying no. She is unsettled when her, normally hands-off dad, insists on taking her shopping against her will; it seems he is trying to get her to change her look, maybe to help her make friends. When she gets into the changing room and sees that she looks different from how she sees herself and thinks about the prospect of having to ask a friend to her house or go to a party, she feels overwhelmed. She notices that her dad doesn't know what to do and she is at a loss as to how to tell him what she really feels inside. She doesn't want to put any demands on him, given that he's already got his hands full with Aron.

Thinking together

The need to keep your own mind in check is even greater when you have a teenager who has a background of developmental trauma. How you think you are coming across will not necessarily be how they see you. Your role is so much more than looking after the young person in your care; it is to teach them an emotional language that they are not familiar with and a means of regulating feelings, which starts with you being explicit about your own state of mind. Eamon and Christopher have responded to Scarlett's quietness and withdrawal with their own withdrawal from her. This has resulted in them failing to mentalize her and show any curiosity about what might be going on inside her mind. It is naturally easier to notice a teenager who's being loud, difficult or demanding, but the need to be curious about what's going on in the mind of a teenager who is quiet and withdrawn is just as great, if not greater. This brings us back to the main tools of reflective parenting: mentalizing yourself and then mentalizing your teenager. Start by being curious about what you are feeling in your relationship with your teen; so in this case Eamon might notice that he is rather cut off and non-mentalizing and he can then start to be curious about why this is. Once you have mentalized yourself and understood where your thoughts and feelings are coming from – how they relate to say, why you became a foster carer or adoptive parent, what your beliefs are about children who have had a history of trauma, how your parenting relates to your own history, and so on – you will then be in a more regulated, reflective place where you can go on to mentalize your teenager.

If Eamon had done some self-reflection first, he then might have been able to be curious about why Scarlett was spending so much time in her room and how she felt about this. Had he understood the fears and anxieties in her mind about the potential for being rejected by friends, he might then have asked if he could help her with this, and it would have allowed him to pause and slow down rather than rush into action to try to fix things (by going to the shopping centre).

Parenting is a lifelong journey, and the only preparation most people have is how they were parented themselves. Parenting a foster child, or adopted child, whose previous experiences have impacted many areas of their functioning, can be much tougher. Therefore, it is even more important that you are aware of yourself: how you parent, what influences you and how you are influenced by thoughts, feelings, beliefs and external events. If you focus on your relationship with your trauma-experienced teenager and less on their behaviour, this will help them to understand themselves better and ultimately manage their feelings and their relationships with others better too. By increasing your awareness of what's going on inside you, you will discover how you can enjoy a better quality of interaction with your teenager. This is because how you feel, and how your emotions influence you with or without your awareness, has an impact on how your teenager both feels and behaves.

Don't forget your own needs, which are separate from your fostered or adopted child's. To be able to connect: to be empathic towards the struggles of a teenager who has been through trauma, it is really important for you to feel connected to other important people in your life – to feel your own needs are being listened to and met. If you're struggling to look after a teenager with a history of trauma, try to reach out to other parents and carers, and to mentalize yourself with other's support if you can. When we know how we feel, and even understand *why* we feel a certain way, we can use our feelings to make good decisions in life and learn to control our impulses.

PAUSE AND REFLECT: PARENTING YOUR TEENAGER WITH A TRAUMATIC HISOTRY

In a nutshell ...

Parenting a teenager who has a history of trauma brings unique challenges to foster carers and adoptive parents. It is harder to mentalize a teenager when you don't understand their full history of experiences, and it is a challenge to keep hold of your own capacity to mentalize in a relationship with a teenager who struggles to understand relationships. Reflective parenting is a useful approach to help you understand the impact of trauma on your teenager and the impact of caring for a traumatised teenager on yourself.

Reflective parenting helps you by ...

Reflective parenting is an approach that gives space for your own feelings as a foster carer or adoptive parent and doesn't just focus on how to support your teenager. You might feel a strong urge to try to fix your teenager who has a history of trauma and has had several family placements in their life. Mentalizing yourself and your teenager can help you learn to deal with the impact of caring for someone who challenges you. It can help you become more aware of how you are coming across and how you can signal your intentions more clearly to your teenager, who struggles to understand relationships. Being aware of your teenager's vulnerability to misinterpreting you will help you to be clear about what you are thinking and feeling.

Mentalizing your teenager helps them by ...

Your fostered or adopted child may not have had an early experience of a secure relationship: one in which they were helped to understand their own feelings and the thoughts and feelings of their caregiver. Understanding their background, and their vulnerability to misinterpreting other people will help you to empathise with their everyday difficulties. By mentalizing them, you will be able to show them you understand that your intentions, for example, to set a boundary around bedtime (so they can get a good night's sleep) are different from how they might see them (for example, being sent to bed as a way of punishing them or sending them away to their room). Past experiences can also cause an overreaction, which leads to an increased risk of conflict.

Mentalizing your teenager – using a parent APP – helps your relationship by ...

By mentalizing your teenager's feelings, you can help them develop a new relationship in which there is trust and validation. Your understanding of the phenomenon of "social thinning" can help you to understand that your teenager *wants* friends and relationships, but struggles to build and maintain relationships, leading other people to pull back. This understanding helps you to resist any urge you have as their carer or parent to pull back and gives them a different experience of someone who is keen to understand their past experiences of relationships and give them a new experience of being understood. By not overreacting to their sensitivity or misinterpretation of your intentions, you keep yourself regulated in their emotions and reduce the likelihood of repeating patterns of conflict between you and your foster child.

Keep in mind ...

- A teenager who has experienced trauma has difficulties understanding their own and other people's feelings at times. You might start to mentalize yourself aloud around your teenager from time to time, to help them understand your emotions and intentions better.
- When your teenager feels confused about your intentions, they might appear to overreact to a situation. Try talking to them about what they thought you meant and listen with empathy. Then, when they are calmer, offer your own perspective on what you really intended. Do the same when you talk with your teenager about their friends and teachers.
- Give your teenager opportunities to develop new relationships by trusting them and talking to their teachers about their history so they can also offer opportunities in school for building friendships.
- Keep your teenager's emotional thermometer in mind – it reacts differently from yours and other teenagers'. Your teenager's emotions might become very intense quickly and it might take them longer to cool down. Take into account that this is a result of their early traumatic experiences, where emotions were often volatile and unpredictable.
- Emphasise the perspective-taking part of your parent APP when you are trying to mentalize your teenager. Their experience may be hard to relate to or outside of your experience and hard to understand, but it's important they feel you take it seriously.

- Notice and name your teenager's strengths and abilities and validate them so you support their developing self-esteem.
- Your fostered or adopted teenager may seem younger than their peers. Understand that they may not have had most of their basic needs met when they were younger and need to experience some of the early parenting they lacked in their birth families. Look for opportunities to offer comfort and soothing that you might give to a much younger child.

10

KEEPING THE CONNECTION

Navigating the transition to adulthood

"I didn't really need them to do anything, just knowing they were there somewhere in the background was enough."

Depending on your cultural background, family belief system, personal circumstances and financial status, you may feel that by the time your teenager reaches adulthood (18 years is the "official" age in the Western world that a young person becomes an adult) they should be learning to be more independent from you. On the other hand, you may believe that your young adult should primarily be living with you and your family; building their life skills from within the family. In many cultures, it is the norm for young people to remain living at home until they build a family of their own, and in some cultures even beyond this. Whatever your beliefs and circumstances, an important task of parenting is to help your teenager grow into a secure adult. We all want our teenagers to flourish into mentally healthy adults. Reflective parenting can be a helpful toolkit to help you and your teenager navigate this transition, crucially helping you to maintain the connection you would like as your teenager becomes an independent, resilient and secure adult (Figure 10.1).

When our children are younger, it might feel easier to notice and praise the times when things are going well, as this is something we've become conditioned to do as part of a "praise and reward" parenting methodology. I often overhear parents saying, "Well done" to their child when they've behaved in a way they approve of, and indeed our whole education system is based on achievement – on getting good grades and being rewarded for good behaviour. Conversely, there is a system of punishing bad or unacceptable behaviour with negative consequences or through

DOI: 10.4324/9780429459245-11

systems such as behaviour points in schools. These methods teach children there is a right and wrong way of doing things and that approval is necessary for them to succeed. But what about learning from our mistakes and failures? And where is the attention and recognition for older teenagers as they start to figure out how to navigate their own way in the world? We tend to pay a lot less attention to the behaviour we want to see in young adults and yet this is an extremely vulnerable time when it's needed just as much as when our children were toddlers.

Ask yourself, "What kind of a relationship do I want with my adult child?" and "What kind of adult or parent do I want *them* to be?" Being a reflective parent is not just about how you interact with your child now, but also how the way you relate to them now impacts the way they interact with other people in the future. If you want a reflective, insightful, emotionally attuned and intelligent young adult, then using the stance of reflective parenting now and modelling a way of relating to other people, will help your teenager use this same set of reflective skills in their own relationships and ultimately (if they have them), with their own children. Your influence as a reflective parent can have huge benefits for the next generation in your family, building on this model of secure attachment relationships.

Throughout this book, we've explored the relationship between secure attachment and reflective parenting, but it's worth reminding ourselves about the practice of reflective parenting as it's in adulthood that your child can reap all the benefits of this approach, even after you've gone. After all, one day your child will need to draw on all that they've learned from you without having you there – we all have a finite amount of time.

How reflective parenting links to secure attachment

Reflecting on the thoughts and feelings of your child teaches them that both you and they have a mind.

In early childhood, mirroring the thoughts and feelings of your child, for example by saying things like, "You're cold, have a blanket," or "You look sad, let me cuddle you," helps them learn an "emotional vocabulary."

Mirroring the thoughts and feelings of your child helps them to understand not only how they feel, but also gives them a sense that *you* understand how they feel and possibly *why*. It helps your child to feel understood.

Having a feeling that their feelings are understood helps your child to manage or regulate their feelings.

Having a parent who helps them understand how they feel and possibly why they feel this way, helps your child to feel they have a parent who has their mind on them and is interested in them.

Learning about feelings in themselves and others helps a child to learn to mentalize. This means they can start to understand the thoughts and feelings of not only themselves but also of other people. They learn to be more in tune with others, empathetic towards others, and appreciative of other perspectives that are different from their own.

Appreciating other perspectives and having empathy for others helps your child to build their relationship skills, so friendships develop easily.

Being able to mentalize is the foundation of secure attachment and instils in your child a feeling that other people are to be trusted, are helpful and available and that they are *worthy* of and *deserve* that helpful response. It simultaneously increases self-esteem and trust in others.

Our attachment to a parent/key carer is a key factor in how we develop resilience in later life. When you take a reflective parenting approach, building up a sense of security in your child, you will find that this sits inside them and will remain with them as they move into adulthood and begin to take on more. In the field of developmental psychology, a helpful concept is the "internal working model" of attachment. This concept can be imagined as a template that you hold onto in your mind and draw on whenever you need it. Our attachment to a parent/key carer is a key factor in how we develop resilience in later life. In fact, it operates unconsciously most of the time without you really noticing it. Think for a moment about what you do when you're stuck, for instance, if you've locked yourself out of the house. Do you stand there helplessly, sobbing on the doorstep? Or do you ask for help, from a neighbour or phone your partner? Most of us in this situation would ask someone else for help. We do this because we've learned from very early on that if we're stuck and need help, we can trust that there will be someone there to help us, and, importantly and hopefully, we've learned that we deserve that help. Not everyone will have this model of secure attachment. Some of you reading this might think you wouldn't feel confident that someone else would be able to or even want to help you. You might think that others might judge you for being so useless that you locked yourself out of the house; thinking this way is probably in part a reflection of your own "internal working model" of attachment. This doesn't mean however, that you can't help your own child to develop a different and more secure model of attachment, so that they learn to expect help from other people and develop their own secure internal working model. Reflective parenting is a tool to help you support your child to develop more features of security in their working models, and it's never too late to start this process.

The transition from teenager to adult

When does your teenager become an adult in your mind? This is a deeper question than it might first appear. It's tempting perhaps to go with the "official" age of 18. This is, after all, the age you can vote and move out on your own. If you think about your teenager at this age, do you consider them to have reached full maturity as an adult? Or is this 18-year-old adult tag actually a pretty unhelpful one, in lots of different regards?

Brain development into adulthood

When we look at brain development, it's factually inaccurate to describe an eighteen-year-old as an adult. Our brains haven't fully developed until we're in our mid-twenties, From the age of 18 until around 25 years old, sometimes even later, our brains are still developing. As discussed in Chapter 1, in terms of neurological development, a critical part of the brain – the prefrontal cortex – hasn't yet fully matured. This is the part of the brain that helps us to inhibit impulses and plan and organise our behaviour to reach a goal. It seems ironic then that this most important part of the brain for organising our lives hasn't fully matured at the age when there are numerous expectations to behave in a more grown-up way. I imagine many of you reading this, who have young adults older than 18, are of course still greatly concerned for their mental health. Furthermore, if you are caring for a young person who has experienced early trauma, for instance, if you are a foster carer or your teenager had a particularly difficult early life experience, the impact of this trauma on the development of their prefrontal cortex will contribute further to the slow maturity of this part of the brain. Somebody who has had an unstable home life is more likely to have trouble with planning and organising and with inhibiting impulses than somebody who has had a stable upbringing. It is important to recognise this isn't their fault but is part of their developing brain needing a longer time period and greater security and support before they reach full adult maturity.

The other part of the brain that is still developing up to the age of around 25 is the reward system which, having become highly active right around the time of puberty, gradually becomes less active, until around the age of 25, when it settles down to its adult level, where it will remain. This means that the risk-taking behaviour we looked at earlier in the book is still part of the post-18-year-old teenager/young adult's way of seeing the world; these young adults are still more interested in entering uncertain situations to seek out possible rewards, often without thinking through the risks. It also means that peer pressure and sensitivity to the views of others, so prevalent in adolescence, is still an important feature of young adulthood; so a 20-year-old will still be 50% more likely to do something risky when they are with their peers than when alone, compared with adults *over* the age of 25. There are some gender differences, too, when we look at brain development and the path to adult maturity, with girls' brains reaching maturity approximately two years before the brains of boys. Many of the risks associated with adolescence, such as driving recklessly, taking drugs, drinking too much, or doing something illegal, still apply to those aged 18 to 25. However, because these young adults have less parental supervision, there is even more opportunity to get into trouble. You are less likely to be vigilant of your 19-year-old teenager than you are of your 15-year-old one, and yet this is the time when the risk is often higher. Of course, this includes being less likely to monitor or even have any insight, into their online life – this may be significantly impacting their mental health. Keeping up a reflective parenting stance, wherein you keep your curiosity and interest in the mind of your teenager, is hugely important in helping your young adult to reflect on their own vulnerability and to access your support and guidance.

The second reason the 18-year-old adult label is unhelpful is that young adults are struggling with their mental health. In many countries, they are deemed too old for children's services but are often highly unsuitable to enter any adult mental health support system, which is set up for mature adults. It would make much more sense for mental health services to support young people up to the age of 25; while in some sectors this is increasingly becoming the case, although sadly this is often not the case in mental health services such as in the UK NHS Child and adolescent mental health service (CAMHS).

The vulnerability of being a young adult

The teenage and young adult years are a crucial time for supporting your young person's mental health. The following statistics can be alarming but being aware of them can help you understand the vulnerability of adolescents and young adults. You can in turn appreciate how using the reflective parenting approach outlined throughout this book can help your teenager through this difficult transition, which can be much harder if left to their own devices. Let's remind ourselves of how long the vulnerability of adolescents and young adults lasts. The latest estimates from 2021 for mental health problems state that 1 in 6 children aged between 6 and 16 experience a "common mental disorder" – which refers to problems such as anxiety, depression and problems with self-esteem. Statistics show that 50% of mental health problems are established by age 14 and 75% by age 24.

Furthermore, in 2020, the leading cause of death for people aged 5–34 was "intentional self-harm," a truly shocking statistic. Rates of hospital admission because of self-harm in children and young people (aged 10–24) are considerably higher for females than males. Between 2012/13 and 2019/20, the rate of hospital admissions for females increased from 508 per 100,000 population to 695 per 100,000 population. Over the same period, the rate for males fluctuated around 200 admissions per 100,000 population. It is obvious to see that our young people are massively struggling, and things have become much harder for them over the past few years. The combination of a global pandemic, with all its missed rites of passage, loss of social relationships, and opportunities for growth; the climate crisis threatening the very existence of the future of the planet and a cost-of-living crisis has left many young people extremely pessimistic about how they can live an independent and financially sustainable future and has had a huge impact on the mental health of our young people. They need our support and guidance more than ever, and not feel that they are left to sort it out all on their own, or that their future needs aren't being planned for.

Parenting a young adult

Just as we instinctively adjust our parenting as adolescents move from younger to older teenagers, we also need to do so during the transition from older teenager to young adult. Some of your young adult's needs will be the same as they were when they were very young: to feel secure, loved and understood. Some of their needs will be different, which means you need to move from being the protector and teacher to something more like an "arms-length" guide, pointing your young adult in the right direction without actually taking them there. It's important to remember that, for all of us, mentalization is fragile and we continually lose the ability to think reflectively; for example, when we are stressed, our capacity to mentalize at the moment is reduced. We have thought about your role as a parent to your teenager, they can turn to you as their secure attachment person when they receive an emotional impact that disturbs their capacity to mentalize – to reflect on thoughts and feelings. At these moments, you can help them to feel calm and recover the ability to mentalize. For young adults, if their "working model" of attachment, outlined above, is robust/secure, this will be internalised and will work even when they are away from you. So if an event has an emotional impact that wobbles their mentalizing skills, their positive relationship with you will mean that they can access this inner resource. It's a form of emotional security, like always having a bit of money in the bank, so that in difficult times, there is an inner resource your young adult can draw on.

Getting the balance right between action and reflection

You will be an effective reflective parent with your young adult if you can apply the different elements of mentalizing appropriately with them. It is a tricky balance as you reflect on what you think and feel and what you imagine your young adult thinks and feels, working hard not to conflate the two, which will lead to misunderstandings between you. The older your teenager gets, the more you will need to step back and reflect on their perspective and way of doing things, and the more you will need to resist the urge to advise as you let them find their way. Parenting is continually challenging your capacity to cope with uncertainty, feelings of helplessness, lack of control and your ability to manage your own overwhelming feelings. As your teenager grows into a young adult, you will be challenged if you see them suffering, whether because of failures at work or in relationships, or because of struggles with their physical and mental health, and your urge is likely to be to fix things and take their pain away. At times like these, you will be tempted to go back to one of the pre-mentalizing modes we described in the introduction to this book. For example, you might want to deploy quick-fix strategies to make your young adult feel better, such as giving them money to make them feel less hopeless. Or you might hold onto an idealistic and unrealistic hope, for example, saying to yourself "When they're older, all this stress and heartache will go away."

We all fall into these unhelpful pre-mentalizing modes at times of high emotional arousal as we lose the ability to think more reflectively. When your mind is dominated by these kinds of thoughts, you start to lose your curiosity about your young adult's thoughts and behaviour as well as your ability to consider different perspectives. This carries a risk of judging their behaviour negatively. For example, if you aren't mentalizing you might think, "They aren't mature enough to handle adult situations, I'll need to step in and sort this out," as opposed to taking a more mentalizing approach, which might lead you to think, "They are obviously struggling here and I wonder what is getting in their way? I wonder if they're worried about not being good enough for that job/course/relationship." Recognising the differences between these approaches – mentalizing and non-mentalizing – can help you see how a reflective approach can help your young adult manage their own emotions through your curiosity about what they're feeling and your message to them that you understand and can respond to how they think and feel. In doing this, you also help your young adult to recover their own capacity to think more reflectively, which, in turn, helps them to problem-solve for themselves, with some support from you or other important people around them.

A young person's perspective

What does a young adult need compared to an older person? I spoke to many young adults as part of my research for this book and found some interesting reflections. A young adult wants to be able to make their own decisions and not have so many boundaries set, so this means they need their parent to be less directive and they want to be spoken to on the same level rather than being talked at or talked down to, and told what to do. They are hypersensitive to how parents and authority figures in general speak to them and say they want the tone to feel less patronising, down to earth, and calm. Generally, it's important to be more forgiving of older teens and young adults because they want to feel older. For example, if your young adult talks to you about a job they are thinking of applying for, ask them for their view of the pros and cons of the position and how they want to approach the interview, rather than start explaining to them what you think they need to do to prepare and whether you think it's a good job or not. If you don't mentalize this need to be treated as a grown-up, you are at risk of talking down to your young person in a way that feels judgemental and critical of their best intentions. For example, a young person is probably aware that they want to be helpful around the house rather than be treated like a kid and told how to behave, so you should assume they will be helpful and be more forgiving when they're not. Young people say they still want to have boundaries, but the way that these are expressed by parents is very important to them.

As part of my conversations with the focus groups for this book, I had these conversations with 20-year-old Liam and 21-year-old Jenna. Let's look at their perspective on how they would like to be treated by their parents.

Liam is 20 years old and has been living at home with his parents and two younger brothers during the Covid-19 lockdown for his gap year. At the release of the Covid restrictions, he's been enjoying going out for nights with his friends and has been partying. He feels secure and happy at home but is keen to move away and start a more independent life. He spoke about what he felt he would like from his parents as a young adult.

"Not being judged is important. If I had a good night and went to a party, had a great time and came back late, rather than knocking something I enjoy by moaning about what time I got home, they could embrace my enjoyment, that would make me more likely to want to talk to them and not close down." I asked him what it would feel like if they were a bit more judgemental, critical or even jokey about his social life. Liam said, "It would kill a bit of the enjoyment and make me wish I had a parent who asked me about something that I'd enjoyed, but not asking too many questions." I asked Liam, "How do parents strike the balance between being curious and just being interested and supportive?" Liam was clear that for him it was about his parents "being understanding rather than making you feel shit; so not saying 'Oh, someone's hungover' making the situation worse by mocking." I asked him, "What about if your parents were feeling anxious or worried about your safety when you're out late with friends at parties, what should they do?" Liam said, "They should hide it. Their anxiety is not going to stop a young person from doing what they want to do but would be annoying and possibly make the young person anxious."

With regard to his parents' role in giving advice, I asked Liam, "What things would he still like advice on?" Liam said that at his age he felt, the only way guidance and advice is going to be taken on is if "the situation is accepted first." For example, "If they want to talk to me about drug use, accept that I take drugs and have a conversation about how much I'm using." I questioned this and asked if everything needed to be led by the young person. Liam said, "No, not everything. With things like work, organisation, money, and structuring life, advice from parents can be useful because this helps with forward planning and organisation. I think you need someone who can help you achieve what you want to achieve, give you a plan to help you get there and then set a plan in place. It's not just about giving a plan, but the way it's communicated is important, so it's rational and reasonable rather than judgemental and demanding."

Jenna is 21 and lives away from home with three friends from school. Jenna did an apprentice internship after she left school and is now working for the business where she did this. I asked Jenna about her experiences and how she thought parents could be most and least helpful at her age. Jenna said, "For the bigger stuff – you just need a parent to be around, be supportive and be present, to literally be close by. If (I'm) going through a breakup or mental health crisis, time alone feels really difficult, so just an invitation to go for lunch would be great." I asked Jenna if it was different now she lived away from home. She said, "When you're away and you've got your friends around you, it's not so much practical stuff then, it's more the knowledge that your parents are there, even if you don't want to visit them. The knowledge of a safe environment with your family – seeing them and even your pets – is a nice thing to have. Distraction can also help, because trying to work through difficult feelings at times can involve going through pain."

Jenna has had a few struggles with her mental health and relationships over the past year but has found her upbringing has helped her to deal with things, to an extent. I asked her if she felt her parents had helped her when she was going through these difficulties and she replied, "I didn't really need them to do anything, just knowing they were there somewhere in the background was enough. Certain thoughts and feelings can't be controlled but I just found myself accepting the terrible feelings and tolerating them."

Jenna went on to say, "A parent will give advice, but ultimately when you're down, you don't want to hear how to get out of it from anyone else other than yourself. Having someone try to fix your pain is only going to make you feel more annoyed, it doesn't work. Sometimes just the presence of someone calm and secure can make you feel better, even without saying anything."

Reflecting on Liam and Jenna

Liam and Jenna both express the wish for their parents to mentalize them – by accepting their feelings, whether positive or negative, and resisting their urge to fix things for their children to make them feel better. Neither of them wants their parents to give them the solution to their problems, acknowledging that no one can know exactly what it feels like to be them. I am struck by the importance for both young people of acceptance and love from their parents, but I also understood them saying that parental words often don't help. Liam told me that in his experience, "going through the pain and learning the strength from your own experience" was important to him. They both underline the point that the parent's job is to steer rather than sort everything out because it's important for the young person to work out for themselves what makes them happy and what direction they should take. These young people are clear that they want to draw on their parents' support to help point them in the right direction and to be treated like another adult rather than a kid. The backdrop to this parenting, however, is a feeling of being looked after and cared for, while also being respected as a separate individual.

Liam and Jenna both seem to have mentalized themselves and their parents pretty well, and they are good examples of young adults who have clear ideas about how their parents can support them. It indicates that they have had a good experience with relatively reflective parents, and a secure relationship, because they can envisage themselves navigating their own way in the world without constant interference from their parents, while also acknowledging that they need their parents as a secure backdrop to their lives, to help them take the right route, but independently. Here's an example of a young adult who is struggling with living independently from her parents.

> Jasmine is 19 years old and has moved away from her family in the town she grew up in, to a university 150 miles away. In the year before she started uni, she had a gap year planned, but the Covid-19 pandemic was ongoing and her options for travel were limited. She had managed a brief trip to Italy but found that most of the time there was spent in lockdown, so she returned home and worked at a local cafe to earn money before she started uni. Her family don't have much spare money and Jasmine felt a bit anxious about heading to uni without any money of her own to support what she expected was going to be a very busy social life. Jasmine is of dual heritage; her dad is Black British of Jamaican heritage, and her mum is White Irish. At school, she had a culturally diverse group of friends and a girlfriend whom she'd been dating since Year 11.
>
> Arriving at uni, Jasmine found herself sharing a corridor with eight people in one of the student villages on the university campus. There were five other young women and two men in the corridor; all of them are white and, to Jasmine, they all seem to be posh compared with the group of friends she had at school. People talk about expensive holidays to places Jasmine has never heard of and use a language that seems almost alien to her. The first night on campus, they suggest a drinking game that goes on until 3 am, by which time Jasmine is desperate to go to bed and get away from them. She texts her parents at 4 am after lying awake crying for an hour and, when they don't reply, she phones her mum to tell her how much she hates it at Uni and tells her she wants to ditch it. She immediately feels bad as soon as she hears her mum's disappointed, anxious voice as she knows her parents will feel massively disappointed as she's the first person in the family to get a place at uni. They were so proud when she got the offer after her good exam results. Hearing her mum's voice just makes Jasmine start crying harder.

Reflecting on Jasmine

Jasmine is feeling completely out of place. She seems to have a strong sense of not being with familiar people. We can understand her gut feeling that she wants to ditch the whole uni experience and go home where she feels more understood and more of a fit. Perhaps she is missing her girlfriend a lot and this strong feeling of being away from all the people she loves might be compounding the feeling of being different from the other students in her accommodation. Is it possible that these feelings are even exaggerating the sense of difference she feels? At the same time, we can empathise with that feeling of being away from home and in an environment where she feels alienated. It must be a lonely and potentially frightening place to be. She is used to having a more diverse group of friends and the visible and invisible differences between her and her uni corridor group are exacerbating her sense of being different and isolated. She has had a year of being locked down and thwarted in her attempts to gain a sense of freedom when she travelled to Italy but found herself in lockdown again. The compulsion to be free to do what she wants and to feel connected to others must be even stronger than it might normally be in this circumstance. Should Jasmine sit it out and hope things look and feel differently in the morning, or run home to her family where she feels she belongs?

Reflecting on Jasmine's parents

What must it feel like for Jasmine's parents to get a call from a distraught daughter in the middle of the night? Her parents found it hard to say goodbye to Jasmine as she's their only child and both had been dreading the day she would leave home, while at the same time feeling a strong sense of pride in her achievements. This is a totally new experience for them; they have no idea what it feels like to go to university and neither of them knows the area at all well: how safe it is, how friendly people are there, and so on. We can imagine how anxious they must feel, being so far away and hearing how much she "hates" it there and how different she feels from the others in her accommodation. They must be torn between wanting to rescue her and bring her back and encouraging her to give it time and possibly explore other alternative accommodations if the situation continues, rather than leave uni altogether. They must have a strong urge to fix things for their daughter. Jasmine's mum

Figure 10.1

is finding it particularly hard to manage her anxiety and lets all her feelings out to her daughter on the phone call. She probably regrets this immediately afterwards but is struggling to let go of her anxious thoughts.

The reflective parenting perspective

This vignette about Jasmine captures the common tension parents experience when they have a young adult in the family: letting go and facilitating independence versus protecting the child and keeping them close to the family. It reminds us of the idea of the parents as a safe harbour, mentioned in Chapter 7, while the teenager/young adult is setting off to sea in a boat without them. If you take a mentalizing approach, you can resolve this internal conflict of holding on versus letting go and achieve both.

This is a new situation for both Jasmine and her parents. They need to listen and empathise with her position and validate her, but not make her feel so different from them. In keeping with the reflective parenting model, it is important for Jasmine's parents first to manage their own feelings and acknowledge they don't know what it is like for her as they haven't experienced going to university. It might be helpful for them to acknowledge that they are more anxious because this is something unknown to them. Even if you did go to uni, it's still helpful to acknowledge that your child's experience is still their own. If they can recognise what they are feeling and then separate out their own wish to pressure her to stay from her experience and the strong feeling that she wants to rush back home, it will make it easier for them to listen and empathise without leaping to a panicky, non-mentalizing response.

Ideally, what will help Jasmine most is for her parents to be supportive and available, but also for them to help her become a bit independent and work out how she is going to navigate her way through the first few weeks at university. This is easier said than done, especially considering the phone call has come in at 4 am and so her parents are naturally going to think that things are pretty serious (Jasmine hasn't previously been someone to call her parents for help at odd hours of the night).

Taking a step back

Regulating your own emotions as a parent is difficult to do when your anxiety is increasing rapidly, so ideally what both her parents and Jasmine need in this scenario is to buy some space and time. Her parents might start by listening empathically, repeating back some of what Jasmine tells them, which is called verbal mirroring. For example, they could say "They are all speaking in a way that's hard to understand. You didn't want to stay up that late, drinking, on your first night. That sounds very hard and confusing for you. I'm really sorry you're so upset." After this, they might move to emphasise their availability and consistent presence in Jasmine's life (underlining the fact that the safety and security of family hasn't gone away just because she's moved out of home). For example, her mum might say, "We are here whenever you need us, Jasmine. If you want to stick it out for the week and then come home at the weekend or want one of us to come up and visit you in a week or so, we can do that. You can ring us or message us any time and we will listen. If you want any help in planning the next week, we can sit together and do that. We trust you to be able to get through this, even though it feels tough right now." Using a combination of a reflective approach with a practical plan that helps Jasmine to feel safe – putting into action the two-hands approach from Chapter 1 – will help Jasmine to feel that they want to understand her experience. At the same time, they will be setting an age-appropriate expectation for her to try to manage and make her way through her first few weeks at uni without coming home too quickly.

As we've outlined throughout this book, one of the most important things a parent can do for a teenager or young adult is to try to listen (despite their rising strong feelings of anxiety) and then to see it from their child's point of view, as well as their own. This perspective-taking approach is one of the most important tools of the reflective parenting skill set, and is even more relevant with young adults than young teenagers because they feel they have formed their own identity and worldview, which needs to be validated and respected. Try to keep in mind that when we're truly mentalizing, we can see the same situation from different perspectives, not just our own. It doesn't mean necessarily agreeing with the other perspective, but it means being able to acknowledge and be curious about it. However hard it is for Jasmine's parents to understand her wish to run away from uni after the first night, it's so important that they acknowledge this is truly how she feels in the moment. Being able to see the situation from her point of view will help her manage the overwhelming feelings she's having at that time. Also, try not to be too defensive if your teenager attacks you when you suggest something. It is quite likely this reaction is born partly out of insecurity and fear and partly out of a need to find a way to deal with things without you. The best thing you can do in this situation is stand very still and solid, offering support and consistency, and then gently steer your teenager in the direction you think they need to travel to find their own happiness.

Staying with the family and living an adult life

Cultural norms or a person's economic situation can mean that some young people stay at home with their parents well into adult life and many young people live with their parents well into adult life for economic reasons. While this has always been the case for many families, more young adults are living with their parents for longer because of the rising cost of living in many countries. This can create a difficult family dynamic as inherent in the situation is the inbuilt frustration of a young person who doesn't want to be living with their parents but independent living is simply unaffordable. However, one advantage to a young adult living at home while they find their way in the world, is that there is an immediate level of support that possibly wouldn't be accessed so readily if the young person was living away from home. On the other hand, easy access to this support can stifle the independence of young adults, leaving them with less developed life skills than their contemporaries who have moved to independent living.

There are also pros and cons for parents in this situation; many parents I've spoken to have said that they frequently vacillate between positive feelings about the intimacy that is still there with their child, and the more negative feeling that parents are needed for support and nurturing (including for cooking and often household chores) long after they had anticipated relinquishing some of these responsibilities. Also, as young adults form their own, often strong, opinions about relationships – including those in the family – parents can sometimes feel judged on their performance as a parent. The roles become confused between parent and child, where the child is taking authority and judging the parent for how they live. The parents' values are no longer the dominant values in the family. One parent in a focus group for this book said she finds it hard to kick back at this judgement because of fear of alienating her child.

Many young adults have left home to go to university (over 50% of the UK school population attend university) and when they return home, on holiday, or at the end of a degree they have set boundaries for themselves that they don't want to lose on their return; they don't want to be infantilised. For example, the time they go to bed and wake up in the morning according to their peer group will not necessarily be something they want, or need, to immediately change when they return home. Also, the privacy a young person has when they are away from home needs to be respected by other family members when they return.

Some parents will try to implement a financial arrangement, whereby their young person contributes to rent and food; your beliefs about this issue will depend on your own values and the economic situation of your child. It's important to draw out the difference between parenting in a way where young adults fit into the parents' lives and where young adults have their own independent lives with parents fitting their needs around this.

The experience of sharing your home with an adult child

Having adult children living at home means sharing your home with other adults, which does bring some joy, but at other times brings pressures. For example, it involves drawing up a new set of guidelines on how you will all live together – whether you eat together, how you share the chores, and so on. Some families will simply maintain their roles as the main carers and providers, but the disadvantage of this is it keeps the adult children in a dependent role where they can potentially stagnate and fail to take the type of risks that involve them having to navigate a way through life's challenges, such as opening bank accounts or getting prepared for an interview. If you stay in the same role you have always had in their lives, the risk is that they will mirror this and stay in their adolescent roles for much longer. It can also send a message to your adult child that you don't see them as being capable of these adult challenges, leaving them feeling helpless and overly dependent. Living with adult children makes it much harder to step back and let them fix their own emotional problems and many parents slip, almost unconsciously, into old roles of parenting a much younger teenager. However, the advantage of having adult children at home means that you have more opportunities for social interaction with them, and can enjoy a sense of closeness and fun. Some parents say they feel it "keeps them young." For others, though, having adult children at home makes them feel they have stagnated in the role of "forever carers" when they want to move on to the next stage of their lives. I recall one adoptive parent of a particularly dependent and anxious young man who was starting to worry that he might not reach independent living until long after she retired, and it compromised her expectations about the plans she'd previously made for her retirement travels. This bred resentment on both sides, with the son feeling resentful and a little ashamed that he depended so much on his mum, and the parent feeling angry and upset at the loss of an anticipated increased independence and new direction in her retirement years.

Maintaining a connection into adulthood

Modelling "safe uncertainty" as discussed in Chapter 3, and curiosity is a key aspect of reflective parenting that continues to be so helpful to your older teenager or adult child. Much of reflective parenting in action is about everyday, mundane stuff, but you may have much bigger, more serious worries about your teenager; for example, what if they told you, "Mum, I sometimes feel really low and I can't seem to shake it off." Your instinct might be to say, "Oh love, I'm sorry. How about we get a takeaway and watch a movie together?" because you want them to stop feeling low and to be happy. Unfortunately, this approach usually doesn't work. Instead, try taking a curious, non-expert approach, that is, one of "safe uncertainty." You could say something like, "I'm sorry you feel low. It's horrible isn't it when you feel like that? Any idea why you're feeling like that? You can talk to me if you feel like it. Or not. I'm always here for you." This won't be any more of a quick fix than getting the takeaway, but it will send a very important communication to your teenager: that although they are forging their own identity apart from you and the family, you are still just as available to them as you were when they were little. It might feel very difficult for you to be empathic, particularly if you feel your job as a parent is to always make your child happy. However, once you recognise and acknowledge to your older teenager or young adult that *all* feelings are important and valid and they can all be tolerated equally, it won't feel nearly as hard for them to name some of their innermost difficult feelings. In turn, this will keep the connection and communication going between you, as opposed to closing it down immediately by not showing any curiosity about what's going on.

When a parent's expectations for an older teenager or adult child don't line up with what the child is thinking or doing, conflict can arise. Here are some tips for maintaining a connection with your teenager into their early adulthood:

- Encourage some independence in your adult child and try not to be over-protective or overly enabling, thinking this will be in their best interests. The problems of being an unmotivated adult child are much greater than the problems of getting a job and learning to live independently.
- Learning new behaviours as an adult child living at home won't happen naturally without you setting expectations and boundaries. For example, an adolescent who has been used to having his clothes picked up off the bathroom floor, won't naturally develop into an adult who picks up his own clothes

unless you make your expectations for a different set of adult-like behaviours clear.

- Recognise that you have a responsibility as your young adult's parent to let them fight their own battles and not blame you if things don't work out for them. Avoid doing everything in your power to protect your young adults from feeling discomfort and know that a little discomfort is not a bad thing.
- One of the best skills you can give your child is problem-solving. Giving them independence and the skills to solve problems will help them become happy and resilient adults. Fixing and solving their problems for them stifles an important developmental milestone and makes your adult child ultimately more vulnerable and unable to cope.
- Set a structure and some achievable expectations for your adult child around things such as applying for jobs, getting up at a certain time, and taking responsibility for the care of the home they live in.
- Think of your adult child's future and not just their current life. You can still offer security and comfort while setting realistic expectations for them. This is how young children need to be parented in order to reach the next developmental milestone, and adult children need the same.
- By failing to set any expectations around their transition from teenager to young adult, you are essentially communicating that you don't expect them to be able to achieve this transition. For example, if you tell your adult child they need to work and they don't and you accept this, you are communicating to them that they aren't capable and you know it. They are getting the message that there's something wrong with them because they don't know how to deal with discomfort and distress.
- Instead, set an example by holding on to the hope for your adult child. When you say, "I think you could go for that job, even though it's probably quite competitive to get shortlisted," you are telling them that you believe in them and think they are as good as anyone else. This supports self-esteem and confidence and nurtures development.
- Keep using your reflective parenting, mentalizing, tools to regulate your own emotions and help your young adult to understand and regulate theirs (using your parent MAP and APP to help remind you when needed).

Your continuing influence on your adult's life

Parenting young adults into their twenties is one of the least written about and researched stages of parenting, but you may find this is one of your most challenging phases, for all the reasons described in this chapter. Whether your adult child is doing well or finding their early twenties are fraught with challenges and obstacles, your role as the taken-for-granted safe harbour to which they can return is hugely reassuring and helpful to their development as adults. You will always be an important influence on your adult child and how they feel about and see themselves will always be partly influenced by the way you have parented them. Never underestimate how important it is for your teenager and young adult to have your interest in them; that need for your attention and curiosity they felt as 3-year-old children is still just as important to them in their twenties. You may express it very differently, but it will always matter to your child to feel your pride, interest and empathy for their thoughts and feelings. This is ongoing until your young adult is your age and older. Knowing that there is always a place they can return to, where a friendly curiosity about them is waiting, is an important buffer to a young adult's life's hurdles. Even if your adult child has physically left home, having an emotional home to which they can return is still important. Your home could be literally the place they return to, or it could be an internalised sense of security they can return to in their minds, even when they are far away from you. If you have taken a reflective parenting stance, the chances are much higher that this sense of your supportive curiosity and interest in them has been embedded in their minds and will help them become independent, happy, and resilient adults.

PAUSE AND REFLECT: KEEPING A CONNECTION

In a nutshell …

Applying a reflective parenting approach to your teenager into young adulthood will help you to have more connected and harmonious times in your family. Keeping a connection means thinking about the thoughts, feelings and intentions of your teenager into their twenties and beyond. Understanding that many of the challenges of adolescence are still present into the mid-twenties will help you to keep using a mentalizing stance and support their mental health.

Reflective parenting helps you keep a connection by ...

Keeping a reflective parenting approach going into your teenager's early adulthood helps you to stay open to being curious and attentive to their thoughts and feelings, even when you think they need you less. You are modelling something just as important to your adult child as you were during their teenage years, perhaps more so as your relationship changes and they look to you perhaps less defensively than in their teenage years.

Mentalizing your teenager/adult child helps them by ...

Mental health difficulties and life's challenges are just as prevalent, if not more so, when your teenager reaches adulthood. The brain is still developing into the mid-twenties and so is vulnerable to impulsive risk-taking, mental health crises and confusion about relationships, decision-making and forward planning. If you show your older teenager that you are interested in understanding their perspective on these things you are still communicating that, "although you are more independent, I understand and am interested in helping you work out things for yourself." The message to your older teenager is that they are capable of making their own choices, but that you still want to help them when they need you. By mentalizing them, you are also communicating that you are treating them as more of an equal and they will feel more confident and competent as a result.

Reflective parenting helps your relationship by ...

Applying a reflective parenting approach and thinking about the mind of your teenager into adulthood will help you to have more enjoyable times together as you will feel close to one another. Reflective parenting – with its foundations in attachment theory – helps build secure and trustworthy relationships and if you keep this going into your young adult's life they will greatly benefit. You will be supporting them from an arms-length but still communicating that you are there when they need you. This sends a message to your teenager that you have confidence in their abilities and maintains a secure base that allows them to assume they can always ask for help.

Keep in mind ...

- Keep an open door of communication between you and your teenager.
- Help your adult child to problem-solve by asking how they see a situation and how other people might think or feel about it – with a focus on a positive outcome.
- Always make time in your life for your adult child, even if you think they don't want or need it all the time. Send the message that your relationship and concern for their well-being is ongoing and show recognition that turning 18 doesn't mean they are capable of organising their own life entirely on their own!
- Encourage your adult child to reflect by modelling and mentalizing yourself.
- The more you show an interest and curiosity in seeing things through your adult child's eyes, the more rewarding you will find your times are together.

REFERENCES

Introduction

1. Bateman, A., & Fonagy, P. (2004). Mentalization-based treatment for borderline personality disorder. *Journal of Personality Disorders*, 18(1), 36–51.
2. Redfern, S. (2016). *Reflective parenting: A guide to understanding what's going on in your child's mind*. Hove, East Sussex: Routledge.
3. Shriver, L. (2018). *Property: A collection*. London: Harper Collins. ISBN: 978000826525
4. Fonagy, P., Redfern, S., & Charman, T. (1997). The relationship between belief-desire reasoning and a projective measure of attachment security (SAD). *British Journal of Developmental Psychology*, 15, 51–61.
5. Blakemore, S. J. (2018). *Inventing ourselves. The secret life of the teenage brain*. New York: Penguin Random House.
6. Fonagy, P., & Allison, E. (2012). What is mentalization? The concept and its foundations in developmental research. In N. Midgley & I. Vrouva (Eds.), *Minding the child: Mentalization-based inter ventions with children, young people and their families* (pp. 11–34). New York: Routledge.

Chapter 1 – Reflective parenting during adolescence: Understanding and nurturing connection

1. Fonagy, P., & Luyten, P. (2018). Conduct problems in youth and the RDoC approach: A developmental, evolutionary-based view. *Clinical Psychology Review*, 64, 57–76. Doi: 10.1016/j.cpr.2017.08.010
2. Blakemore, S. J. (2018). *Inventing ourselves. The secret life of the teenage brain*. Penguin Random House.
3. Carey, S., Diamond, R., & Woods, B. (1980). Development of face recognition: A maturational component? *Developmental Psychology*, 16(4), 257–269. Doi: 10.1037/0012-1649.16.4.257

4. Hauser, S. T., Allen, J. P., & Golden, E. (2006). *Out of the woods: Tales of teen resilience*. Cambridge, MA: Harvard University Press.
5. Suchman, N. E., DeCoste, C., Leigh, D., & Borelli, J. (2010). Reflective functioning in mothers with drug use disorders: Implications for dyadic interactions with infants and toddlers. *Attachment and Human Development*, 12, 567–585.
6. Suchman, N. E., Decoste, C., McMahon, T. J., et al. (2011). The mothers and toddlers Program, an attachment-based parenting intervention for substance-using women: Results at 6-week follow-up in a randomized clinical pilot. *Infant Mental Health Journal*, 32, 427–449.
7. Suchman, N. E., Decoste, C., Rosenberger, P., & McMahon, T. J. (2012). Attachment-based intervention for substance-using mothers: A preliminary test of the proposed mechanisms of change. *Infant Mental Health Journal*, 33, 360–371.

Chapter 2 – Reflecting on yourself as a parent

1. Fonagy, P., Target, M., Steele, H., & Steele, M. (1998). *Reflective-functioning manual, version 5, for application to adult attachment interviews*. London, UK: University College London.
2. George, C., Kaplan, N., & Main, M. (1985). The adult attachment interview. Unpublished manuscript. Department of Psychology, University of California at Berkeley.
3. Suchman, N. E., Decoste, C., Rosenberger, P., & McMahon, T. J. (2012). Attachment-based intervention for substance-using mothers: A preliminary test of the proposed mechanisms of change. *Infant Mental Health Journal*, 33, 360–371.
4. Baumrind, D. (1991). Parenting styles and adolescent development. In J. Brooks-Gunn, R. M. Lerner, & A. C. Petersen (Eds.), *The encyclopedia on adolescence* (pp. 746–758). New York: Garland Publishing.
5. Asen, E., & Morris, M. (2020). *High-conflict parenting post-separation. The making and breaking of family ties*. Abingdon, Oxon: Routledge.
6. Suchman, N. E., Decoste, C., Rosenberger, P., & McMahon, T. J. (2012). Attachment-based intervention for substance-using mothers: A preliminary test of the proposed mechanisms of change. *Infant Mental Health Journal*, 33, 360–371.

Chapter 4 – Autonomy: Your teenager's need to separate

1. Fonagy, P., Redfern, S., & Charman, T. (1997). The relationship between belief-desire reasoning and a projective measure of attachment security (SAD). *British Journal of Developmental Psychology*, 15, 51–61.
2. Blakemore, S. J. (2018). *Inventing ourselves. The secret life of the teenage brain*. Penguin Random House.

Chapter 5 – Autonomy: Your teenager's social world

1. Allen, J. P. (2008). The attachment system in adolescence. In J. Cassidy, & P. R. Shave (Eds.), *Handbook of attachment: Theory, research, and clinical applications* (pp. 419–435), 2nd ed. New York, NY: Guilford Press.
2. Ciccetti, D, & Toth, S. L. (2005). Child maltreatment. *Annual Review of Clinical Psychology*, 1, 409–438.
3. Fonagy, P., Redfern, S., & Charman, T. (1997). The relationship between belief-desire reasoning and a projective measure of attachment security (SAD). *British Journal of Developmental Psychology*, 15, 51–61.
4. Leonardt, M., & Overa, S. (2021). Are there differences in video gaming and use of social media among boys and girls?—A mixed methods approach. *International Journal of Research in Public Health*, June, 18(11), 6085. Published online 2021 Jun 4. Doi: 10.3390/ijerph18116085
5. Festinger, L. (1954). A theory of social comparison processes. *Human Relations*, 7, 117–140. Doi: 10.1177/001872675400700202

Chapter 6 – Your risky teenager

1. Galvan, A., Hare, T. A., Parra, C. E., Penn, J., Voss, H., Glover, G., & Casey, B. J. (2006). Earlier development of the accumbens relative to orbitofrontal cortex might underlie risk-taking behavior in adolescents. *Journal of Neuroscience*, 21 June 2006, 26(25), 6885–6892. Doi: 10.1523/JNEUROSCI.1062-06.2006
2. Casey, J., Getz, S., & Galvan, A. (2008). The adolescent brain. *Developmental Review*, March, 28(1), 62–77.
3. Drazenovic, M., Rukavina, T. V., & Poplasen, L. M. (2023). Impact of social media use on mental health within adolescent and student populations during COVID-19 pandemic: Review. *International Journal of Environmental Research and Public Health*, February, 20(4), 3392.

Chapter 7 – Understanding self-harm

1. Gillies, D., Christou, M. A., Dixon, A. C., Featherston, O. J., Rapti, I., Garcia-Anguita, A., & Christou, P. A. (2018). Prevalence and characteristicts of self-harm in adolescents: Meta-analyses of community-based studies 1990–2015. *Journal of the American Academy of Child and Adolescent Psychiatry*, 57(10), 733–741.
2. Gillies, D., Christou, M. A., Dixon, A. C., Featherston, O. J., Rapti, I., Garcia-Anguita, A., & Christou, P. A. (2018). Prevalence and characteristicts of self-harm in adolescents: Meta-analyses of community-based studies 1990–2015. *Journal of the American Academy of Child and Adolescent Psychiatry*, 57(10), 733–741.
3. NHS Digital/The Independent. (January 2020). 'Number of children admitted to A&E with mental health problems jumps 330 per cent over past decade'. Available at: https://www.independent.co.uk/news/health/children-mental-health-hospital-suicide-nhs-ae-a9255626.html
4. Young Minds. (Summer 2020). 'Coronavirus: Impact on young people with mental health needs (survey two)'. Available at: https://www.youngminds.org.uk/media/355gyqcd/coronavirus-report-summer-2020-final.pdf
5. NCB and UCL Research. (November 2020). 'One in six report severe mental health difficulties by age 17'. Available at: https://www.ncb.org.uk/about-us/media-centre/news-opinion/one-six-report-severe-mental-health-difficulties-age-17
6. ONS: Deaths Registered in England and Wales. (2019). Section six: 'Leading causes of death'. Available at: https://www.ons.gov.uk/peoplepopulationandcommunity/birthsdeathsandmarriages/deaths/bulletins/deathsregistrationsummarytables/2019#leading-causes-of-death
7. NHS Digital. (2018). 'Mental health of children and young people in England, 2017'. Available at: https://digital.nhs.uk/data-and-information/publications/statistical/mental-health-of-children-and-young-people-in-england/2017/2017. Based on 46.8% of 17 to 19.
8. Masten, C. L., Eisenberger, N. I., Borofsky, L. A., Pfiefer, J. H., McNealy, K., Mazziotta, J. C., & Dapretto, M. (2009). Neural correlates of social exclusion during adolescence: Understanding the distress of peer rejection. *Social Cognitive and Affective Neuroscience*, 4(2), 143–157.
9. Motz, A. (2009). *Managing self-harm - Psychological perspectives.* London: Routledge.
10. Rossouw, T. I., & Fonagy, P. (2012). Mentalization-based treatment for self-harm in adolescents: A randomized controlled trial. *Journal of the American Academy of Child and Adolescent Psychiatry*, 51(12), 1304–1313.
11. Rossouw, T. I., & Fonagy, P. (2012). Mentalization-based treatment for self-harm in adolescents: A randomized controlled trial. *Journal of the American Academy of Child and Adolescent Psychiatry*, 51(12), 1304–1313.

Chapter 9 – Foster carers and adoptive parents: Parenting your teenager who has a history of trauma

1. Lewis, S. J., Arseneault, L., Caspi, A., Fisher, H. L., Matthews, T., Moffitt, T. E., Odgers, C. L., Stahl, D., Teng, J. Y., & Danese, A. (2019). The epidemiology of trauma and post-traumatic stress disorder in a representative cohort of young people in England and Wales. *The Lancet Psychiatry*, 6(3), 247–256.
2. McCrory, E., & Viding, E. (2015). The theory of latent vulnerability: Reconceptualizing the link between childhood maltreatment and psychiatric disorder. *Developmental Psychopathology*, 27(2) 493–505.
3. Ensink, K., Begin, M., Normandin, L., Godbout, N., & Fonagy, P. (2017). Mentalization and dissociation in the context of trauma: Implications for child psychopathology. *Journal of Trauma & Dissociation* 18(1), 11–30. doi: 10.1080/15299732.2016.1172536. Epub 2016 Apr 12.
4. van der Kolk, B. A. (2005). Developmental trauma disorder: Toward a rational diagnosis for children with complex trauma histories. *Psychiatric Annals*, 35(5), 401–408.
5. Midgley, N., Cirasola, A., Austerberry, C., Ranzato, E., West, G., Martin, P., et al. (2019). Supporting foster carers to meet the needs of looked after children: Afeasibility and pilot evaluation of the reflective fostering programme. *Developmental Child Welfare*, 1(1), 41–60.
6. Redfern, S., Wood, S., Lassri, D., Cirasola, A., West, G., Austerberry, C., Luyten, P., Fonagy, P., & Midgley, N. (2018). The reflective fostering programme: Background and development of a new approach. *Adoption & Fostering*, 42(3), 234–248.
7. Sroufe, L. A., Egeland, B., Carlson, E. A., & Collins, W. (2005b). Placing early attachment experiences in developmental context: The Minnesota longitudinal study. In K. E. Grossmann, K. Grossmann, & E. Waters (Eds.), *Attachment from infancy to adulthood: The major longitudinal studies* (pp. 48–70). New York, NY: Guilford Press.
8. Trickett, P. K., Noll, J. G., & Putnman, F. W. (2011). *The impact of sexual abuse on female development: Lessons from a multigenerational, longitudinal research study*. Cambridge: Cambridge University Press.

INDEX

Note: Page numbers in *italics* refer to figures.